THE
SCARIEST
PLACE
IN THE
WORLD

ALSO BY JAMES BRADY

Further Lane
Gin Lane
The House That Ate the Hamptons
Hamptons Christmas
The Coldest War
The Marines of Autumn
Warning of War
The Marine
Superchic
Paris One
Nielsen's Children
The Press Lord
Holy Wars
Designs
Fashion Show

THE
SCARIEST
PLACE
IN THE
WORLD

A Marine Returns to North Korea

JAMES BRADY

Thomas Dunne Books ✹ St. Martin's Press
New York

THOMAS DUNNE BOOKS.
An imprint of St. Martin's Press.

www.stmartins.com

Map by Mark Stein Studios

Library of Congress Cataloging-in-Publication Data

Brady, James, 1928–
The scariest place: a Marine returns to North Korea / James Brady.—1st ed.
        p.   cm.
Includes index (p. 269).
ISBN 0-312-33242-4
EAN 978-0312-33242-6
1. Korea (South)—Description and travel.   2. Korean Demilitarized Zone (Korea)
3. Brady, James, 1928—Travel—Korea (South)   4. Korean War, 1950–1953—Personal
narratives, American.   I. Title.

DS902.4.B73   2005
915.1904'43—dc22

2004051491

First Edition: April 2005

10   9   8   7   6   5   4   3   2   1

This book is dedicated to the late Senator John Chafee of Rhode Island, the captain of Dog Company, and to the men I first wrote about years ago in The Coldest War. *And to all the Marines and other Americans who fought the Korean War.*

It is also for my daughters, Fiona and Susan, and for my grandchildren, Sarah, Joe, and Nick Konig, so they will know something about my friends, living and dead, who fought in Korea.

And for the great Eddie Adams, with whom I traveled back in time.

I am grateful to U.S. Army General Leon LaPorte, officer commanding in Korea and northeast Asia, for granting me an on-the-record interview, and for facilitating my travel through Korea and allowing access to sensitive areas. I am also in the debt of Army Colonel Matthew T. Margotta and Marine Colonel Michael A. Malachowsky, and of the Marine detachment serving in Korea in 2003. My thanks to the men and women of the United States Army in Korea who made my return possible. With special thanks to Lieutenant Colonel Steve Boylan, Major Holly Pierce, and Sergeant Russell Bassett, and to First Lieutenant James Gleason for his personally guided tour of the DMZ and for permitting Eddie Adams and me to bunk in with his recon troopers at Outpost Ouellette.

CHINA

Yalu River

NORTH KOREA

Taedong River

Sea of Japan

⊛ Pyongyang

● Hill 749

38TH PARALLEL

● Hill Yoke

⊛ Seoul

DMZ
(Demilitarized Zone)

Inchon ●

Han River

SOUTH KOREA

Kum River

Yellow Sea

Naktong River

N
W   E
S

| 0 | miles | 60 |
| 0 | kilometers | 100 |

© 2005, Mark Stein Studios

THE
SCARIEST
PLACE
IN THE
WORLD

CHAPTER 1

YOU NEVER SAW SUCH A THING,
SAID GAUCHE, IMPRESSIONABLE LEFTENANT HOOPER.

In the opening pages of Evelyn Waugh's *Brideshead Revisited,* a wartime detachment of Royal Marine Commandos bivouacs in the moonless night on the grounds of some vast but only glimpsed and half-suspected English country house. When the troops are roused at dawn, disoriented by the long train ride, by fatigue and the morning mists, and harried by their corporals and sergeants, Hooper, a gauche, easily impressed young leftenant from the unfashionable Midlands, hurries to wake the world-weary and Old Oxonian protagonist of the novel, Captain Charles Ryder, an older man disillusioned with the army.

Atwitter about their lavish new surroundings, the provincial Hooper rhapsodizes about what he's seen so far of the strange estate, its palatial extent, its wonders and splendors, its supposed riches.

" 'Great barrack of a place. I've just had a snoop around. Very ornate, I'd call it. And a queer thing, there's a sort of R.C. church attached. I looked in and there was a kind of service going on—just a padre and one old man. I felt very awkward. . . . There's a frightful great fountain, too, in front of the steps, all rocks and sort of carved animals. You never saw such a thing,' he assures Ryder.

" 'Yes, Hooper, I did. I've been here before. . . .'

" 'Oh well, you know all about it. I'll go and get cleaned up.' "

Ryder had been there before, we realize; he did know all about it. The great estate was called Brideshead, and it was there that Captain Ryder had been young and in love.

Like Charles Ryder, I too was an aging former captain of Marines who had once gone to war, and there found love.

Ours wasn't a towering and noble crusade such as World War II, but small and brutish, rather old-fashioned, on the other side of the world in the mountain snows and stinking paddies of a strange, antique Asian land, a long-ago little kingdom invaded and ransacked by marauding enemies over the millennia, and left lone and forlorn. By today's high-tech, more discriminating standards, it was a primitive war, to which half a century ago some of us went almost eagerly and with a certain dash, having missed the "Big War," and feeling left out. I fought there, in Korea both North and South, as a twenty-three-year-old infantry officer of American Marines.

It was hard fighting by foot soldiers, often at hand-grenade range, against the tough little peasant army of a local warlord named Kim Il Sung, who'd learned his trade as a battalion commander in the Soviet Red Army in the Nazi war. For three years we fought Kim and his allies, the forty divisions of Chinese Communist regulars, killing plenty of them, and saving the marginally democratic country of South Korea, enabling its economic miracle.

But we took our losses.

In the three years of that war, from June of 1950 to July of '53, thirty-seven thousand Americans were killed, infantry soldiers and Marines mostly. Thirty-seven thousand dead in thirty-seven months. Put it in context. While this is being written in the summer of 2004, the Iraq war has been on for eighteen months and a thousand Americans have died. In Korea, a thousand of us were killed every month, month after deadly month for three years.

This book is about that war and the Marines who fought it.

It is also about a college kid from the Brooklyn fishing village of

Sheepshead Bay and his love for the Marine Corps and the men with whom he campaigned: the classy university types, the roughnecks and the poets, the sophisticates and the hicks, the salty regulars and the freshly graduated, and what the Marines called "the Old Breed," the hard old China hands. It is about those who died, those who lived, some of them scarred forever, and the happy few who survived Korea and went on to fortune and occasionally to fame.

The kid, as he was then, was a Marine rifle platoon leader, a member of an exclusive fraternity.

In the entire Marine Corps of two divisions and 175,000 men, there are only 162 rifle platoons, each of them commanded by a young second lieutenant, for it is the most lethal job description in the Corps, a young man's work. After enough combat, men grow too wise to want to command a platoon. When Marines assault a beachhead or a hilltop or a fortified position, it is the rifle platoons that lead the way, that attack and smash, and sometimes break against, the enemy lines. The mortality rates are such that some of his forty-five men may never even get to meet their platoon leader before he is wounded, killed, or replaced. This is about one of those replacement lieutenants, who arrived Thanksgiving weekend of 1951 in the Taebaek Mountains of North Korea, and was given a Marine rifle platoon to lead.

And it is about the place where he fought as a boy, the auld enemy he fought against, about his comrades in arms, and what happened to them after the fighting, all of this now seen through the focus of age at his house on Further Lane, where the lovely three-centuries-old beach town of East Hampton borders the ocean and where, in the night, he can hear the Atlantic combers crashing on the sand.

The kid survived the war to become a newspaperman, covered the Senate during LBJ's era, came to know Jack and Bobby Kennedy, became a foreign correspondent, got to live in Paris and London, was an editor and publisher, went on television, learned about fashion, and about life, at the knee of Coco Chanel, knew Joe Heller and Truman Capote and Mailer, worked for Rupert Murdoch and had breakfast with Kate Hepburn, met the Queen, once rode in an ambulance with a badly burned Kurt Vonnegut, watched Dali having cocktails at the Ritz, interviewed Malraux, and attended Ike's and de Gaulle's press conferences. On a Budget Day, from the press gallery of the House of Commons, he actually saw Churchill, bent and fat, deaf and very old. And at Cape Kennedy covering the *Apollo 11* launch, he attended in one of those mammoth, echoing hangars a cocktail party with von Braun and Charles Lindbergh, the entire history of manned flight in the same room, the German mobbed by flatterers and Lindy in his muted gray business suit, alone and unnoticed, but graciously willing to chat when a journalist approached, bashfully, to say hello and talk a little about flying.

Yet nothing he ever did in his life, except for having children and making a life as a writer of books, quite matched the intensity, the gravitas and sheer excitement of fighting in North Korea as a rifle platoon leader of Dog Company Marines under Captain John Chafee in 1951–52.

It all happened a long time back when he was young, and half a century later in his seventies, listening to the sea at night, he remembers.

CHAPTER 2

A JOY IT WILL BE ONE DAY, PERHAPS,
TO REMEMBER EVEN THIS.

The story of Charles Ryder's return to Brideshead was fiction, elegant, delicious fiction. But in real life, how many of us get to turn back calendars? To thrill again to first loves and grand adventures?

In the fraying ends of winter two years ago, it appeared that I might be given just such an opportunity. I was a working New York newspaperman who had cunningly achieved the American dream (hardcase Marine buddies, even as they muttered, "That son of a bitch!" vicariously enjoyed the notion) of a five-day weekend in the Hamptons, writing books and weekly magazine columns. Now came suggestions I travel back in time, to write for Sunday newspaper readers about the war we fought and the men who fought it. Surely a tale worth telling, but an opportunity I would ruefully have to decline.

This despite the fact what most Americans had taken to calling "the forgotten war" was in 2003 and 2004 unexpectedly being remembered, back on the front pages and leading the evening news.

In his presidential campaign John Kerry would cite North Korea, contrasting it to the mess in Iraq, calling the North Koreans "a far more compelling threat," but offering no solutions. A *New York Times* editorialist grumbled that a notorious homicide in California was getting "more attention than the North Korean nuclear program." In September of '04, the South Koreans admitted that they too had an enriched-uranium program. And then, promptly, denied any such thing. The Bush administration seemed honestly confounded, perplexed, and dithered between negotiating with the North Koreans and freezing them out, leaving the diplomatic heavy lifting to Beijing. Mr. Cheney, pugnacious if not very helpful, declared: "We don't negotiate with evil, we defeat it." Bill Clinton, who knew little of war, for once got it precisely right, when he said of Korea, and of the Demilitarized Zone that separates North and South Korea: "This is the scariest place in the world."

In the past year or two it had gotten scarier. The North Korean army of 1.2 million men was twice the size of our own. The United States had ten times as many people and half the number of soldiers. North Korean artillery and missiles easily ranged Greater Seoul with its population larger than New York's. Their weird and nepotistic "Dear Leader (only son of Kim Il Sung)" was a recluse, unpredictable, loopy, and surrounded by sychophants. (Their official press agency reported that in 1994 Kim Jong Il had taken up golf and, in his first round ever, was thirty-eight under par! Tiger Woods should do as well.) But shrewdly noting our bizarre obsession with Saddam and Iraq, and with their accustomed lack of grace, the North Koreans announced they now had a couple of nuclear weapons, were producing more, and for the right price would barter or sell them in the international arms bazaar to other rogue states or even terrorists.

One headline writer nailed it: "Nuts with Nukes."

Would there be a Second Punic War? Would we have to fight the North Koreans again? That was really up to the loonies in Pyongyang, wasn't it? Though to an extent the decision might also lie with Mr. Bush and those whose advice he listened to: Cheney and Rummy, Condi and Wolfowitz and Perle, those warriors who had never fought.

These ominous and unsettling developments were sufficient and valid reasons for a journalist to journey to Korea. It could be a wonderful assignment.

Though not for me. Why would I even consider revisiting a place I'd sworn never to see again? Still, in the winter of 2003, the idea tugged at my journalist's sleeve.

Perhaps it did so because I was growing old, and it was in Korea that I had been young and in love. Less discriminating and sophisticated than Charles Ryder, I'd not come under the spell of a great estate and its aristocratically dysfunctional family, had not fallen for tipsy, beautiful, and doomed Sebastian Flyte, or for his lordship's unattainable sister Lady Julia.

No, my boyish infatuations were quite different. My love affair, set against the background of a nasty little Asian war, was with the United States Marines Corps.

Nothing unusual about that, I suspect. Plenty of fire-eating kids feel that way about the Marines. The odd thing: I was the most hesitant of warriors. As a boy I don't believe I ever won a single fistfight. Later on, when I pulled on the forest green uniform, I was quite sure I would be killed and was terrified at the prospect. At the same time I was romantically drawn to the Corps, fascinated by its history, its pantheon of heroes, thrilled by its glorious martial traditions. And being a nosy kid, I feared I might be missing something.

In the end, I hoped that if I did actually get into battle, the bravery of other Marines might somehow rub off on me.

Perhaps explaining the paradox, a fearful boy volunteering for the Marines, my youthful passion was less with the Corps itself than with an extraordinary crew of young officers—we were all young then—who passed through and came out of the Marine Corps Schools of Quantico, Virginia, in 1950 and '51. Well-bred college boys, most of us young gentlemen flavored by a handful of old salts and the inevitable rogue, largely middle-class but a number raised in privilege and graduated from the top universities, all being trained to command rifle platoons in combat.

And quite a crew we were, the Marines of our generation.

There was the Boston Brahmin, big, redheaded Douglas H. T. Bradlee, the Harvard tackle (and first cousin of Ben Bradlee of later *Washington Post* and

7

Watergate fame); Bradlee's teammate the Harvard linebacker and captain, Phil Isenberg, later a famous surgeon; Kenneth "Gunny" Arzt, who owned a car dealership in Yakima, Washington, and spoke airily of his "sixty-three landings on hostile beaches"; George Paterno of Brooklyn and Brown, a football player and later coach (brother of the more celebrated Joe), who suffered maybe the worst case of poison ivy the Naval Hospital at Quantico had ever seen; Arthur Ochs "Punch" Sulzberger, future publisher of *The New York Times,* an enlisted man during the Big War, gone on to Columbia University after, and in 1951 back in uniform at Quantico; "Wild Hoss" Callan, the New Mexico rancher's son saving his Marine Corps pay to stave off bankruptcy for his daddy's ranch; Dick Bowers, the Yale tailback who never played an Ivy League game as tough as Friday night high school football in the coalmining towns of his western Pennsylvania.

And there was John Warner, a future United States senator and Liz Taylor husband; "Taffy" Sceva, who'd fought the Japanese under the legendary "Chesty" Puller, and raced yachts across the Pacific; Pete Soderbergh, who would serve a great university (provost of LSU, I believe) and whose son makes wonderful movies. There was Bjornsen the giant forest ranger who'd fought as an enlisted man and then, as a "mustang," was commissioned an officer; Chuck Brodhead from the famed Michigan marching band ("We've got more members in our band, Brady, than the student body of your whole damned school!"); Al Myers the lacrosse all-American from RPI who once played at Wembley during an Olympic exhibition; Lew Faust, who broke a man's nose in a barracks brawl and later became a broadcasting executive for Capital Cities; Joe Buscemi of Illinois, who blocked for all-American Buddy Young and played in the Rose Bowl.

And young Allen Macy Dulles, Princeton '51, whose uncle would become secretary of state and whose daddy would run the CIA; decathlon champ Bob Mathias of Stanford; George Eversman, who would prosper as an ad agency head; Bernard "Mick" Trainor, who would eventually be promoted to lieutenant general, serve as military affairs correspondent for *The New York Times,* and be elected a Fellow at Harvard; Chuck Bentsen, who rowed for Wisconsin; and Redskins quarterback Eddie LeBaron. There was also the immortal Adams from the University of Georgia, a large, drawling young collegian with angry red pimples on his buttocks, who strode through the barracks in his wooden shower clogs, idly scratching himself, buck naked and uncaring. No American serviceman, ever, didn't know at least one guy like Adams.

Oh, yes, add Pat Robertson to the roster, the future TV evangelist who ran for president and admitted holding conversations with God. Pat's daddy was Senator A. Willis Robertson, the junior senator from Virginia (apple-cheeked, whispering, senior senator Harry Byrd was the real power), but with sufficient political muscle that his son hinted the brass would sort of look after him, which stirred resentment among fellow officers and led to tribulations of near-biblical proportions for young Lieutenant Robertson.

Think of our bunch as you might of Beau Geste and his brothers, joining the Foreign Legion for the defense of Fort Zinderneuf, and falling in with martinets, thieves, fierce Tuaregs, and mutineers. John Buchan, eloquently describing our British counterparts in the First War, young subalterns fighting on the Western front, wrote of them as "debonair, brilliant and brave."

It was these young men of Quantico I would come to love, with whom I wanted to go to war, despite my appalling lack of heroism.

Later, our class of green lieutenants would be leavened by less debonair officers who had fought against and defeated the empire of Japan, and by the first officers rotated home from the early fighting in Korea at Pusan and In-chon and Chosin Reservoir, and by others who came up through the enlisted ranks as commissioned "mustangs." All of us, the Old Breed and the college kids, were being trained up to the same intensely focused purpose: to lead Marine infantrymen in deadly fights and kill the other fellow.

Most of our generation, the college class of 1950 that fought Korea, children of the Great Depression, boys who had just missed World War II, couldn't wait to go to war; no self-loathing, no guilt or equivocation, a few nerves (the handful of fainthearted like me) but fewer doubts. We were in the Marines for the excitement, even if sometimes we would get more than we needed. The draft was on, the 1950s were a different time, and Korea was just maybe the last war Americans fought in which everyone went, the rich and the poor, the Harvards and the high school dropouts, the cowboy and the rancher's son, a war that almost no one, not even in the moneyed classes, ducked or bought his way out of. If at Quantico we weren't yet Nathan Bedford Forrest as professional killers, we were ambitious to get there, and believed we were closing fast.

My own aspirations had been more modest: don't get myself, or anyone else, killed through my own fear or folly.

As we get older, we tend to live increasingly in the past, which is all very pleasant but not very realistic. That's why one of the great things about newspaper and magazine work is the unbending deadlines. So that in early 2003, with Korea newly simmering, I followed the current, round-the-clock news cycle with more than professional interest, fretting about a troubled and contemporary world in weekly columns while indulging myself in remembering what Korea had been fifty years before. Not the narcotic grip of brooding memory but cheerful recollection of those gallant and colorful young platoon leaders in training at the Marine schools, and how well most of us had turned out.

If only I *were* sufficiently fit for a last adventure, a return to the old battlefields, journeying back in time to the only war I ever attended.

The men of those battles were real, the place exists, the war was heroically fought though not neatly or dramatically won, the enemy was turned back, the far-off, long-ago little kingdom saved. How, I wondered, if at all, would our war be memorialized by the ages?

Robert Fagles, translator of the famously pessimistic Virgil, provides a possible text from the *Aeneid*. In an interview with the *Times,* Fagles cites what he calls one of "the most beautiful" lines ever written in Latin.

Aeneas is mourning the war he has just fought, the horror, the cruel losses, the deaths of friends, when in summoning up hope out of grief, he says of his war: "A joy it will be one day, perhaps, to remember even this."

Is that how men really think of their wars? Was that how I felt? Or could even Aeneas be mistaken? Maybe our recollections should instead be summed up to the more cynical beat of the bittersweet old American marching song:

The men will cheer/the boys will shout,
The ladies, they will all turn out.
And we'll all feel gay,
When Johnny comes marching home.
Hurrah, hurrah.

CHAPTER 3

THE GENERAL, SMOOTH AND SMUG,
WAS CONDESCENDING AS HELL.

As the United States prepared to go to war yet again in the Middle East, those surly bastards the North Koreans were making mischief on the far side of the world.

Which was why in February of 2003, Brian Williams of CNBC had sent out a camera crew to my house on Further Lane in East Hampton to set up an interview.

Since I'd fought in Korea and had written a couple of books about it, I was to be on Mr. Williams's show that evening as one of two experts du jour on the North Koreans, the other being a retired Air Force three-star general. Through the clever techniques of split-screen video Brian Williams was in his studio, the general was somewhere else, Washington, I supposed, and I was propped cheerfully on a kitchen stool set up in my living room (the cameraman didn't want me slouched on a couch and liked my wall of books as background) four hundred yards from the Atlantic Ocean. As you might imagine, I was enjoying the moment; lieutenants and captains love getting equal billing with generals on TV.

As we gathered electronically for our triangular chat, the Communist North was threatening the uneasy truce which had held since July 27, 1953, when the Korean War came to its equivocal close and the guns fell mute after three years of hard, cruel fighting. The Koreans and the Red Chinese had killed thirty-seven thousand Americans and left another eight thousand Americans missing in action (MIA). Their own losses in men and treasure had been enormous. The general and I were to discuss all this. And wanting to clear my head, think about it a bit, to get it right, I settled into my lurching gait for a stroll along the beach while the crew set up in my living room. A cold wind came off the water, turning my face ruddy and my hair tousled as I stared out at the winter ocean at dusk, thinking meaningful thoughts, and I came back windswept, but alert and refreshed, to be hooked up to a mike, ready for the general at his best. I probably should have changed from sweater and leather jacket into a proper shirt and tie, combed my hair, but, to hell! I wasn't sitting for a portrait by Karsh of Ottawa.

Mr. Williams introduced us both to his audience, deftly summarized the situation. The North Koreans were making ugly noises at the back of their throats about, just maybe, being quite willing to use nuclear weapons against their neighbors. Or against their favorite devils (the Americans). The threat hung there, ominously vague, on the diplomatic air. The show's producers ran some grainy black-and-white file tape from the actual war of 1950–53 and then some current video of monolithic Red Guard battalions goose-stepping in Pyongyang, and of anti-American riots in Seoul.

Given a cue, I blathered on for a time about the North Korean soldiers, how tough they'd been fifty years ago, how the Marines pretty much had to kill them to stop them, and how implacable a foe I presumed they would still be, especially with a huge numerical advantage over us in the relative size of our armies. They had little effective air in my time, most of their tanks had been destroyed, but their foot soldiers were some of the best light infantry in the world, and their artillery, old and outmoded as it was, had been deadly, especially the mortars. Today, in 2003, I assumed the SOBs could still fight. The general, smug and smooth, found my anecdotes charming, the colorful reminiscences of an old foot soldier, but lost little time putting me in my place. When in the spirit of full disclosure, I admitted that I'd left Korea as a first lieutenant in the summer of 1952 and had never gone back, the three-star pounced.

How could I possibly know anything about what was going on over there now?

His disdain for a mere junior officer, and a crude infantryman at that, was palpable. I bit back a wiseass riposte. Had the three-star ever fired a round, lugged a dead man back to the lines, seen a lobbed hand grenade tumbling toward him? I kept my mouth shut.

The general instead favored us with a recitation of his own credentials, a chronicle of top military jobs he'd held in the region, the time he'd spent in South Korea, rattled off statistics, dropped names. It was all very impressive.

I thought to myself, This bird had done everything in Korea but fight.

This went on for a while, the urbane Brian Williams officiating, the Air Force officer becoming more condescending. As our time ran out I played the only card I really held.

"General, you flyboys tend to see the world from thirty thousand feet. Infantry officers see it as it really is, crawling around in the mud, on our knees, flat on our bellies."

What was he going to do, have me court-martialed?

I don't know how that played across America, but the boys in my living room, the camera crew, liked it. After we went to black, I wanted to pour all of us a drink. Or might that get them into difficulty with the network? But I did appreciate their taking a rooting interest, even if it was just the usual working stiffs' resentment of big shots, enlisted guys versus the brass. I was still steamed about the general. What did that arrogant bastard know about fighting in a summer's heat that stupefied and prostrated healthy young athletes? Or on winter nights when the glass fell to twenty below and men lost toes and fingers and ears to frostbite and others died of exposure? I resisted the urge to tell the cameramen about what it was really like, combat in Korea, to tell them about the firefights, the primal scream of combat on the ridgelines, fighting as men had done ten thousand years before. The hell with that! They'd seen the tape, had gawked at the fading photos on my wall, and that was sufficient. They didn't need an old fart's war stories. It was a long time ago and what did these kids care? And why should they?

Reluctantly, and only to myself, I had to concede the three-star was right. It had been presumptuous of me to go posing as an expert with the most minimal of credentials. I didn't really know a damn thing about today's Koreas, North or South. My lack of knowledge was, in fact, purposeful. Some years ago in a book about Korea, reviewed by *The New York Times* as "a superb personal memoir of the way it was," I'd concluded by saying I'd never go back, that I'd never sign up for an old soldier's tour. I wrote:

"I didn't want to see the hills again or feel the cold or hear the wind out of Siberia, moaning. I didn't want to disturb the dead."

On that chill winter's night in East Hampton as the camera crew loaded into their van and I waved them off for the drive back into Manhattan, and despite my embarrassing national display of ignorance, there were no regrets. I'd done my Korea tour, I'd fought my war. I'd thought the matter through and had never returned. Like Waugh's Captain Ryder, I knew the place. I'd been there before.

Now, of course, there was no longer any possibility of my going back.

Just over a year earlier, December 11, ninety days after the World Trade Center attack, I left my East Side flat in the cool, sunny late morning to stroll over to Saks Fifth Avenue for some Christmas shopping when I encountered author Dominick Dunne on the sidewalk across from the great store, and paused to chat. When Nick left, I suddenly went spacey, unsteady on my feet. No pain, no nausea, but alarmed by this unexplained weakness, I cut short my errands to go home. If you collapsed in Saks during Christmas shopping season, you might be stowed away in a stockroom until the January clearance sales. En route, I cashed a check at the bank (you don't want to be short when you're sick), canceled lunch with Marty Singerman, publisher of the *New York Post,* made a few calls, actually did a previously arranged phone interview with a young actress, Natasha Lyonne, and tried to nap.

The next few hours were a jumble. An old friend from Washington, Kandy Stroud, was in town and called, suggesting cocktails. For some reason I lied and said a movie actress (Miss Lyonne) was then at my apartment and I couldn't talk. I phoned my brother (the monsignor) who suggested I go to the ER. No, I was going to sleep this thing off. It was probably the flu and I'd feel better in the morning. A persistent tingling, left arm and left leg, woke me again and I called my internist, David Globus. The good doctor listened to my symptoms, seemed to know from my layman's description just what was happening to me, and asked with some urgency if I could get a cab. I said sure. He told me not to change clothes or do anything else but to go to the ER. In the taxi, a pointless, stupid vanity took over and I remember assuring the cabbie I was fine and just visiting a sick friend. What the hell should he care? I ended up early that evening at New York Presbyterian surrounded by neurologists and hooked up to machines all of which agreed on the same diagnosis.

I was seventy-three years old and I'd just suffered a stroke.

I didn't want to die but I wasn't afraid of dying. If you consult the actuarial tables for twenty-three-year-old second lieutenants, I'd already lived half a century on borrowed time, and pleasantly so. Naturally, there were people I loved and would miss, and any number of places and things. What did frighten me was the very real prospect of a half-life. Of surviving but not being able to think, to reason, to communicate and make judgments, and to write. If I could retain those powers, and be able to hobble about, if only marginally, then I would be able to maintain my quality of life in Manhattan and out on the beach, writing columns and publishing books, playing grandpa, broadcasting, and raising modest and occasional hell.

A small blood vessel at the back of my brain that controlled the motor functions on my left side had become partially clogged. At first I could neither walk nor raise my hand off the bedsheet, there was a curling at the left side of my mouth, and my speech was somewhat slurred. A lugubrious and not very promising state of affairs.

The physical and occupational therapists went to work, and a speech therapist urged me to recite poetry or the Gettysburg Address at the top of my lungs, enunciating with exaggerated jaw and mouth movements.

"People will think I'm crazy," I said, slurring the words.

"Half the people in hospitals are nuts," she said. "Start shouting."

It was at that doleful moment that the Marine Corps reentered my life.

General Jim Jones led the charge with a cheering phone call. The general, six five, raised in France and fluent in the language, a Georgetown graduate and Vietnam combat veteran, is these days supreme commander in Brussels of NATO forces, customarily addressed by me as *"Mon Général"*; but in 2001 he was commandant of the Marine Corps. The call from this somewhat overwhelming figure was echoed by similar greetings from retired Marine General Martin Steele, who ran the Intrepid Air and Space Museum aboard the storied old aircraft carrier moored on the Manhattan waterfront.

This was followed by a bedside visit by Marine Major Dave Anderson and a captain I didn't know. There they were in their blues at the foot of the bed as Dr. Alan Z. Segal, my neurologist, came in, his eyes widening. The Marine Corps does things like that routinely, visiting the sick, burying the dead. But to Dr. Segal, a great doctor freshly arrived in New York as a highly touted hotshot from Mass General, uniforms in the sickroom may have been a novelty. He was smooth, very cool, but curiosity got the better of him.

"What was that all about?" he inquired after the Marines had left and he'd done his poking and prodding. Until now I'd been just another anonymous patient.

With mock solemnity from my bed of pain, I informed Doctor Segal, "Marines never abandon their wounded, Doctor."

The neurologist, seeing my crooked grin, mocked me right back.

"I hadn't realized you were such a celebrated figure, Mr. Brady."

It was my first laugh since the stroke, and my recovery may be dated back to that moment.

I was hospitalized for three weeks, rehabbing, and a year later was still doing outpatient therapy at Mount Sinai for a gimpy left knee and a balky rotator cuff. No novelty in that, nor disgrace, not in being a crip. I'd known plenty in the Marines. Bum legs, no arm, an eye wandered off somewhere, a limb or a couple of fingers gone missing, the usual scars. Trademarks of the business. A knee was derisory stuff.

And except for that and the daily popping of a few pills, life had returned pretty much to normal. I was writing again, had finished one book and begun another, had flown about the country, dutifully taking off my shoes at airports. All these things considered, life was far too comfortable to put aside for stupid, quixotic adventures based on the mere resentment of generals. Going back to Korea simply to spite a supercilious three-star—that would be stupid, wouldn't it?

Spring wasn't far off, there would be kayaking on the ponds, surf casting off the beach near my house, my grandchildren would organize foot races which, for the first time, they shrewdly calculated I was now odds-on to lose. Friends in Sag Harbor would forgive me my bum knee and allow me to play genteel mixed doubles on the local courts.

In Manhattan I was already impatient with inquiries about my gimp, and instead of being civil, going into courteous detail about strokes and rehabs, and grown a bit cocky about having survived, I snarled away curiosity with a throwaway and curt, "Damned Commies!" Liz Smith, on a slow news day and to my secret pleasure, got a line out of that for her column.

Thanks to long walks on the beach, trots along Further Lane past Jerry Seinfeld's fancy new $32 million house, and discreet trespassing on the out-of-season fairways of the posh Maidstone Club, my legs had strengthened to an attempt at ice skating on the town pond where Main Street abuts the local graveyard. On a good day with smooth ice, the pond was a bustling, colorful scene by Currier & Ives out of Brueghel (the Elder or the Younger, I'm not sure which). So I chose an early January morning with only the cemetery dead as witnesses, unwilling to make a fool of myself before an audience. I was all alone out there, tentative and stumbling, crawling back to the bulkhead to regain my feet each time I fell, when I noticed a car idling by the graveyard. As I struggled to get up, the driver, an unimpressed local, watched for a time, then rolled down his window and shouted out at me.

"Ya write better than ya skate!"

He was right about that and I waved a hand in acknowledgment.

I was writing (and hadn't missed a deadline!) for *Advertising Age,* for *Crain's New York Business,* and every Sunday for *Parade,* was alternating serious novels about Marines and their wars with screwball comedies set in the Hamptons, a few of them optioned by Hollywood, making some pretty good money, reading a lot and falling asleep to the metronomic thud of the big waves breaking, knowing just how fortunate I was to be neither paralyzed nor brain-damaged.

I was too smart to hazard all that, wasn't I? Too smart, and too old. On the coming November 15, 2003, the feast day of Albertus Magnus, the teacher of Thomas Aquinas, I would be seventy-five years old.

CHAPTER 4

A DEAD MARINE WAS LAID AT THEIR FEET IN AN OLD
PHOTO OF A SHOT-UP RIFLE PLATOON.

I'd had my war and, like most soldiers, didn't really want to fight another,
yet Korea continued to exert its pull.

It was where boyhood ended, where I learned to fight, where I really
became a Marine. Half a century after the war we fought to save Korea, we
still had thousands of Americans stationed south of the DMZ. Were these GIs
infantrymen? Or specialists operating radars and listening posts? They could
hardly defend in depth. Did they simply man a few outposts, just a political
force the Communist North would have to take into account if another war
began? Were American kids out there as a tripwire, "raw meat on the end of
a stick"?

What did they think about it, being raw meat? What was duty like for
those GIs still in Korea, manning that long and wandering line? Did the
troops think another war was coming to "the scariest place"? And the generals, what were they saying?

No one in the States seemed to be asking those questions, writing or
broadcasting that story, not with a second Iraq War about to break out. My-
opic, perhaps, but for me Korea remained in clearer focus than the Middle

East. And as a newspaperman, I thought Korea was a badly underreported story.

But then, I had my biases.

On the wall of my house in East Hampton hangs an old, water-damaged black-and-white photo dating to September 1951. It is an informal portrait of what was left of the 3rd Platoon of Dog Company, 2nd Battalion, 7th Marines, a rifle platoon I would later command.

There are about twenty Marines posed against a steep hillside of shattered, shell-splintered trees, the Marines crouched or kneeling, some standing, armed and several helmeted, a few in "go to hell" caps, one or two smoking, all of them young but wary, hollow-eyed and gaunt, as drained and worn down as young men in their teens and twenties could be and still function. To their immediate front on the bare, dusty ground is a USMC-issue stretcher on which, snugly lashed by cord and web belts, lies the poncho-wrapped body of a dead Marine.

Over the years it had become something of a "cause" to me, finding out the identity of the dead Marine in the poncho. I long assumed this was their platoon leader, killed in a fight famous among Marines for its singular savagery, on an obscure little piece of North Korean high ground called, for its height in meters, Hill 749. When I sent a copy of the photo to check with my onetime squad leader, Sergeant John Fitzgerald, wounded in that fight, Fitz phoned to say that the dead man in the poncho was probably an assistant machine gunner named "Hollywood," attached temporarily to the 3rd Platoon. An assistant machine gunner is the guy who lugs the metal ammo boxes and who feeds the belt of cartridges into the gun and takes over if the gunner is hit. In combat, there is understandable confusion about casualties. And, wounded himself, Fitz didn't know Hollywood's last name, couldn't even be sure he was the "stiff" in the poncho. "Stiff" being the operative word in the combat Marine's jargon.

But Charles Curley, a machine gunner in that same fight, insisted the dead man was Joe McKenna of Elizabeth Street, San Francisco. Curley said McKenna of the 3rd Platoon was KIA September 13, 1951, on Hill 749.

"They were isolated on another knoll, ran out of ammo but still held the position."

Curley, and Dick Curtin and Lee Wimpee, all of whom fought in the Dog Company assault on Hill 749, fleshed out Joe McKenna's story. He was the third of three McKenna brothers killed in action in American wars. First Lieutenant Frank McKenna, USAF, was shot down over Germany in February 1944. PFC James McKenna, USMC, died fighting the Japanese on Saipan in June of that same year. Another McKenna brother lived to retire from the Marine Corps as a lieutenant colonel, and another boy, a sailor, was wounded by the Japanese but survived. And Joe died on Hill 749.

Dick Curtin said it was a war correspondent, arriving after the fight, who got the Marines to pose with one of their dead. It turned out to be Joe McKenna, whose corpse had conveniently just been brought down off the hill. The correspondent needed a stiff as centerpiece to his photo, and McKenna happened to be it. Wimpee told me that Artemise McKenna (Joe's mom) had regularly sent cookies to her boy, and continued to bake and send cookies to Marines of the 3rd Platoon even following Joe's death.

Three McKenna boys dead and the mother was still sending cookies. Dog Company Marines remember those cookies.

The normal Marine rifle platoon numbers forty-five; there are only twenty men in the photo—the rest were dead, or wounded and evacuated. In the otherwise unremarkable four-day fight for Hill 749, ninety American Marines died, 714 were wounded. A nothing fight for a lousy no-name ridgeline, hardly rating a footnote in history books, and we took eight hundred casualties.

To the extreme right front of the picture is the platoon sergeant, Ronald E. Stoneking, a tall, rawboned, and very hard man, seated on a rock and looking at the camera, his mouth flat and unamused, his eyes narrowed, both big hands easily around the barrel of his carbine.

Stoneking lives now in North Carolina in a town called Swansboro, on VFW Road, but as a teenager he drove a bootlegger's truck in dry Oklahoma, running illegal hooch. He was married to an attractive brunette Wave who sent him sexy photos of herself. He had fought the Japanese all the way across the Pacific, had lost platoon leaders before and, presumably, would lose platoon leaders again. Platoon sergeants knew those were the odds on rifle platoon leaders, those were the ways of the Corps, of the goddamned world.

And, at Thanksgiving of 1951, I would inherit the 3rd Platoon from, and replace, tall and balding Lieutenant Clair "Ed" Flynn, who had also been hit on 749 and was being rotated home (Dog Company was going through platoon leaders pretty fast that season). An unimpressed Sergeant Stoneking regarded me narrowly, a green lieutenant fresh out of Quantico, a skinny, wide-eyed kid, looking about seventeen and puffing a cigar (I imagined it lent me the authority and maturity I sorely lacked). Flynn had led them on Hill 749, the men knew his worth, they knew and trusted Stoneking, and who the hell was I?

For the next months up there on the line, and despite whatever doubts he may have had, Stoney and I shared a small, low, cramped log-and-sandbag bunker, into which we had to crawl, and in which neither of us could stand up, and where we slept head to toe at night in our sleeping bags. Two grown men, sleeping in their clothes (only the boots came off and wet socks exchanged for dry), carbines stacked, revolver worn even in the sleeping bag, grenades piled with the ammo in a corner, our only light a candle, augmented at mealtimes by a Coleman stove or a purple-flamed sterno can. Simply stated, we lived like animals, stinking, itchy, smelly, covered with scabs, minor sores, rashes, and abrasions. Dingleberries? The reek of filthy bodies? Don't ask.

A sergeant we both knew that winter, a good man, maddened by the incessant wind whistling through his firing port, cracked and began firing a BAR inside his own bunker, shooting at rats that weren't there. If the Reds didn't get you, the cold, the wind, the weather, would. The battalion's three rifle companies once went forty-six days without changing clothes or taking a shower, hundreds of healthy young men living in holes in the ground. In our bunker, between my cigars and the smoke of the Coleman stove and the candles we burned, when we spit, the phlegm came out sooty, suggesting lamp black, and you wondered about the state of your lungs. Healthy young men, by civilian standards very young men, hacking and coughing, old and rotten before our time.

And though he may have only tolerated me, as a city boy, I came to enjoy Stoneking's homespun style. We swapped bootleg yarns. How the Baptists and the bootleggers teamed up down in Oklahoma to vote against Repeal, since both the church and the bootleggers relied on Prohibition. He had colorful stories of bootleg drivers, illegal stills, and revenue agents, of shootouts and jail sentences.

I tried to keep up by telling Stoney about Sheepshead Bay, where they brought in the illegal by boat at night or in the fog (there was a John Garfield movie about it, *Out of the Fog*), landing it out of rowboats on the beaches or at the piers along Emmons Avenue. I told him how one of the Lundy brothers, the family that owned the biggest restaurant on the waterfront, was killed in a shootout with the feds. In Sheepshead Bay rum-running wasn't considered a mortal sin, and they named the Lundy Memorial Chapel in our local Protestant church after the late, lamented Lundy.

"I didn't know you were Protestant, Lieutenant."

"I'm not. But I once went there for a wedding. Pete Lundy, who was a Marine during the war, seagoing, aboard a battleship of Task Force 58, came home on leave and married Dorothy Geistweit, prettiest girl on our block."

"Seagoing?" Stoneking shook his head. No seagoing bellhop of a Marine deserved the prettiest girl on the block. Infantrymen think that way.

But it was my story; I'd gone to the wedding. Even though the nuns at Saint Mark's warned us that if a Catholic went to a service in the Protestant church, he'd go to hell.

"And you went?" Stoney asked.

"I did. I was thirteen or fourteen years old and I took the chance."

Stoneking perked up. Maybe this Brady wasn't just another big-city phony or a New York sharper. Anyone who stood up to the Roman Catholic Church to defy nuns and the pope, and was willing to risk hellfire to attend a Protestant service, maybe was okay. And gradually, we grew on each other. The sergeant even showed me some of the sexy pictures his wife sent him.

I learned from Stoney, as I did from the platoon guide, Wooten. He was older than Stoneking, much older than I, and had been up and down the promotion ladder several times, a grizzled career Marine who took a drink, and if you asked about the state of the food supply, Wooten was capable of lines such as: "Lieutenant, we got rations ain't never been eat!"

But it was the cynical Stoneking who informed me of a reputation I'd earned suffering from diarrhea my very first week as platoon leader. There had been shelling through heavy snow one night and probing by the North Korean infantry. So much so that after my third or fourth precarious trip down the icy reverse slope in the dark to the holed and creosoted ammo box that served as a toilet, I simply gave up. I didn't intend being killed maintaining the niceties, and distinguished myself ever after by taking a frightened crap on sheltered ground at the bottom of a trench.

"You know, Lieutenant, when you first got here, they had a nickname for you," Stoney said months later.

"Oh, what was that?"

" 'Shit-Trench Brady.' "

It had been uncharacteristically thoughtful of Stoneking not to share that intimate little disclosure until I'd earned a small measure of respect from the platoon, who might justifiably have been thinking, We're short an officer and they send us this jerk kid?

We would fight in North Korea the rest of that fall and winter and then in defense of Seoul the following year. Captain Chafee would go home, Stoney would be rotated to the rear, green replacements would come in, and I would be promoted but stay on with the battalion, fighting up there on the line. No one laughed at me anymore, no one coined nicknames. I was smoking cigars only because I enjoyed them, not as part of a costume. There was no costume any longer.

And I enjoyed the irony that I was still here, and in combat, while that decidedly hard man, Sergeant Stoneking, was back there in some cushy billet, playing rear-echelon pogue. Please do not inquire of me what "pogue" means; if you are a Marine, you know.

CHAPTER 5

THIS IS ABOUT ARMS, AND THE WAR. BUT MOSTLY ABOUT
THE MEN.

So I'd sworn never to return? I had indeed, and between hardcovers,
which is even more binding than the swearing of oaths.

In the chill midwinter of 2002–3, the rogue regime of Kim Jong
Il was recklessly aprowl. Their country was broke, their people starving, their
only exports drugs, counterfeit U.S. dollars, and armaments. They had little
else to sell, nothing to lose.

Skeptics and his political enemies inquired of Mr. Bush's administration
why he was invading Iraq when North Korea might be even more menacing?
The answer, wise men said, was that Iraq was "doable." Left unsaid, because it
was embarrassing to say so, that maybe North Korea wasn't.

With a presidential election campaign firing up, there were solemn editorials in *The Times,* think pieces in *The Washington Post* and the *L.A. Times,*
cover stories in *Time* and *Newsweek.* Would Bush hang tough on Korea, a
Democrat be more deft? But why was North Korea so dangerous?

Where do I start?

Maybe in a sort of iron triangle of Northeast Asia, a cold, hostile, and
largely empty place of wind and mountains, where there meet within a hundred miles North Korea, the Chinese province of Manchuria, and Russian

Siberia. And with Japan just to the east, a fifteen-minute jet flight or an intermediate ballistic missile downrange.

About 1,300 years ago, there existed in the region a scatter of hunting tribes which called themselves the Kingdom of Koguryo, and occupied a big chunk of what is today north China. In AD 668 Koguryo was conquered by the Tang dynasty, and ever since then the area has been frequently in dispute, what *The New York Times* has called a "Once and Future Kingdom" which "China fears."

The ancient rivalries and hatreds, the ambitions and insecurities of four nations that go back centuries to Genghis Khan, the czars, the shoguns, come together there at a corner of modern North Korea.

You think the Middle East is volatile with its imams and its tribalisms, Sunnis versus Shiites, Kurds versus Arabs, Jews and Palestinians, fanning embers into flame? But the Middle East has no big armies. Communist China has the largest army in the world. The Russians, for all their problems, remain a considerable regional force. The North Koreans have 1.2 million men under arms. (The U.S. Army has 480,000! Throw in our Marine Corps of 175,000 and we are still outnumbered two to one on the ground.)

And just why had I fought there? people asked, their memories short. Couldn't you dodge the draft in those days, pull strings, go to Canada? Why had I, with no family military background or apparent qualifications, joined the Marines? Why had any of us gone to war willingly, even eagerly?

Because we were raised in "hard times" amid slight hopes and slim expectations, and because we came of age during World War II, when our role models, our dads and older brothers and young men down the street or on the next farm, were going to war. And we felt somehow cheated and left out, suspecting we had missed something rare. Maybe that's why we went to Korea, a romantic yen of sorts.

When I finally got to the war I realized that despite boyish illusions, combat wasn't all that romantic. Only the men were that, were truly worth remembering. Men whom I love to this day.

As the poet wrote, "I sing of arms and the man." Shamelessly poaching, so do I. Less about arms than about the men.

As winter wore on into early 2003, the two Koreas were making news and I was a newspaperman. Some in Congress wanted to bring home the troops. In South Korea radical university students and intellectuals wanted us out. At the Pentagon, Donald Rumsfeld hinted of a tactical pullback, distancing ourselves from the DMZ. And you know Rummy—his "hints" usually portend much more. The paranoid North fretted that we might attack them! Nuclear buzz intensified. And the fiftieth anniversary of the 1953 Korean cease-fire was coming up.

You understand better what is going on over there if you look at a famous photo taken from a satellite in outer space during a Korean night some years ago. The South is ablaze with light, the whole country; the North, by contrast, is totally dark except for a flicker at their capital city of Pyongyang and another at Panmunjom, the trucial town. That's all there is; most North Koreans to this day do not have electricity.

I thought there must be a story in all this for *Parade,* a story I could write from Manhattan or East Hampton. With the anniversary impending and talk of a new war, did the magazine want me to write something? A reminiscence? Maybe a phoner with a GI serving up on the DMZ. Or a profile of some old guy who'd actually fought there. A story like that would be easy.

Managing editor Lamar Graham wasn't impressed, said they might want something "bigger." Magazine editors actually talk like that, in terms of "big" pieces. And "bigger" pieces. Weeks passed, and I was called in from East Hampton by the editor in chief, Lee Kravitz. I half suspected what he was about to propose and was conflicted, not sure if I would be depressed. Or elated. Kravitz didn't waste time.

"Would you think about going back to Korea?"

It was still winter and on icy Further Lane I'd already gone on my ass once, fracturing a finger breaking the fall. I remembered the Korean winter all too well, I was still doing outpatient physical therapy, and wasn't I getting just a bit old for this sort of caper? I stalled by saying I'd have to think about it, talk to my daughters, consult my physician.

Stupid of me, but I was tempted. How often do old men get to revisit boyhood?

We spoke again and I leveled with Kravitz. I didn't want to interview politicians or marvel at the Korean "economic miracle" or do a "big-picture" overview. But if I could write the piece as an old soldier going back, sure. I'd consider giving it a shot. There was little significant Marine presence over there anymore, so I lacked leverage. Could *Parade* sweet-talk the Army into getting me back to the places where I'd fought? Hill 749 in the mountains of North Korea? The low sandstone hills masking Seoul where we fought the Chinese? Could I hang with and interview the young GIs holding those same positions today?

Kravitz liked the idea. "Write it with the novelist's eye, write what you feel, what you think, what you remember."

When the editor is saying yes to every one of your suggestions, it's difficult to say no. Needing a sounding board, I phoned Pierce Power.

Pierce is a lawyer who plays golf half the year on Long Island and the other half in Florida. But we were at Regis High School and then Manhattan College together, enlisted in the Marine Corps the same day, and fought as rifle platoon leaders. In the assault on Hill 749, it was Pierce's platoon of the 1st Marines that got to the top. Getting up there Pierce was wounded—on his birthday, September 13—and for Marines of our time, a crappy little ridgeline became something of a holy place.

"I might be going back to Hill 749, Pierce. What do you think?"

If you've gone to war with a guy, you can speak candidly. Pierce did.

"I think you're nuts," he gleefully informed me.

He was right, of course, but as Gerry Byrne, a Marine lieutenant in Vietnam and longtime publisher of *Variety*, likes to say, "all Marines are crazy."

Personally, I prefer "high-spirited" or "colorful" to "nuts" and "crazy," but I'm not one to quibble with lawyers like Pierce or with a publisher who "helmed" *Variety* for ten "boffo" years.

And doesn't every Marine have a tale to tell?

At Camp Pendleton in December of 2000, the Corps marked the fiftieth anniversary of the epic fighting march by the 1st Marine Division from the Chosin Reservoir to the sea through twelve divisions of Chinese regulars.

"The Chosin Few," the Marines who fought that battle, are fierce and troublesome men held in considerable esteem by the rest of us.

They held the ceremonies on the Camp Pendleton football field with maybe five thousand of "the Few" up in the bleachers, and because I'd written a novel about their fight, I was the speaker. But preceding me on the program there were far more celebrated Marine figures: General Jim Jones, commandant of the Marine Corps; three winners of the Medal of Honor; the commanding general of the British Royal Marine Commandos; a chaplain who prayed over us; and the event's MC, Colonel Jerry Coleman, a Marine fighter pilot in two wars (like his pal Ted Williams) who had played second base for the Yankees. Everyone had mustered but Montezuma himself.

Knowing I was outgunned, I contented myself with slandering the strategy and reputation of General Douglas MacArthur for about ten minutes and sat down, to enormous applause. Marines disliked MacArthur and loved hearing him trashed. The commandant pumped my hand. Even the British general wagged his swagger stick jauntily in my direction. And the chaplain murmured a pious blessing. The late MacArthur, who spoke directly to the deities, would not have been pleased.

That evening, mustering at the bar of a San Diego hotel, I fell in with a salty NCO of the Chosin Few.

"You remember," he began over a drink, "how we were always either constipated or had the runs?"

It was typical of a Chosin Few to start off in medias res with a story about bowel movements, and I agreed this was so.

"Coming down from the reservoir one of the boys hadn't taken a crap for maybe four days," he said. "Two hundred thousand Chinamen were just behind us and coming fast. The trail was pinching out, we were tired, and this boy just couldn't shit."

I bought us another round and the NCO went on.

When the inevitable finally happened, along a snowy mountain trail, the young Marine called out in exultation, drawing the usual, nuanced Marine witticisms: "Kill that thing! Kill it! The son of a bitch is still moving!"

The sergeant hustled up to get his men back on the march, but found himself staring. Fresh and unbroken, the turd just lay there on the snow, steam rising.

"Hell of a thing, ain't it, Sarge?" men murmured reverentially.

"Yes, it is," said the sergeant, not easily impressed.

Pleased at the attention, the young man modestly began policing the area, scuffing snow over his production, when the sergeant grabbed him.

"What you doing, boy? Don't nobody cover that thing up, you hear me? The Chinese will be coming along here inside of an hour, maybe less."

"Yes, Sergeant?"

"And they see that there turd lying there"—he paused a perceptible beat— "they'll think we're giants!"

So, while recognizing at my age it was "crazy" to do so, and that I was probably "nuts," I told the editor that I'd take the assignment; I'd go back to Korea. What I didn't tell him was that in ways, I missed the war. Never again would I live as completely on the edge, and come out the other side alive and almost swaggering. I'm not a great one for introspection, pondering the essential meaning of life. But not long before, I'd been paralyzed, and now along came this gloriously cockeyed opportunity, to go again where I'd gone at twenty-three.

And which of us wouldn't seize the day?

My doctor nodded approval and said he'd find out what shots I needed. My daughters voted yes, Fiona with reluctant and loving concern, Susan (who had three small children and might have considered Korea a break) asking if she could go along.

There would be the usual visa and passport complications (where was Senator D'Amato when you needed a pol to cut through the red tape?), e-mails back and forth with the Pentagon and with U.S. Army officers in Korea, plane reservations to be made. These turned out to be anything but routine, the military buildup around Iraq diverting some commercial jets to troop-ferrying duties. If I reached Seoul and the Persian Gulf exploded, could I get home? To complicate matters, SARS had broken out in Asia and quarantines loomed.

Then there was Hill 749, which I wanted to see again. But the Pentagon didn't want "civilians" going up there. They couldn't take responsibility. The hell! I'd been there during a shooting war. A Marine Corps general, Drew Davis, went down the hall and spoke to another general, an Army colleague. Reluctant at first, now I was eager to go, and impatient. But not before Lee Kravitz, reading the ominous e-mails, sent me a handwritten note warning he wasn't willing to put me in harm's way.

Oh, for God's sake!

The editor had also lined up a companion. I would be retracing a wartime journey, revisiting a Brideshead of my own, accompanied by a contemporary, though cannier, Hooper, the photographer Eddie Adams, a strange and talented man, impatient, angry and profane, who won his Pulitzer for one of the most famous war photos ever taken. You remember it, the Associated Press shot he'd made on a Saigon sidewalk as a South Vietnamese officer blew away the head of a captured Vietcong.

With Eddie, of course, nothing was simple. He had a shot lined up, for which he'd had to rent a swimming pool in Southern California in which to pose Arnold Schwarzenegger swimming with a yellow rubber duckie. I canceled a family ski trip to Vermont and, while waiting for Adams to clear his dance card, did a little research. In the South, great cities had sprung up, and freeways supplanted ox-cart tracks through the rice paddies; desolate empty spaces given way to the twenty-first-century traffic jam, and the rivers were bridged by suspension steel and not the inflated rubber pontoons on which I'd crossed. But behind the barbed wire, the old hatreds seething, what would we find in the North? There was little informed data. North Korea, where the DMZ meandered miles above the Thirty-eighth Parallel, remained an enigma.

I could imagine the mountains, where snow would still drift, the ridges still rise as steeply out of the narrow valleys through which the mountain streams rush, and the gunmen of each side roam and contend. The North would remain as bleak and chill as I recalled it, ominous and full of menace. While the same wind blew out of Siberia, moaning.

Not, I agree, the most propitious place for fighting a war. Or for falling in love. But it had happened. It was the romantic in me, I suppose, the twenty-three-year-old naïf in an alien place. Quite possibly, it hadn't even been true love; I had simply been hoping to be found worthy of the Corps, and not at all sure the Marines loved me back.

That was then. What was my motivation today?

An irresistible reporting assignment? The damn fool caperings of two old soldiers on a pass? Or something deeper, the inexplicable pull, perhaps, of a war Adams and I fought there? Maybe this was all perversity on my part, a show of defiance, because I'd had the stroke and might have died, and that was why I decided to go back. Or were we going simply because, in Korea, I once fell in love?

Couldn't tell Eddie that, could I?

CHAPTER 6

Kurt Vonnegut once wrote of one of my books, overgenerously to
be sure, "The Korean War now has its own *Iliad*."

An English major, giddy at such praise, I tend to go all literary,
thinking of our trip as a blend of James Michener and Geoffrey Chaucer,
with a dollop of Kipling thrown in. You know, the Canterbury pilgrims meet
Tales of the South Pacific, with regimental beastie Gunga Din providing inci-
dental music and the bugle calls.

Ours was to be a serious affair, but with an undeniably jaunty element of
lark, the suggestion of "gentlemen-rankers out on the spree."

Perhaps it had been like that, too, for pilgrims on the fourteenth-century
road to Canterbury Cathedral: there was a solemn, even saintly, purpose to
their trip, just as there was purpose to our assignment, but along the route,
there might be opportunity for a colorful yarn and a glass before the tavern's
fire, a game of chance, a little randy work with a lusty serving wench.

Consider the ironies. Here were a couple of old gyrenes who'd fought
there, heading back to Korea to interview today's GIs. Adams, as a young Marine combat photographer in 1953 when the truce took effect, had, on assignment, actually photographed the DMZ from one end of the country to the

other, all 155 miles of it, a monthlong project. On that same line I'd fought for months as an infantryman. Our return to the DMZ was the assignment.

But not exactly the story I meant to write.

That story waited for me up on the obscure and barren ridgelines and hillsides on which I'd fought. My hope was to find a young Army rifle platoon leader, about the age I was when I was there, and to write about him and his men while Eddie photographed them on the job. Fifty years had gone by, and I wanted to see if the high ground had changed. Find out, too, how the young men-at-arms had changed. I hoped to draw conclusions, make comparisons. Could the Pentagon find me such a guy, a twenty-three-year old infantry lieutenant? E-mails were sent, ranking officers hemmed and hawed. I don't mean to read too much into the assignment. It was what it was, a magazine job. But one with very personal aspects.

One of those ridges, Hill 749, was thirty or forty miles above the Thirty-eighth Parallel. People seemed dubious about getting us that far north. Do you guys want to get killed? Still worse, create an international incident? Officials blathered on.

During the Iraq campaign, a good deal would be written, much of it rubbish, about the changing nature of war correspondence. Some of the press agentry from the networks and print media seemed at times to suggest their embedded correspondents were fighting the battle as well as reporting it. Despite the inarguable courage and resource of reporters covering Iraq, or any war, soldiers do the fighting; reporters write or broadcast about it.

I know plenty of professional and quite wonderful journalists, some of them friends, a few close friends. But only a handful (David Douglas Duncan, Walter Anderson, Jim Webb, Jack Jacobs, and Adams himself, among them) have ever fought a war, have ever tried to kill a man. Which was part of what made Adams's and my assignment different. Because we had fought. There was nothing heroic about our trip; war nerves, after all, weren't a shooting war. And it never occurred to Adams or me that we were at risk. War correspondents get killed by accident. Soldiers die because that is the work they do, killing and being killed.

This is a major difference in job descriptions.

Our road to JFK was sinuous and exasperating. The usual red tape, of course, having to deal with the Korean authorities as well as the American. Did a reporter need a tourist visa or a business visa? I had little patience for consular waiting rooms. A First Lieutenant James Gleason was proposed to us as the platoon leader I'd asked to meet and hang out with. Were there any options? No. Was this Gleason the Army's programmed poster boy, the one carefully tutored junior officer they trotted out, the one they could let the press get at? Growing antsy over delays, I started to identify with Ronald Colman in the early reels of *Lost Horizon,* firing his revolver and herding missionaries and Englishwomen into that old DC-3 and off as rioters storm the tarmac. What Shangri-la awaits us? I wondered.

In Manhattan, sophisticated eyebrows were raised. Do Brady and Adams have any notion of just what they are doing? Do you realize how old those two guys are? Is this some publicity stunt whipped up by *Parade?*

I was fed up with bureaucrats, with red tape, with e-mail. The latest query from Seoul, would Adams and I agree to have a U.S. Army reporter from the division newspaper go along? One guy? Okay, then. Could South Korean reporters come along? A television crew? Hell no. We didn't want an entourage. I began telling myself I didn't need this crap.

Adams had even less patience. When I called to report on the latest, niggling roadblock, he'd had enough. Furious and profane, he was speaking for both of us when he demanded: "You really want to make this effing trip?"

"Yes," I said. "They've got me so pissed off, yes, I really want to do it."

"Okay, Lieutenant," said Eddie, the old sergeant. "Then let's go! Just effing go!"

So on March 26 we took off for Korea. And since I was still a working newspaperman, I left behind a column, written just before the second Iraq war began: "This is being written in the final hours of peace. I do not like this war. Our soldiers are so good, our power such, that this may be a short and happy war. But I think it is the wrong war in the wrong place at decidedly the wrong time. A war that promises a hard and bitter peace."

I wish I'd been wrong, but I'm glad I wrote it.

The Korean Air 747 to Inchon left New York at noon on a cold, clear day for the fourteen-hour flight through fourteen time zones. So we were forever chasing the sun, and just about keeping pace, and were in brilliant daylight all the way. The flight was almost full, lots of businessmen, but Adams and I were topside, so each of us had a row to himself. A Korean business type sat next to me and tried to practice his English, but I gave him scant encouragement and he moved. I'm known to be grouchy that way, wanting to be left alone. As for Eddie, balding (so sparse that he may have known each hair by name) but for a long, stringy white ponytail, I let him be. He was anything but soft and cuddly, impatient with me at the best of times, and I saw no need to rile him on airplanes.

On the other side of the world American Marines and paras, with their embedded press, were rolling through a falling-apart Iraqi army and driving hard on Baghdad.

CHAPTER 7

That plane ride in March of 2003 really began halfway through the last century. The cold war was on, East versus West, this country versus the Soviet Union, Congress had reinstituted the military draft, and I'd joined the Marine Corps during my sophomore year at Manhattan College.

Until a shooting war came along, the 1950s were going to be maybe the best time there ever was in America. Optimism was chronic; you couldn't avoid it. Everything was possible, and we twenty-year-olds were all going to live to see the year 2000.

The country was big and booming and at peace and unless the Russkies went bonkers, there would never again be another world war. Food and clothes and rents were cheap and new jobs were hiring. The first veterans on the GI Bill were graduating from college and Mr. Levitt was building dandy, affordable little houses for them, wall-to-wall carpeting, with washers and dryers thrown in. The girls were prettier and the Hollywood flicks better, *South Pacific* was going to run forever on Broadway, and you could hum the songs on *Your Hit Parade*. In the White House a bow-tied Harry Truman played show tunes while his wife, Bess, beamed as leggy Betty Bacall lounged on the president's piano. New cars rolled out of Detroit (the Japanese and Germans were only just starting to make automobiles again), sleeker and faster than ever, and they were even getting the bugs out of the new automatic transmission. A factory-fresh Ford convertible cost about two grand. Some of the neighbors had seven-inch black-and-white Dumont televisions, and if there were a big fight or an important ball game, you might be invited over. Everyone liked Ike and there was talk he might run for president. If they could only figure out if he was a Democrat or a Republican.

Nineteen fifty was a swell year. And when I graduated from college early that June, I bought myself (for 350 bucks) a beat-up old 1939 Buick convertible, the model with the two-part windshield that Bogey drove around Paris in *Casablanca* with Ingrid Bergman. I was looking for my Bergman, and life was going to be roses all the way.

Instead, that same June, the Korean War happened.

By profession, being a newspaperman and a onetime Marine, I am supposed to be pragmatic and cold-eyed, a skeptic and, at bottom, a sensible sort of fellow. In actuality, I am a romantic of the worst sort, given to unrealistic dreams, the saving of old letters, the pressing of memory between the pages of favorite books. Maybe I'd been waiting for a war of my own, waiting for a Korea.

In its way, Korea would be the first hot battle of the cold war. An "Iron Curtain" (Churchill's phrase) had slammed down across Europe, Mao and his Reds were booting Henry Luce's poster boy, Chiang Kai-shek, out of mainland China, the Berlin blockade had thrown a scare into Washington (Stalin, that bastard, was still alive). In America, eighteen-year-olds like me went looking for legal ways to dodge the draft (no collegian wanted to peel potatoes at Fort Dix). So in early 1948 I enlisted in a reserve officer candidate program, spending college summers in uniform and cleverly insulating myself from the draft, as a flirtation began, tentative and unsure, between me and the Marines. I can assure you it was hardly love at first sight.

And then, suddenly, on another Asian Sunday, June 25 of 1950, almost nine years after Pearl Harbor, the Soviet-backed North Koreans invaded our client South Korean state; we were again a nation at war.

Until the shooting started, I had been a lousy peacetime Marine. All that saluting and white-glove inspections and standing at attention at Quantico, Virginia, where the Marines train their future officers in a super boot camp. Where, once commissioned, they shove you into a military finishing school they call the Basic School, polish to a high shine, and turn you loose on innocent and unsuspecting enemies abroad. Or so went the theory.

To a kid like me, there was an irresistible "Charge of the Light Brigade" glamour to the Marine Corps, one of dashing lives and glorious battlefield deaths (that death might hurt rarely occurs to the young). Instead, the between-the-wars Corps was, though few would say so, stupid and boring. I'd expected more out of the Marines, or my boyish, Hollywood version, and like all young men, I was impatient.

My disillusionment had nothing to do with the men, the future lieutenants with whom I served. We ranged from raffish to sophisticated, and even from the very first, raw weeks in the late forties, were a sort of roll call of American college boys ranging from preppy Ivy Leaguers, to farm state kids (known invariably as "shitkickers"), to Southern Californian surfers and land grant college students, to big-city Catholic school dayhops like me. Just imagine all these educated (well, some of us!) young boys off the college campus, with its free and easy ways, suddenly harnessed into the taut and disciplined structure of the gloriously tradition-bound and legendary Corps.

During those college summers at Quantico, we played at being Marines, undergraduates pledging a cool fraternity, going out for the varsity. But once Korea began, as newly commissioned officers training for combat in a wartime Corps, and joined by an influx of "real" Marines, World War II reserve officers called back for a Quantico refresher, we came together in the Basic School, the boys from the campuses, and our slightly older brothers in arms. And what a powerful kinetic mass was produced by this unexpected melding, shortly and thrillingly to be released! We were the men who would fight the Korean War, a "best and the brightest" of that pre-Halberstam era. Intelligent young men eager to serve, to fight, to command, to defeat an enemy in combat, and to have some fun doing it. Even the few like me wondering privately if we were good enough, if we really belonged.

In Virginia where we trained, the Marine Corps still smacked of Dixie, and maybe half of us were southerners. In my time, there were no black platoon-leader candidates or black lieutenants. No black officers I ever saw, a Truman-ordered military integration progressing sluggishly. And for all of what we considered our racially enlightened and superior ways, we Yankees lacked their songs, had to admit that when it came to music, we weren't in a league with our southerners, that they were just singing fools. And in the end, their songs became ours. Maybe it would be the last American war where guys sang.

The North Carolinians sang, and we enthusiastically pitched in, and loud:

> *I'm a tarheel born*
> *And a tarheel bred*
> *And when I die*
> *I'll be a tarheel dead.*

The boys from Georgia Tech taught us every verse of their great drinking song:

> *Like all good jolly fellows*
> *I drink my whisky clear*
> *I'm a Rambling Wreck from Georgia Tech*
> *And a helluva engineer.*

Even the tin-eared among us, like me, essayed close harmony to some of the old, sweet, and politically incorrect songs of antebellum Dixie:

> *In the evening by the moonlight*
> *You can hear the banjos ringing*
> *In the evening by the moonlight*
> *You can hear the darkies singing.*

Further redolent of the Old South, there were Confederate flags every-where. Even some of us empty-headed Yankees tied one to the car antenna, unaware of the symbolism and thinking it was cool. Later, of course, we came to understand it was anything but, and the Rebel battle flags were stowed with old fielder's mitts and wooden tennis racquets in dusty closets, and forgotten.

That was hardly all that would change with Korea.

College days and pranks, Rebel flags and fight songs and close harmony were put behind us. Those second lieutenants' commissions and gold bars we sported, but were never going to have to do anything about? Suddenly, we did. Thousands of reserves (even Teddy Ballgame, Ted Williams of the Red Sox) were called up, and it turned out a reserve commission carried obligations beyond impressing girls and the neighborhood guys. Suddenly we were taking classes with postgraduate scholars, with the hard men who had fought on Iwo, on Okinawa, on Saipan, who'd waded the bloody lagoon at Tarawa.

We hung on their war stories, and I believe they were a bit startled and unsettled by our sheer, youthful energy.

And then, home from Korea to take over our instruction, came the first of the 1st Marine Division officers, from the Inchon invasion and the epic battle of the Chosin Reservoir. And life grew serious, as tough, combat-hard men like Ike Fenton came among us.

Ike was something. Francis I. Fenton, a regular and a captain, had been on the cover of *Life* magazine, fighting at the Pusan Perimeter (where he lost dead or wounded half the 190 men in his rifle company), his story chronicled in words and photos by the great David Douglas Duncan. Ike's Marine brother had been killed on Okinawa during the Pacific war, where their dad, a Marine brigadier general, also fought. There is a memorable photo of General Fenton kneeling in prayer beside a stretcher, on which lies the body of his boy Michael. So Francis I. "Ike" Fenton had the bloodlines, was all Marine, all fighter, though with an unexpected wit and sense of the absurd. He and his fellow veterans back from the division didn't lecture at us from a detached, academic distance but told us about what life was really like, "up on the line" in combat, in an actual war.

To a brash, untried, and newly minted second lieutenant like me, Ike was the dashing heroic role model I wanted; he was also the bracing splash of reality I needed. Consider the gist of a typical Ike lecture, pithy, sensible, pragmatic:

War doesn't work a forty-hour week. You'll fight all night and then fight all the next day. You never get enough sleep. So let your men "crap out" whenever they can. That goes for you, too. The North Koreans are good soldiers. A lot of their officers and NCOs fought in the Soviet army against the Nazis; that was the major leagues. The food is lousy, the meals irregular; get your folks to send you One A Day brand vitamins every thirty days. Stuff toilet tissue into every pocket because you'll always have the runs. Carry a couple of pencil stubs; ink runs in the rain, pencil lead doesn't. It's always dark or raining and you have to read maps, write messages, find a spot to take a crap; pack a rubber-encased hardware-store flashlight. Carry a nail clipper in every pocket; if a nail gets too long and is torn off, you'll be fighting one-handed. Lug a good pocketknife. Tape your dog tags together so they don't jangle and give you away at night. Change your socks every day so your feet don't freeze or blister, and don't concern yourself about urine-soaked or shit-caked underwear: in combat everyone stinks, the dead worst of all.

But they don't care about it anymore.

Ike Fenton's talks were precise, unimpressed; they made cold sense, and came from a man who had actually been there, had fought and defeated the North Koreans. At Waller Hall, the officers' club, where an Old Forrester and branch water or a Tom Collins cost twenty-five cents, the men home from Korea did a little drinking. A few, more than a little. I stood there, a boy nursing a Coke, and watched them. And for the first time I heard the phrase "a thousand-yard stare." You saw that stare on some of the men at Waller Hall.

And you wondered what such a man had seen over there; what he was still seeing. It was from those men that the kids among us, like me, began to learn how to become rifle platoon leaders.

That "how" is significant. In the Marine Corps they drill into you a very simple system, starting at the bottom with the nine four-man fire teams in a platoon. No one man really controls those nine teams in combat; you can't. Each fire team leader controls his three men, each squad leader keeps an eye on his three fire team leaders, the platoon leader watches over his three squad leaders, and this is how a Marine rifle platoon goes into a firefight. Each one of us has only three other Marines to command. Simple and effective. But if you screw up, the Marine Corps is merciless. It will sack an incompetent or lazy or gutless rifle platoon leader instantly. Those forty-five men of his deserve the best leadership possible; the Marine Corps sees to it that they get it from their platoon leaders, at whatever cost.

No one has ever properly defined the Marine Corps. I've written of it as a sort of violent priesthood. Others speak of warrior monks. Some think of it as a professional society like the AMA or the bar association. In some ways it resembles the Catholic Church or the Old Confederacy, certain of the righteousness of its cause, unforgiving in its zeal. The more literal characterization is as an elite corps fighting the country's wars with a lethal ferocity, a professional competence. The historical-minded return for a definition to its founding by the Continental Congress as "soldiers of the sea." Cynical enlisted men call it "the Crotch." In ways it is as quaint and dashing (and some feel as anachronistic) as the Foreign Legion; every definition falls annoyingly short of definitive.

Ironically, it was in the midsummer of 2003 that the United States Army (hardly fond of the Marines) may have come up with something close.

It was then that a committee of generals, doing a Pentagon postmortem on the Iraq butchery still being waged months after the "official" end of hostilities, labored and brought forth a startling new idea.

"Every soldier a rifleman!"

The Iraq guerrilla experience, where truck drivers and cooks and electronics specialists, even young women soldiers like Jessica Lynch, found themselves ambushed, cut off, battling for their lives in firefights, had convinced the generals.

Too many of these young GIs, unexpectedly in combat, couldn't fire a weapon, couldn't even load one, hadn't the vaguest idea of how to defend themselves, to fight back. Their exotic specialties, at which they were very good, had allowed insufficient time for elementary-school weapons training. From this, the Army generals concluded with stunning insight, "We should be more like the Marine Corps. We ought to teach our soldiers how to shoot."

Teach soldiers how to shoot?

Not even the apostle Paul, struck from his horse on the Damascus Road, had experienced such a startling epiphany.

CHAPTER 8

THIS IS WHERE I BELONG, WHAT I WAS MEANT TO BE.

On my first full day as a Marine in the peacetime summer of 1948, a New York kid dropped into a milieu as alien as the Gobi's, I was issued a rifle. It was the first killing weapon I'd ever touched.

It was a Garand M1, a gas-operated, clip-fed, air-cooled, semiautomatic shoulder weapon. It weighed 9.5 pounds, carried eight cartridges in the clip, had an effective range of 600 yards, and a maximum range of up to 5,500 yards, about three miles. The *Guidebook for Marines* urges the young Marine, "Treat it well. Your life and the lives of your buddies may depend on the way you use it." This particular M1, when the Japanese war ended three years before, had been packed in a heavy protective grease called cosmolene, had been in the gunk ever since. The rifle was slammed into my hands, I was ordered to memorize the serial number, and we were trotted out behind the Quantico barracks to a sun-baked concrete alleyway to clean up our newly issued M1s, polish them to a high shine.

We wore boondockers (field shoes) and skivvies (why get grease on a clean set of fatigues?), and, both arms aching from the morning's half dozen shots, the sun beating down, we laboriously fieldstripped ("What's that mean, Sergeant? And where do I start?") our weapons and cleaned out the grease, to the cheerful, affectionate patter of affable DIs ("get effing going on that there weapon, boy!") and a vulgar little ditty intended to educate us into the nomenclature of weapons (a rifle was always a rifle or a weapon, never a "gun"):

This is my rifle
This is my gun [a grabbing of the crotch],
With each I shoot
With this [more crotch-grabbing] I have fun.

In barracks each man was issued a combination lock and a short length of chain used to secure the weapon lengthwise under the bed by locking it to the steel framework of the bunk. If you dropped a rifle, you slept with it that night, with the chamber locked open so that if you rolled over and disturbed it in your sleep, it could slam shut, maybe catching your testicles or another sensitive portion of your anatomy in its powerful steel grip. It was one of the terrors of a Marine boot camp for officer candidates and recruits both.

And then after a month, they turned us loose on the rifle range.

Until then my Marine Corps career had been one of sullen distaste for dawn, for being shouted at and cursed, for saluting, counting off, and obeying idiotic orders mindlessly. Even our weapons training seemed dull and sophomoric, snapping in with unloaded rifles, shooting practice at very short range with .22s. Now, on the firing range, with a loaded M1 in his hands for the first time, a nineteen-year old college sophomore stopped feeling misused and sorry for himself, and things began to change, to fall logically into place.

But maybe you've fired the range, you know how it is there. The purposeful bustle of the NCOs preparing the day's shoot and calculating the windage, the men marching out just after dawn, rifles slung, platoon by platoon, from the redbrick college-campus-looking dormitories, the sense we were finally going to do something constructive.

At the range in the predawn the sergeants had already lighted the smudge pots where we blackened our sights. I remember the smell and the sound of it: the smudge pots, the smoke in the morning air, the whiff of gunpowder and reek of the sheepskin shooting jackets, the furious shouts of the range sergeants, the sharp, instant crack of a round fired from a good rifle. The shooting itself, the businesslike jolt of the M1 rifle against a young Marine's padded shoulder, the whining song of a ricochet, the pure, animal elation of being able to put a round at three hundred yards, or even at five hundred, into the middle of a bull's-eye. And do it over and over and over again.

I had 20/15 eyesight and the doctors told us Ted Williams was 20/10, so 20/15 wasn't too shabby, and building on good eyes, the instructors were able to cobble a city boy into a sharpshooter, something even I considered little short of alchemy.

I loved it all, including what most considered drudge work, pulling targets in the butts while others fired, hearing the shots ripping through the cloth-and-paper targets a few feet above your head, the odd ricochet off the steel frame of the targets, the misshapen bullet falling at your feet, too hot to pick up, or whining off spinning into the distance. I liked hoisting a circular marker to signal a hit, joyously waving the red flag for a complete miss, the derisive "Maggie's drawers," even liked the gunnery sheds where they marched us after a shoot, where we swabbed out our rifles in steaming water and then dried with the small cotton patches and oiled them, the smell of the steam and the oil, the slithering metallic rasp of the ramrods scouring out the grooved, rifled barrels, the easy chat and banter, the macho boasting about hits scored, the coarse joshing of men who had shot badly.

It was the second week of live firing exercises and we were firing for the record (scores would go down in our service record books: marksman, sharp-shooter, expert). We'd just finished off a series of shots from the various positions, kneeling, sitting, then prone, and I'd pumped shot after shot into the black. That was the bull's-eye. And from a sun-weathered range NCO behind me watching my gunnery from under the brim of a campaign hat, came a low, appreciative growl.

"That's well."

The standard but ungrammatical Marine Corps phrasing invariably annoyed the English major in me, but now for the first time I stopped acting like a sophomore, took the compliment with a tangible satisfaction. And having been raised on the tales of James Fenimore Cooper, I privately began to think of myself in terms of Natty Bumppo, "the Deerslayer," and blood brother to Uncas and Chingachgook, the last of the Mohicans.

That was the beginning.

Two years later, in 1951, my third year at Quantico, I was a second lieutenant, no longer playing at being a Marine, the college summers of the Platoon Leaders Class fading into memory. The country was at war, we would soon be going to it, and in the Basic School attitudes had changed. Once more, we were on the rifle range, marksmanship having become second nature, shooting once more for the record.

We were firing a final set from the standing position. And I stood there with a lightly oiled and loaded M1 rifle, warm from the firing, cradled easily in my hands, looking left and right at a long straggle of other young men with rifles, all of us armed and ready, sporting those salty, smelly leather-padded sheepskin shooting jackets. Not all the marksmen were college kids now; some were old salts, hard men who had shot it out with "the damned Japs." I wasn't yet quite one with them, but I was holding my own, putting rounds into the black. College boys didn't put it into the black; Marines did. The blue-gray smoke and acrid smell of earlier volleys still hung on the morning air, after we'd fired and some of us had scored well, and without overanalyzing or thinking about it too hard, the whole thing felt right, felt natural. No more doubts or hesitations about the Marines, about why I was here. Startling even myself, I thought: Yes, I really am a part of this. This is where I belong. This is what I was meant to be.

I recognized infatuation for what it was. There was plenty about the Marine Corps that still drove me nuts. But it was on the rifle range where love first called, where I started to feel a part of the Corps, the genuine, the wartime Marines.

As an effete city boy who'd never even owned a Daisy BB gun, I can only suggest that having been surrounded for three years by shitkickers, cowboys, good old Southerners and Western kids who'd been firing rifles and shotguns from boyhood had somehow rubbed off. As I hoped Marine heroism also would.

We fired the light and the heavy machine guns, bazookas and mortars, those crappy carbines almost no one liked, the .45 automatic that couldn't hit anything, the wonderful Browning automatic rifle, the BAR, so steady on its bipod that a good shot could put a bullet through a man's head at a thousand yards. If you could see a man, you could kill him, that's how good the BAR was. But it was the M1 rifle, the Garand, that we loved. Every Marine, at bottom, is a rifleman; that's where it starts. Maybe that's where it ends.

Eventually and essentially, of course, it would be combat, the genuine stuff, that would put an end to youthful flirtation, would consecrate the religious vows between me and the Corps. War itself that would close the deal.

CHAPTER 9

And then, in the autumn of 1951, where the rest of America ends, California shouldered its brawny way into my affair of the heart. I'd never seen California until the Marines sent me there en route to Korea as a replacement. As what the troops amusingly called "fresh meat."

It was a funny sort of war I was going to, not ha-ha funny, of course, but strange. Nowhere near as big or significant as World War II, as bloody as Vietnam, but not as long-lasting, or as bitterly divisive here at home. Since it fell between the "Big War" and Vietnam, it tended to get lost. Korea didn't inspire the best love songs ever written, as World War II had done; it didn't even have a protest song, as Vietnam did. We had no Bob Dylan. All we ended up having was *M*A*S*H*, and that was really Bob Altman and Ring Lardner Jr.'s allegorical take on Vietnam.

And it was mainly the white American middle class that fought the Korean War. Almost no one dodged the draft. The Ivy League and the men of Cal Berkeley joined up.

Marines still wore those old-fashioned yellow canvas leggings, still fired some weapons, like the Springfield rifle our snipers used, the .45 pistol, and the .30 caliber heavy machine gun, that dated back to the First World War or before. There were, as I mentioned, no black officers (at Quantico, a mere thirty-five miles from the White House and the Lincoln Memorial, black Marines and their families and girlfriends were still sent to sit upstairs at the base movie house). No one—well, maybe the occasional medic on morphine—did drugs. Officers weren't fragged. The French were on our side. The Russians were the bad guys. And we assumed it was Russkies who flew the enemy jets, fired the enemy's more sophisticated big guns. The Chinese regulars, hundreds of thousands of them, walked across Manchuria to the war, as if the internal combustion engine had never been invented. South Africa was still largely governed from London, and the dashing Boer fighter pilots, with their funny names, sounded Klaxon horns when they dove on the Reds. The Belgian detachment of Flemings and Walloons spoke two languages. The Aussies wore those funny, lopsided campaign hats, and sang "Waltzing Matilda," verse after verse. The Greeks and the Turks both fought gallantly, but had to be kept apart lest they fight each other. The Irish lent a hand, in the form of the Ulster Regiment. The Brits in summer wore shorts like Monty's men in the desert fighting Rommel, and had an endless supply of vulgar songs, my own favorite being the one about

> *Three Old Ladies*
> *Locked in a lavatory.*
> *They were there*
> *from Monday to Saturday.*

As I say, a funny war that was, in weird ways, possible to enjoy.

A week after Bobby Thomson hit his home run against the Dodgers, I flew west out of New York for L.A. I was to report in at Camp Pendleton to FMF PAC, Fleet Marine Force Pacific, clutching orders to what they called, in a rare official poetry, "duty beyond the seas," in the 1st Marine Division fighting in Korea. And, having a few days of leave remaining, and like the bumptious young Hooper unexpectedly exposed to Eden, I decided to have a snoop around.

Being ignorant of Los Angeles (where some were still sounding the hard *g* in Angeles, as "AN-guh-less") and touchingly innocent, I permitted the cabbie from the airport to recommend a clean but dull commercial hotel in the absolutely wrong part of town, the seedy downtown, near city hall and the *L.A. Times* building, and being fresh out of college, I thought I might stroll over in the bright, fresh October morning to UCLA and look at a California campus. The sort of jaunt you take routinely in Manhattan when walking from midtown down to Greenwich Village and the NYU campus or uptown to Morningside Heights and Columbia University. But when I asked an L.A. cop for directions, he regarded me as if I were mentally defective. Things were different out here, he said, the distances! UCLA was in Westwood, perhaps twenty miles west of downtown, and I'd best take a city bus.

I spent the hour's ride staring out at Beverly Hills and Hollywood and Sunset Boulevard, looking at those great, tailored emperor palms and the whisper of luxurious homes behind their discreet hedges, at sleek, tanned people in open cars, hoping to see a movie star or possibly a great director in his beret and ascot, Howard Hawks, Cecil B. DeMille, Capra, someone like that.

The lovely green-grassed and palm-treed UCLA campus with its vaguely hacienda-type architecture was a stunner. How far I'd come from that small redbrick and ivy-covered but hardly Ivy League school of mine in Riverdale. For sightseeing, I was dressed not in uniform but in khaki trousers, a Brooks Brothers button-down blue Oxford shirt, and white bucks. I was suntanned from Quantico, clean-shaven with a crew cut, and as I strolled about UCLA, it occurred to me that while all the girls seemed to have been sent over by central casting, I looked pretty much like these boys, and they all looked like me. Except that I was pulling on an incongruous cigar. And that while those boys were going to class, I was going to the war.

Funny, I didn't feel put upon or resentful, just a touch wistful with a vague sense of loss. That maybe I never would get to say hello to, never mind sleep with, a golden girl.

The morning train rolled south out of Union Station for Oceanside and Camp Pendleton on the day I had to report, and I got a window seat, enjoying a fresh and wonderful country, the great Pacific rollers coming up on the golden beaches to the right, the low brown hills of the sprawling Irvine Ranch and the working oil wells of Long Beach to my left, and beyond them in the distance, snowy mountains against the sky. I was liking California better with each passing hour despite the callous disinterest of their golden girls! And when I reported in at Pendleton, I even liked the sentries saluting smartly at the main gate, the exciting wartime bustle of the base, the look of the great, sprawling camp, the dark green trucks hurrying past, the detachments marching in cadence, the big new barnlike wooden barracks of a suddenly expanding wartime Marine Corps, smelling sweetly of freshly sawed wood, in which we were quartered for our last month in the States. And starting the next morning at dawn, I would be commanding troops of the replacement draft, running field problems in the hills, splashing ashore in the Oceanside surf, firing the range.

It was all brisk and purposeful, so different from the gentler, collegial atmosphere of Quantico, where one evening a few of us new lieutenants were invited home for dinner by Colonel Kaempfer and his wife. The affable colonel had a dozen brown glass quart bottles of home-brewed beer regimentally lined up along the hallway outside their apartment door in senior officers' quarters.

"A hobby of mine," said the colonel expansively over dinner. "The beer ferments best in dark places as the yeast works."

Several times during the meal, with Mrs. Kaempfer generously urging second helpings on her husband's "young men," there was a muffled explosion out in the hall.

"During fermentation, gases tend to build up," placidly explained the colonel.

Another bottle blew.

"The yeast is working," his wife informed us.

The California weekends were different, too. Saturdays they let us go at noon, and we drove up to Laguna Beach, an hour north and a world away, four Marine lieutenants sharing a room at one of the funky pastel stucco hotels along the beachfront, swimming and bodysurfing, playing beach volleyball ("Raiders' Rules," which meant anything goes, short of tearing down the net!), and chasing girls. The girls taught us about surfing, we tutored them on Raiders' Rules. The day began with breakfast (they served "breakfast" all day long), eggs and coffee with hot breads and rashers of bacon for fifty cents at the formica-topped tables of a little clifftop restaurant run by a bustling soul everyone called "Mom," where the waitresses were cute local teenagers, and from which you could watch the surf rolling up on the sand. I'd never seen a surf like that, had never seen a seal sunning itself on the kelpy rocks. The big football games back east were on the radio and we lay in the sunshine listening as the announcer, it was always Bill Stern, would be talking about how it was getting darker and colder at the Yale Bowl or Pittsburgh or high above Cayuga's waters at Cornell, and starting to sleet, and here we were in swimsuits, smearing zinc oxide on our noses against the California sun.

Late afternoon meant beers at My Place or the Coast Inn, where tropical fish swam just beneath your drink under the glass-topped bar, and which was known locally as "the body exchange." We chatted earnestly with girls with long sun-streaked hair and told them lies about the Marines and exaggerated our lives back home, the places where we lived and had gone to college, and sat close to them on the sand or up on the cliffs as we watched the red ball of the sun fall toward the western sea, the Pacific we would soon be crossing. Most of it was awfully innocent. I don't remember where we ate dinner, or if we did. Maybe the girls we met on the beach cooked for us. Laguna girls were swell and they were nuts for Marine officers going to the wars. It was all pretty sweet.

But we knew it wouldn't last; that the war was waiting for us.

At Quantico we were newcomers prepping for war; at Pendleton, in Fleet Marine Force, we were replacements actually going to war. There really was a distinction. Bored in Virginia, here in California there was a lovely and palpable tension, an awakened, Scott Fitzgerald sensitivity to life, and to its possibilities. On my twenty-third birthday, November 15, no longer a college boy, but a lieutenant of American Marines, the real goods, going overseas, off to the wars, I flew out of Pendleton for Asia.

CHAPTER 10

CUSTER WAS A GENERAL AT TWENTY-THREE AND DEAD AND
MUTILATED BY SQUAWS AT THIRTY-SEVEN.

In late March of 2003, half a century after the fighting ended, I was once more flying to Korea, like Charles Ryder returning to a place where he'd been young and in love. And, like Ryder, I too knew all about it.

Or thought that I did.

I'd taken along, like a well-thumbed guidebook, a sort of Baedeker, a copy of my Korean memoir, *The Coldest War,* and a couple of paperbacks for the long flight to Inchon out of New York, Joyce's *Portrait of the Artist* and a Conrad novel, *Lord Jim.* I always read Conrad when heading out to Asia. Most of us do, don't we?

Our trip was to be a sort of cool pilgrimage, with digressions and grand adventures.

The distinguished Mr. Adams, with his restlessly focusing eyes, his white ponytail out of the lofts and studios of Greenwich Village, and his black leather gear out of the *Matrix* films, looked as if he, too, like Keanu Reeves, were battling evil forces for the future of mankind. Adams and I would spend ten days visiting old battlefields, bunking in with today's heavily armed young U.S. Recon scouts on ranging duty, along and inside the rugged no-man's-land of the DMZ. The soldiers we would be meeting, GIs and generals both, wouldn't be the men setting policy, coping with the crazies of the North and their nuclear ambitions. They would simply be soldiers. They would do what soldiers always do, take their orders, do their duty, fight and die, if they had to, questions of war and peace not up to them. But they were the men I wanted to see, theirs the places I hoped to go.

Such was the plan.

That first flight to Korea I'd taken only one book, the paperback edition of a novel by Budd Schulberg about Scott Fitzgerald's decline, getting stewed at the Dartmouth Winter Carnival, embarrassing some Jack Warner–like movie studio tycoon. It was a novel I'd already read and very sad, but, as I say, I read favorite books a second or third time. When you are young you can afford a sad book. Because tomorrow, and there are plenty of tomorrows, will be happier. If you are old, spare yourself the sad books; you already have sufficient troubles.

But in the sleek 747 of today, I found myself drifting, and turned from books to the frost-laced porthole as at thirty-seven thousand feet snow-covered Canada gave way to even snowier Alaska and then the bleak emptiness of the Arctic Ocean ice. I kept trying to see polar bears down there so I could tell my grandchildren in a postcard, but no such luck. Then after an endless, dull, featureless stretch, we were crossing a sullen shoulder of Siberia, brushing Kamchatka and Sakhalin Island.

I wasn't drinking much that spring, being on assorted medications, so when the stewardess came around I took a glass of red wine and passed on the cocktails. It was a nice flight, very smooth, the stews fed us every few hours and new movie followed old movie on the little armrest screen. I skipped the flicks and instead kept switching to a channel that had plucked at my interest. It had a kind of miniature diorama showing our speed and altitude and the course we were flying and how far ahead Korea might be. I like to keep track of things like that; Eddie didn't care, hunched up asleep, since there was nothing he could do about it. But as I saw Manchuria approaching on the display, that pulled me up short, I can tell you.

Manchuria! I'd never seen it before, but I knew about Manchuria. It was out of there that had come the Chinese armies, half a million men, camouflaged in white, bugling and blowing whistles and determined to trap and kill, which they damned near did, the twenty-five thousand men of the 1st Marine Division up at the reservoir. It was into Manchuria that our POWs would vanish, some never to be seen again. And it was against those same Chinese that I would fight in the spring and summer of 1952. When you competed with the Chinese army, you were in with the professionals.

Somewhere halfway across and nearing the pole, and with Adams asleep, his baseball cap tugged low, I put Joyce aside (I was deep into *Portrait of the Artist* by now, the fire-and-brimstone sermon) and stared through the port at sky and snow, thinking about the Korea I remembered, about the men I'd fought alongside. I could see their faces out there somewhere just beyond the Plexiglas, silvered with its ice particles. They weren't booze memories either, not on a red wine or two, but real memories, real faces remembered. Though I did find it odd, how young we all were. Even the dead were young.

I'd flown across that first time, too, November of 1951, being pulled almost literally off the troopship at San Diego to fly the Pacific, one of maybe twenty officers and thirty or forty senior NCOs, the kinds of replacements the division needed after the hard mountain fighting of September 1951, rifle platoon leaders and NCOs of various talents and specs.

We left Pendleton by puddle jumper on my birthday, and when I remarked to a man in the next seat that I was just twenty-three, he looked at me unimpressed. "At twenty-three George Armstrong Custer was a brigadier general. Temporary wartime rank, of course." Marine officers are punctilious about such matters, but I resented the pedantry and ventured a retort.

"Yes," I said, with considerable satisfaction, "and at thirty-seven Custer was dead and mutilated by squaws."

That shut him up but also got me to wondering, would I live to Custer's thirty-seven? Would I see twenty-four?

We flew the feeder plane north to Alameda, outside San Francisco, for a Navy C-4 to island-hop our way across the Pacific to the war. The plane did round-trips, flying casualties back and replacements out, and instead of airline seats was rigged out with stretchers affixed lengthwise to the bulkheads and double-decked. The stretcher canvas, I noticed when we got to sit on it, was spotted with brownish stains, the dried blood of wounded men, dead men. They flew out the replacements, they flew home the wounded, some of them dying en route.

Maybe some of them were men that I knew as Quantico classmates who had gone out earlier to the division and were already dead. What would Korea be like? I wondered. Would I get a rifle platoon to lead? Was I ready for command? For combat? Would I live up to my company commander's expectations? And it was the rifle company captain who could make or break a young platoon lieutenant. I had no basis for comparison or true experience in any of these matters to call upon for reassurance.

I'd never gone to war before.

CHAPTER 11

They sent me as a replacement to Dog Company of the 7th Marines, which had in September of 1951 helped to capture, and was now holding, a North Korean ridgeline called Hill 749. The fighting, which continued through November and into the winter, was at close range, so close that the Marines shared with the North Koreans a stretch of ridgeline from which we had been unable to dislodge them, a rocky spur called "Luke the Gook's Castle." The commander of Dog Company was a captain named John Hubbard Chafee. Because he did not talk about such things, I did not know Chafee was from a wealthy Rhode Island clan, that he was a Yale man and a Harvard Law graduate. Nor did I know he was an Old Breed Marine who'd fought almost four years against the Japanese during the "Big War."

But some of the old-timers in the company knew Chafee's story, the Marine part of it.

Chafee had fought as a private on Guadalcanal from August 8, 1942, into February of '43. The Canal, as they called it, was the first big offensive campaign of the Marine Corps in the Pacific. It was also the longest. And some said the worst. The Japanese threw a major battle fleet into the campaign (in a single night sinking four U.S. and Australian cruisers) and tens of thousands of their best troops. Malaria, jungle, snakes, crocodiles, headhunters, fever, quicksand, and sharks made Guadalcanal worse.

Okinawa, in 1945, was the last and largest Marine battle of the war. By then Chafee had gone through officer candidate school and been commissioned a second lieutenant, and on Okinawa he commanded troops in tough, slogging combat.

Chafee fought both those battles, and then, six years later, when Korea came, a married man with a kid and a law practice, he was called back to active duty by the Marine Corps, this time to command a rifle company up in North Korea.

I mentioned that Korea might have been the last war where the Marine ranks, and certainly the officer corps, cut across class lines. The best families, the best schools, the old-guard names, the moneyed, what they used to call "the blue bloods," served alongside working-class kids like myself—cowboys and refrigerator repairmen and forest rangers and salesmen and cannery executives, all together. And those were the officers.

When you speak of class and privilege, people like the Chafees come to mind. The family was prominent: both of his grandfathers had been governors of the state, and he would himself in future serve as governor and secretary of the navy, and be four times elected to the Senate; but he first came to note as a Boy Scout.

In winter there was skating and hockey on the local pond and there were strict rules. If a boy fell through, there was no going out on the ice trying to save the lad; that was how dreadful tragedies occurred. The boys all knew and understood the rule. This was in the 1930s when John Chafee was thirteen or fourteen, and on this winter's day the ice had marginally thawed and a fat boy broke through. The others sprinted away, shouting for help. Young Chafee should of course have gone with them. Instead, he remembered advice about using a hockey stick in an emergency, and squirmed and slid across the bending ice to where it had broken and where a cold and frightened kid was desperately holding to the edges of the ice, quite literally hanging on for dear life. And when Chafee got there to the hole, he extended his hockey stick and began to tug.

As the first adults arrived at the scene, Chafee and the other boy were painfully but gamely edging their way back toward shore, where John was promptly chewed out for his audacity.

In an interview much later Senator Chafee was asked if any book he read as a boy helped shape him as a man. *Yankee Ships in Pirate Waters,* he responded with some alacrity. This happened to be a book of which I myself was an enormous fan, colorful tales for boys about early-nineteenth-century American merchantmen sailing out of New England ports bound for the Pacific and Indian Oceans in search of spices and profitable trade, but encountering en route typhoons, tiger sharks, treacherous maharajas and crafty lascar seamen, reefs, waterspouts, and piratical cutthroats.

That young John easily imagined himself sailing into such swashbuckling adventures goes without saying, and anyone who knew his taste in reading realized that the lad was destined for something more than a nine-to-five desk job in the city.

In the autumn and winter of 1951–52, I was one of Chafee's three rifle platoon leaders in Dog Company.

Despite a lengthy and impressive combat record dating back almost ten years, the "Old Man," as we thought of him, wasn't yet thirty and approachable, easy to talk with and to, but businesslike. He never spoke of his war against the Japanese or his origins, so I only learned these things much later.

Chafee had considered Brown but, like most of us, wanted to get away from home, and he ended up at Yale. He'd wrestled in prep school, and at 165 pounds and growing bigger, he swiftly made the varsity at New Haven and by sophomore year was one of their stars. When Pearl Harbor was attacked Chafee went down to the recruiting station and enlisted in the Marines, not as an officer candidate but as an ordinary recruit. He trained at Parris Island boot camp, fought his way across the Pacific, and was one of the Marine officers sent into north China at war's end to accept surrender of the Japanese army there.

After the war, First Lieutenant Chafee returned, still a sophomore, to Yale and went out again for the wrestling team, where, the 1947 *Yale Banner* reported, he "advanced to the finals of the eastern intercollegiates" and was awarded "the James Getz Trophy," apparently something of a big deal. He was tapped for Skull and Bones, greatest of all the Yale honor societies and one so secret that a "Bonesman" must immediately leave the room if a nonmember utters its name. On graduation from Yale, Chafee studied at Harvard Law and, after passing the bar, went into private practice in Providence.

A reporter for the *Providence Journal* years later asked then Senator Chafee where he was when Korea was invaded in June of 1950.

Chafee's response (this was in his Senate office and I was there) says something about the man's style and how he ordered his priorities.

"I didn't know anything about it," John said. "I was sailing in the Newport-to-Bermuda yacht race and a special girl [later his wife, Virginia] was waiting for me at the dock in Bermuda. That's all I cared about. Getting to Bermuda and seeing Ginnie again."

When the Marine Corps in 1950 called up the reserves for Korea, Captain Chafee, married and with a baby on the way, was among them. Bitter, was he? Lots of reservists were.

"No, I wasn't making that much money practicing law and Ginnie and I thought, well, a captain's pay isn't bad and maybe we'll be stationed someplace pleasant, such as Southern California."

Instead, after a refresher course at the Junior School, he arranged to get himself shipped out to North Korea to a tank outfit and then to command a rifle company. Other men pulled strings for cushier jobs, but not Chafee. A man with family money and political connections, a graduate of both Yale and Harvard, he saluted and went to war. For a second time.

Perhaps Chafee was always destined for fame, for position. Some may have predicted the political career he would craft. But neither Yale nor Harvard nor all those local connections could possibly have predicted what a man he was in a tight spot, what a terrific soldier. The Ivy League knew John Chafee could wrestle; only the Marines knew how he could fight. That was the Chafee we knew.

My first glimpse of him was Thanksgiving weekend of 1951 on Hill 749 in the Taebaek Mountains of North Korea when I reported in as a replacement. I was skinny, green and awed, and the captain was tall and tough, splendidly mustachioed and with a high color (his tan and coloration as well as his name suggested to me he might be a French Canadian; he was really a good old-fashioned New England Episcopalian), a graceful, loping figure wielding a sort of alpenstock as he sped along ridgelines and vaulted over trenches, stooped to peer into bunkers to greet his men and question them about their night's action, about enemy sound or movement anywhere along the line, a raid, an ambush, a patrol perhaps, inquire about the state of their provisions and ammo, chew out this man and compliment that. Competent and efficient, a tireless and cheerful, yet quite serious, figure to whom we all looked that winter, especially on the bad days and worse nights, when the going was hard.

In a firefight or under a mortar or artillery barrage, Chafee was always Chafee. The situation changed, conditions worsened, the enemy threw us a curve, someone screwed up, an operation was falling apart, he maintained control, he was still the same, was still "the Skipper," our commander. He didn't fluster, didn't anger, didn't pass the buck when an unpopular order came down from battalion or regiment, but saw to it that the order was carried out. Whatever the hour of night, when a nervous platoon leader called on the field telephone or the radio about mysterious noises out there, it was always Chafee, and not the first sergeant or the exec, who picked up and listened, patiently. And if he sensed there really was trouble coming, he would soon be heading your way, ignoring danger and the dark, loping long-legged along the trench, that silly alpenstock in his paw. Only half a dozen years older than we were, he was the big older brother or the father figure some of us had never had.

Did he ever sleep, was he sometimes confused or afraid? Whatever the deal, Chafee seemed always, in the words of basketball's Al McGuire, "as cool as the other side of the pillow."

Even today, Dog Company men publish a little newsletter through which they stay in touch and in which men often cite their memories of Chafee. There are also, in the occasional letter to me, mentions of the Skipper, routine and even banal, nothing really significant, just fifty-year-old stuff, remembering things Chafee said or did or didn't do, and how it was when we were all young and he was our captain.

In those weeks and months of 1951 and '52, up on the line and in combat, with never a hint of the rich life he had already led or suspecting the political career he would one day fashion, I thought Captain Chafee was approximately God.

CHAPTER 12

"MOUSE" BRYDON KNEW OF A GEISHA HOUSE
CATERING TO MARINE OFFICERS.

On that first crossing to Korea, the Navy got the division's new replacements delivered, but they took their time about it, the Alameda
C-4 quite thoughtfully, we felt, breaking down on a regular basis
along the way, giving us a day and a night in San Francisco, a magical city I'd
never seen, a weekend in Hawaii on the beach at Waikiki, and various South
Sea coffee breaks. That first breakdown, we spent a glorious afternoon at
Stanford, guests of Bob Phelps, like me a young lieutenant, unlike me a
wealthy, powerful young man who'd played varsity football, and who shep-
herded us over to their big football stadium and introduced us to coach
Chuck Taylor and his team, including those fleet, and unpronounceable, Ar-
menian running backs out of Fresno, and the strapping all-American end (and
future Olympic decathlon champion) Bob Mathias, who would himself become a Marine officer.

Stanford that week was the number one team in the country and Taylor's
picture had been on the cover of *Life* or *Time,* I forget which, so we were
somewhat wide-eyed. While, in their turn, the college boys seemed rather
awed to meet Marine officers on our way to a shooting war. The coach broke
practice to let us mingle with the players and talk football. Then we visited a

student hangout under some big shade trees where a pretty waitress served up cold steins of beer. First the campus at UCLA, then the sun-bronzed surfer girls of Laguna Beach and now the groves of Palo Alto. Was everyplace out here this beautiful? I began to think seriously about the merits of a relocation to California after the war. You know, when and if . . .

The evening was passed at the Top of the Mark, drinking and staring out at the lights of fishing boats on the bay and freighters steaming beneath the Golden Gate and out onto the Pacific that I would be crossing, maybe (don't young men always think such thoughts?) never to return.

In Honolulu the plane failed again and we had two glorious days ashore on leave, four young officers sharing a suite at the Royal Hawaiian, the days spent as guests of the very posh Outrigger Canoe Club, being paddled about in canoes and trying to surf. You couldn't buy a drink. Suntanned gents with graying hair kept buying rounds and telling us war stories of their own, and there were some very pretty girls. Everything was gorgeous, the people, the place, the weather.

You had to say this, when you went to war in the Corps you traveled first-class.

We didn't break down during a refueling on Johnston Island, where there wasn't much to see, but we enjoyed a sunset evening at Kwajalein, where I strolled the beach and stared out at the lagoon, still studded with rusted-out American landing craft and tanks, thought long and hard about the young men of both sides, a lot of them Marines, who'd died here. There was a night on Guam at the officers' club, pretty dull garrison types. And a weird refueling stop on Iwo Jima, maybe the dreariest place I'd ever seen.

Of course I knew about Iwo, could tell you how many thousands of Marines died there, how fiercely the Japanese fought and for how many weeks, how many of the enemy died. It's all part of Marine lore. You learn it by rote, as Catholic children are taught to pray the rosary by Sister Michaela, how you memorize the Spiritual Works of Mercy. But now for a few hours I was confronted with the reality of Iwo, how small that lethal Mount Suribachi really was, how empty and barren the island. They told us to stay close to the airstrip, but I chose to walk around a bit, do some thinking. I was still in high school when the Marines took this place. I owed those men a few thoughts. The wind moaned dolefully as it blew across the volcanic ash. Then the refueling was finished and we were called back to the plane.

Years later I interviewed Joe Rosenthal, who took the famous flag-raising photo. He was an old man and sick, living in San Francisco. He sent me a copy of the photo, gilded, which wasn't necessary, and signed, which was. I was glad I had once seen his island, I told Joe. I don't know that it meant much to him but I wanted him to know.

There was a night and day in Tokyo, where the postwar American occupation had just ended. And being the product of a misspent boyhood watching too many B war movies pullulating with menacing Japanese (most of them played by our wartime allies the Chinese or by Filipinos), I went sightseeing on the Ginza with a loaded .38 Smith & Wesson revolver stuffed into my trouser belt. I don't know what I expected of the Japanese six years after they surrendered (some samurai with a grudge, wielding a sword and yelling, "Joe, you die!"), but I intended to be ready for it. Thinking back on it now, we were such kids, wanting desperately to be as hard and tough as the Marines of the Big War had been, and, in my case, not at all sure I would measure up.

The whole long flight across the Pacific, with its breakdowns, its layovers and refueling stops, made me think that, in a small way, we too now had our *Tales of the South Pacific,* had in small ways brushed against Ensign Nellie Forbush and "Bus" Adams, Marine Lieutenant Joe Cable, Emile de Beque and Bloody Mary.

A final night in Japan was passed at a geisha house near Itami, the big American airbase located between Osaka and Nagoya, guided there by Ernie "Mouse" Brydon. He was a first lieutenant we'd known at Quantico, a fast-talking little guy whose acolyte was a big young football player, a big crew-cut blond second lieutenant from Philadelphia named Baker, who double-soled his shoes and wore them with metal taps fore and aft, which enlisted men do but not usually officers. You could hear Baker coming a hundred yards off but he didn't say much. His customary opening remark was "Where's the Mouse? The Mouse okay? Anybody seen Mouse?" For Baker, life revolved around Ernie the Mouse.

Brydon sold real estate in Philly and was a hustler, furtive, cunning, a survivor. He'd been in Korea a couple months and was in Japan on "a liquor run." His battalion's officers, forty of them, had put up the dough, and Brydon was here to buy maybe fifty cases of booze, bourbon (the Marine Corps being still very southern), gin, and Scotch, and then get the stuff back via bribery (malleable pilots and truck drivers would get a case or two for their cooperation), cajoling, and sheer nerve. Mouse's forest green uniform blouse was emblazoned with ribbons, at least one Purple Heart, Bronze and Silver Stars, even a Navy Cross. We were all impressed. The Cross was just below the Medal of Honor.

"Mouse, where the hell did you get a Navy Cross?" Brydon had never before been suspected of heroism. But what did we know; maybe in Korea, heroes came in all sizes.

"Borrowed it," he said, unashamed and rather pleased with himself. "The boys all chipped in their medals. Thought it would help me getting through with the hootch."

The geisha house and its girls, all of them artistically and gently reared and delicate of feeling, were representative of an ancient culture. ("So," Brydon cautioned us, "don't call it a whorehouse. They're very sensitive.") This particular establishment, he explained, was operated by the *tres soignée* widow of a famous Japanese admiral, catering to a clientele consisting of senior American officers of the Army and Navy and Air Force, colonels and above. Or United States Marine officers of any rank.

So we were assured first by the Mouse (you began to appreciate how good a real estate salesman he must have been) and later by the admiral's widow, whose gallant husband we had killed. Suffused with good feeling, I wondered if we ought to pay our condolences as we left.

The next morning, in a snow squall, we flew out of Itami across to Korea, encouraged on our way by a helpful ground officer who ominously informed us, "There are MIGs out over the Sea of Japan. They'll go for a transport plane if they can."

Swell! A hangover wasn't bad enough?

It was Thanksgiving and at home they would be marching in the Macy's parade, which I'd done a year earlier, dancing the Charleston in a raccoon coat and white bucks with Pete Oldham and a couple of lovelies from the Art Department, and Cornell and Penn would be playing football at Franklin Field. That weekend was when we joined the 1st Marine Division and went to war alongside the Marines of Dog Company.

Half a century later, I recalled in rather startling detail the Hollywood soundstage setting of our gorgeously manic November flight across the Pacific, the sunset beaches of the coast and then the Pacific and the islands, the flight across time zones and hemispheres, the thrill of joining a famous Marine division on the battlefield, of being among the chosen, the few, the elect. Surely not everyone went to war as glamorously, as memorably, and with such undeniable dash (what the French call élan) as did our platoon-leaders class from Quantico in the golden late autumn of 1951.

Everything about our journey to war had been cool. That final night at Top of the Mark. Waikiki and the Outrigger Canoe Club and the rusted tanks in the lagoon at Kwaj. Mouse Brydon from Philly and the Japanese admiral's widow. The backdrop of Mount Suribachi and, in counterpoint, the geisha girls. Even the Smith & Wesson jammed melodramatically into my waistband for a stroll along the Ginza. All of it seemed precisely right. I thought about that first crossing of the Pacific in November of '51, and of those men and my own youthful innocence, as our Korean Air 747 bore steadily west toward Asia.

CHAPTER 13

SERGEANT FITZGERALD OF DOG COMPANY SHOT IT OUT
WITH A LOCAL BAD MAN UP IN MICHIGAN.

The purser broke into my reverie to inform us Japan was somewhere to the left, China to the right, and in two hours we would be descending to land between them in Korea.

I'd been daydreaming, recalling the men, not that any of them had ever vanished entirely from the screen of memory. How could they?

Few of us were elected to the Senate. Or ever ran *The New York Times*. Or became TV evangelists who spoke directly to God. Or got to be writers who lived in Paris. Still fewer grew up to marry Elizabeth Taylor. Most of us, and they included the finest we had, were just plain Americans who had gone to war, done some fighting, and returned home to a more or less pleasant anonymity.

Take Fitz, my best squad leader, maybe my best Marine, period, a natural at war, a gifted warrior, and a man I'd once gotten blown up. We'd stayed in touch for half a century. John Fitzgerald of Flint, Michigan, twice or maybe three times wounded in Korea, once told me his ambition was to get a job as an armed guard at Ford Motor Company. It was very simple, he said. "I've got used to wearing a uniform and carrying a weapon. And I'm good at it."

Like so many modestly educated men, I was convinced everyone deserved some higher learning.

"How about college, Fitz?"

"I never did have the grades, sir, and don't think I could cut the books."
"Cut" in our lexicon meant "handle," as in "Can you cut the hills?"

Fitz was a handsome, husky blond kid, sturdy and tough, who joined the Marine Corps out of high school so he could play football. His best-laid plans for football had gang somewhat agley when he was dispatched to Key West, one of the few Marine bases that didn't field a team.

In Korea, Fitz got something of a reputation for freelance scouting, wild midnight capers, going out alone or with a couple of other inspired madmen on ambushes. They worked light, they worked quiet, no ammo belts or canteens or helmets, just their weapons and maybe a knife and a compass, nothing to clank or clang. They were pretty good at it. Fitz seemed actually to enjoy what he was doing.

"Lieutenant, I love this shit."

Fitz was one of seven hundred Marines wounded in September capturing Hill 749, and had been repaired and returned to Dog Company, where I made him a squad leader, promoting him and getting him another stripe.

I told you how I wrote asking him what he remembered about 749 and sent along a copy of that platoon photo.

"I know they called it 749 later," Fitz said. "But when we were going up we called it 'Bunker Hill.' "

I understood why; the south-facing forward slope of the entire Kanmubong Ridge was simply honeycombed with North Korean bunkers, many of which we would later use, living in them that fall and winter. What I couldn't grasp was how Marines ever made it up that hill under fire and at that degree of slope. I asked him to tell me whatever he remembered.

Maybe Fitzgerald couldn't understand it either, his account a stream of consciousness, diffuse and jumping about, like sound bites without benefit of segues.

"I was a fire team leader and we were tied in with Fox Company," Fitz said. "You notice in that picture there's almost no one from the First Squad.

We pretty much got wiped out. So was my fire team. There was a bright moon and McClellan was shot through the mouth and Mr. Flynn was hit and suddenly I found myself alone with Luke [the enemy, for 'Luke the Gook'] for company and I saw two Lukes standing there and I got them both with my M1 and then I threw a grenade into one of their bunkers. Then there were a couple of us sheltering in the shadow of a bush against the moonlight, you know how moonlight throws a shadow, and just the other side of the bush was another Luke. I jumped out and gave him six rounds to the gut and he went down and was lying there gurgling and I got out my knife to cut his throat, but then suddenly they were all around us and firing. And I'm standing there looking stupid with a knife in my hand.

"Godsey, the machine gunner, got hit, Bobby Knight told me. Bobby's still alive, lives in Grand Blanc, Michigan. I'll ask him for you, Lieutenant. But that was when 'Hollywood' was killed, the assistant machine gunner attached to us. I don't know why we called him 'Hollywood.' They said I killed nineteen. I was written up, big time, but the company commander had something on me and I ended up with the Bronze Star with combat V."

If "Hollywood" and Joe McKenna were two different men, both of them dead, Fitz couldn't say. Chuck Curley says the only "Hollywood" he knew in Dog Company was Bobby Knight. And he's alive and well and living in Grand Blanc.

So don't let anyone, even as good a man as Fitz, tell you he remembers what happened and when in a firefight. Much of combat is pure chaos and even after the fight no one is quite sure exactly who did what and just where and what happened next. Memory plays tricks, you're scared or badly hurt, things happen too fast, the noise of firing and the yelling, the unfamiliar terrain, smoke and the night confuse and disorient you.

I asked Fitz how he got wounded. "Lieutenant, I've been burp-gunned and bayoneted and blown up, but that night it was a grenade that went off near my ankle that got me, and they shipped me out."

"To Japan?"

"No, to the *Haven,* the hospital ship."

Then, on January 13, 1952, I got him wounded again. That was what he meant by that crack about being "blown up." Sergeant Fitzgerald, understandably, was miffed at the time, though he didn't hold a grudge, and I don't blame him for being sore.

It was only our third day back up on the line after a wonderful Christmas 1951 reserve and this was another stretch of the same Kanmubong Ridge but new to us. So we were feeling our way, trying to get a grip on the ground, the draws and hillocks, the dead zones up which an enemy patrol might advance, the places masked from machine-gun fire, the defiladed places only a mortar might be able to reach. Sometimes I thought topography was a science overlooked at the Basic School. If you could appreciate the terrain, you had a discernible edge. And in combat, you wanted the edge.

So Chafee had each of his platoon leaders take out daylight patrols to scout out the ground just in front of us and on each flank. It was Chafee's thesis that if you knew the ground like the back of your hand by day, you had a better chance of handling it in a firefight and by night. On the thirteenth I was with Fitzgerald's squad heading down a steep draw, out of sight of the North Koreans, but with the deep snow, almost two feet in the drifts, and how steep the slope was, we went gingerly. I had the point. Why not, we were totally in defilade and hardly likely to come under hostile fire. Night ambushes and combat patrols were trouble; a little jaunt like this on a pleasant morning was a walk in the sun. We were thirty or forty yards down the forward slope when I tripped and found myself flying briefly through the air. I don't know if the blast or the noise came first but there I was, sprawled facedown in the deep snow, stunned but not hurting anywhere. I'd never been wounded before so maybe that didn't signify. I felt around with both hands and I seemed intact. No blood, either, not that I could see.

Somewhere, someone was yelling. I didn't recognize the voice.

"A mine! They hit a goddamned mine!"

"Fitz?" I called out.

"Okay, Lieutenant." But I didn't think he was. Not the way his voice was different, kind of muffled, so he hadn't been the one yelling. There were men coming toward us now, glissading downhill and shouting at us.

"Don't move! You might set off another one."

"Okay," I said. "But get a rope down to us and you can pull us out.
"Fitz?"

"Got my arm," he said. He didn't sound happy, so I tossed in a sincere "Sorry about that, Fitz."

He was equally sincere. "Forget about it, Lieutenant. Could have gotten you instead of me."

He couldn't get his other arm out from under the snow and asked me if he looked all right. I thought about crawling over to him, but there might be more mines, so maybe that was a bad idea.

"Fine, Fitz. You bleeding anywhere else?"

"Don't think so."

I was feeling okay now, a little dizzy. The company runner, a big black kid named Duke, was coming down to us with some rope. Duke fancied himself a boxer and had balls.

"Toss it down, Duke. Don't come any closer."

Duke ignored me, kept coming. Ignored the mines. He had the rope and helped get Sergeant Fitzgerald to his feet. He looked okay except for the bloody forearm. Topside three or four other men were hauling on the rope, and Duke had a big arm around Fitz's waist, and slowly they made their way up. I started to follow, staying right in their tracks in case there really were additional mines. Up there on the trail I could see Red Phillips and Chafee. They were both staring at me.

The captain had a look on his face. Part concern, part amusement. He seemed to be wondering about me, with the jury out and Chafee a lawyer.

Since I'd just gotten one of his best NCOs hurt, I could understand why. The corpsman checked me out by looking into my eyes and asking me to count numbers backward. He took care of Fitz with a tweezers and iodine, pulling bits of metal out of his forearm, swabbing out the wounds and painting it. "Shrapnails," as Sergeant Wooten, the salty platoon guide, called shrapnel. Then they wrapped some bandages around Fitz's arm and pronounced him fit for duty. If a touch cranky.

If you were still walking, could see, and weren't concussed or anything, a little wound like this didn't qualify for evacuation. Captain Chafee said we were lucky the snow was so deep that it smothered the explosion. I guess so. But it puzzled me that Fitzgerald, so much better a soldier than I, a regular, a football player, a tough young veteran of the fight to take 749, had been hurt while I, the new boy on the block, unsure of himself and untested, even though I set off the mine, was simply knocked on my ass. Fitz was hurt, I wasn't.

The following May I was in another fight where forty-eight of us attacked a Chinese hill and thirty-two or thirty-three were hit. Again, I wasn't. Why was that? I wondered. Was this what they meant by "fortunes of war"?

A few days later a new order came down from division. Platoon leaders weren't to play point man on patrol. We were to stay back where we could control the squad leader or leaders and not lead from the front.

"It's called the 'Brady Rule,'" Mack Allen wisecracked. "You'll be famous yet. They'll write about you in the training manuals."

"Sure." I knew how lucky I was not to have lost a leg or two.

Sergeant Fitzgerald did eventually hire out as an armed guard, at one of the big Detroit auto companies, and then after another tour in the Marines in Vietnam, ending up as a gunnery sergeant, he became a cop up in Flint, Michigan. One night, Fitz went alone into a basement after a gunman.

"It was about two thirty in the morning when we get a call. Sounds to us like a drunk call. My partner Tony and I go over, it was on Grace Street, I remember that. This woman meets us and says this fellow's been threatening them. 'He's downstairs in the cellar,' so we go around into the backyard, and I go into the basement, the cleanest basement I ever saw, I remember that. And there's this guy with a wild look in his eyes and I say, 'Oh, shit.' I turn and he slams the door and it knocks me back and he jumps toward me and I see the pump gun. We had cross-style holsters and I didn't want to shoot off my arm by mistake in hurrying the shot. Then I saw the blue flame and it hit me and drove me back against the wall but I got off two shots.

"He's still up, standing in front of me and he says, 'Okay, you got me. I'm going down.' But I feel the pain and I think maybe he's still got a gun down there and so before I passed out and went down myself, I shot him again.

They told me later any one of the three shots might have killed him. He was a guy with a record but it was really just a family deal with him. I think they were all related. He'd been threatening two women including the woman who let us in."

The shotgun shell carried much of Fitzgerald's leather duty belt and bits and pieces of metal into his guts. That, and the usual infections and succeeding operations, took considerable time afterward. But Fitz was alive and the other guy dead.

Which is what they pay off on in wars or police work, and that was always Sergeant Fitzgerald's style.

He's living now in a town called Byron, with his wife, Theresa, whom he calls "Sam" and who's written a quite wonderful book about how to get kids hooked on math. They had one child, a college student named Amanda, a girl who was one of the best high school softball players in the state and won a partial college scholarship for her ball playing. Fitz phoned me about her, sent local newspaper clippings about Amanda, her strikeouts, the velocity of her pitches. She was, quite clearly, the center of his universe.

Fitz has a boat, too, a forty-one-foot ketch-rigged sailboat moored near Port Huron that they take out on the larger lakes for extended summer cruising. "We were cruising forty days last year. I'm going out into Lake Superior next summer for the first time," he told me last time we spoke. Nice sort of retirement. Still has all his hair and looks very fit. Just a year or two younger than I but you'd take him for a guy in his fifties. Like a tougher Tab Hunter with scars.

A few years back when Greyhound went on strike and there was industrial sabotage with violence, John answered an ad for armed guards to ride shotgun on buses breaking the strike and defying picket lines. The money was pretty rich, but at his age, was it a terribly good idea? I called Fitz and asked. But he shrugged it off.

"It's the work I'm good at, Lieutenant. Wear a uniform, carry a gun. No strain." Eventually the strike was settled and Fitz didn't have to shoot anybody or get shot again.

Couple of years ago at Easter he phoned from Michigan. I thought he was asking after my health following the stroke and wishing me a happy holiday, so I went on for a bit and then asked how he was.

Not so good, Sergeant Fitzgerald said. There'd been a car crash during spring break. College kids out driving, driving fast. His Amanda was in the car. She was dead. His only kid. The daughter who was so good at softball that she won a college scholarship. And now she was gone and John Fitzgerald and his wife Sam were alone. But carrying on, he said, the two of them, trying to handle their loss and planning to sail Lake Superior this summer.

We talked about Amanda for a time. With two daughters myself, I kept attempting to say something that made sense, to a man who'd just lost his only girl. I didn't do it very well. And this was a man I'd gone to war with, had put into a book. A man who'd lived his entire adult life with death, killing and not getting killed. Yet he was alive while, home in Michigan, his little girl was dead. Try to make sense of that. In the Marine Corps, in a couple of towns up in Michigan, they knew about John Fitzgerald, surely they mourned with him.

Few other Americans know of the wars he fought or the bad men he went into cellars after, or maybe that Fitz ever even lived. Or that his kid was dead.

CHAPTER 14

MARINES AT THE "21" CLUB, WITH FRENCH MOVIE
SEX BOMBS IN PURSUIT.

O ur bunch from Quantico began taking casualties early. A few never even got to the war.

Most of us would reach Korea, some of us to die there, others to return whole, some carried to the naval hospitals, all of us to do some fighting, and a few turning out to be naturals who earned serious medals and an undeniable celebrity within the very exclusive set of Marine gunslingers.

Marines are snobs; if you haven't fought, you don't really belong. It has nothing to do with money or origins, all that socioeconomic stuff, with class or caste. Only if you fought or not. Of course, there were some who through no fault of their own didn't get to the division. These were men who wanted combat but who drew the wrong cards.

Men like Carly Rand and John Ledes.

Carlton Rand was a member of the Rand McNally clan, the mapmakers, a sleekly black-haired gent who'd just graduated from Harvard (did EVERyone at Harvard join the Marines?), had plenty of what Philip Marlowe called "the folding," and a glorious and socially well-connected young wife, Edie ("she's a Pratt, you know," said Ledes, who was our one-man *Almanach de Gotha*). Ledes himself was related to the Skouras family, wealthy Greeks who owned

20th Century–Fox. He'd been with Carly and Edie in that chartered plane to Reno the night before they were scheduled to fly out of San Francisco for Korea in the May of '51.

I lunched with John recently at the Yale Club in Manhattan to get straight just what happened that last night. Things are rarely dull chez Ledes, and just as we ordered lunch, a kitchen fire broke out and we had to walk down twenty-two flights of stairs to the lobby, where we were assured the Yale Club wasn't really burning down, and we returned (via elevator) for lunch.

A few in our class (including me) had stayed behind pro tem at Quantico to help train the next class; the rest were ticketed as replacements in Korea. They were at the St. Francis Hotel, jovial and flush, even boys who didn't customarily have much money, like Jimmy "Wild Hoss" Callan, whose ranch was going bust, and Champion, who repaired refrigerators in private life. But in this instance, everyone had a little dough because, in Marine parlance, they'd all "taken down a dead horse," drawing three months' pay in advance of going overseas.

Someone at the St. Francis got the brilliant idea of chartering a plane to fly them up to Reno for an evening's gambling and then back in time for breakfast and the flight out to the war.

Wild Hoss said no, saving his dough, and Doug Bradlee (the big tackle for Harvard) was off to Palo Alto for dinner. But the others, including Ledes and John "Dusty" Rhodes from Short Hills, New Jersey, were game for the casinos.

"The pilot never filed a flight plan," complained Ledes over our Yale Club lunch, "or he would have known there was a spring snowstorm coming." It was fifty-four years later and Ledes was still ticked off. "Carly was sitting in the copilot's seat, but when we hit turbulence and the snow began he went back to sit with Edie, so I took the copilot seat. And when the plane started to descend I knew we were in trouble.

"We crashed into the Truckee River, and the pilot, that son of a bitch, was okay, sitting up there, dumb and happy, but the ball of my right shoulder was smashed and I'd need one hundred ten stitches in my head. I would have bled to death except the Truckee was so cold it clotted the blood. Carly was dead and Edie's back was hurt but Dusty had only a sprained ankle, and he and I dove underwater and got the others out somehow, and he climbed up the riverbank to a road. It was Dusty who saved us.

"There was a bar down the road and he threw open the door in his soaking uniform with the blood all over it and started yelling for a phone. And the barman was shouting at Rhodes, 'I told you drunken Marines to stay out of here!'

"Dusty just grabbed the phone and called the state police to report a plane crash."

They were all carted off to a local hospital; Ledes eventually transferred to St. Alban's Naval Hospital in New York. It was there they formed an ad hoc group of rehabbing Marine officers, each with "a wounded flipper."

John Ledes was the only New Yorker and the one with connections. More important, he had an apartment on the posh Upper East Side just opposite Gracie Mansion where the mayor lived. Other wounded Marines coalesced around Ledes. "Joe Owen's right arm was burp-gunned at the Chosin Reservoir. Ace Parker had been arm-shot in April. Dick Brennan was shot [also an arm] leading his platoon in an assault on a hill. They awarded him a Bronze Star but Dick turned it down. Said leading a platoon up the hill was the job he signed on to do. Some people thought he rated the Medal of Honor."

Each day, following physical therapy, the boys checked out of the naval hospital in uniform, gorgeously complete with medals, and boarded the subway for their command post at Ledes's ground-floor apartment in an elegant town house. I'd been there to parties and was curious.

"How'd you ever find that place, John?" I asked at lunch.

The response was pure Ledes. "Vincent Astor owned the whole block and Minnie Astor told me about the apartment."

John Ledes had at age seventeen entered Columbia University and, despite being too small, gone out for football. With World War II on, the Navy had a V-12 program which trained future officers at civilian colleges, and when Ledes turned eighteen, he joined up and was transferred to Yale, where he took engineering and went out again for football. He claims to have played against one of the great West Point teams of Blanchard and Davis (I'm still unsure if he was playing for Yale or Columbia). John was perhaps five eight, barrel-chested but not bulky, and he was playing football against all-Americans?

He was eventually commissioned, and at war's end in 1945, John was one of those thousands of American Marines training to take part in the final assault on the Japanese home islands.

"Then Truman dropped his hand grenade [the A-bomb] and saved my life. Saved all our lives."

Since the Marine Corps was going to make up the first waves of the invasion, all six divisions landing abreast, Ledes may not have been exaggerating. After the Big War he went to law school, became a lawyer at the SEC (to study loopholes he might later exploit in corporate life), bought and sold radio stations, married well (Sally is from Baltimore), and today owns beauty and fashion trade publications, hosting each October on his birthday a lavish black-tie dinner in Paris.

But it was his bachelor apartment on East End Avenue that we recall, with its cocktail parties, gorgeous young women, decorated Marine officers, and White Russian aristocrats. Prince Serge Obolensky, who had once served the czar, was now running the Hotel Astor for the Astor family, and his son, Ivan, was a book publisher and Ledes's pal. The nobility embraced us all as Ledes's friends, and I spent glorious evenings with the Obolenskys, their friend Count Vava, assorted barons and other grandees, and the beautiful women who trailed in their luminous wake. Joe Owen, one of the St. Alban's wounded, somehow came up with a length of good black silk and fashioned it into slings for their wounded arms when they went out into Manhattan society, the black silk setting off elegantly the forest green of uniforms and the gaily colored campaign- and combat-ribboned decorations. Wounded Marine officers from the untutored corners of rustic America, recently returned combat officers of no especial background, arrivistes like myself, there we were hanging with a Prince of all the Russias, cracking Easter eggs and hurling champagne glasses into fireplaces. Ledes introduced us to these giddy circles, and impertinently informed the nobility that they were fortunate to have as their guests heroic officers of the United States Marine Corps.

A number of Ledes's friends, discharged Marines and unemployed White

Russian aristos both, made their money selling expensive perfumes wholesale to Bergdorf Goodman and Saks, and spent it squiring Broadway ingenues and fashion models about Manhattan. The St. Alban's wounded, John's intimate circle, were held in the highest esteem. Following a night on the town, one of the Marines who'd forgotten his key entered John's apartment through one of the ground-floor windows and was very nearly shot as an intruder by another damaged Marine officer with the shakes, who couldn't sleep without a loaded revolver under his pillow.

I'm unsure if Dusty Rhodes figured in that episode but I wasn't able to check, since he died in 2000 on November 10, birthday of the Marine Corps, which is always among Marines considered good form, and exquisite timing. Ace Parker worked at J. Walter Thompson and so did Dick Brennan; Ace flourished, becoming something of a big deal in their Mexico City offices, but Dick put more of himself into his unproduced play about U. S. Grant than he did into efforts on behalf of JWT's clients. This did not mean that Dick, tall, lean, darkly handsome, lacked a fan club.

Few people really knew Brennan, an ascetic loner who resembled the actor Stewart Granger but with crow's-wing black hair. He was from Natick, Massachusetts, a relative of Admiral Alfred Thayer Mahan, the "sea power" strategist, and had been a Marine in the Big War. In Korea, his arm was badly shredded. After the war Dick got a copywriting job on Madison Avenue while he kept trying to write that play. One evening Bob Kriendler, who owned the "21" Club, had a bunch of us from Korea in for drinks. Kriendler had been a Marine colonel during the war. I believe that because of his expertise in operating a saloon, he ran all the PXs across the Pacific. Nice man. We were impressed to be in his wonderful club and I think he was impressed by us. Because while he'd been overseeing post exchanges, we were out shooting people. Colonel Kriendler made a little speech in which he urged Marine officers to consider the "21" Club our headquarters. I did so enthusiastically over the years, but found I still had to pay for the drinks.

It was that evening at "21" when Dick Brennan caught the discerning eye of the current French cinema sex bomb, Denise Darcel. We were all squeezed into one of those tiny club elevators and Mademoiselle Darcel kept staring up into Brennan's handsome puss (he was about six four) as he towered above her, "Ooh la la!" When we arrived at the ground floor, old Denise kind of enlisted in the Marine Corps, joining our ranks for the evening. I never quite figured out with whom she came in but it was obvious she planned to leave with Lieutenant Brennan. Dick, ever the gentleman, deferential and calling her "Miss Darcel," shyly passed, attracting good-humored abuse from the rest of us. Several others made a run at the Frenchwoman but Denise fended us off.

Few of Brennan's nights were that glamorous. He drifted into lesser copy-writing jobs at lesser ad shops, then out of the advertising business entirely, and ended working for an insurance company. He always dressed the same, a navy blue suit, business shirt and tie, as neat as you'd want, still polishing both his black wingtips and that stage play of his. He was drinking a bit, didn't wear a topcoat in winter, and some people put that down to whim and not economics, but I didn't think he owned a coat. Some of us took turns taking Dick to lunch and checking in on him. Dick insisted everything was fine.

I don't know about anyone else, but I had the guilts about Brennan, that I didn't do more. Last thing I knew, he was reduced to staying in an SRO hotel on Lexington Avenue near Gramercy Park, where one night he collapsed. John Ledes and his boy George and some others went down there and got Dick out, packed up his one suit and a few books (his favorite, *The Killer Angels,* among them), and summoned an ambulance. When some of the dump's staff turned surly, the Ledes boys began to take the place apart. Threatened with bodily harm, the staff swiftly sprang to it, helping gather up Dick's gear. Those bastards would have let him just die there if it weren't for Ledes.

No trace of Dick's DD214, the official Department of Defense service record a veteran needed to get into a VA hospital where they would know how to take care of an old soldier with problems. Whom did we know, what strings could we pull? I called northern Virginia, where retired colonel Stew McCarty, with whom I'd fought in Korea, went into action. McCarty had never heard of Dick Brennan, but he got onto the military records department in St. Louis and came up with the DD214, which got Dick into the hospital. It was sufficient to McCarty that a Marine was in trouble, and he did what Marines do—we bring home the wounded.

Dick ended sadly, wasting away in the VA hospital at West Haven. We sent books and *The New Yorker* and *Time* and *Newsweek,* and tried to cheer him, but he didn't read much anymore. Didn't seem anxious to get out of there or get better. Even quit working on his play about U. S. Grant. His last employer, a good man who ran the insurance company, was a fan of Dick's, and faithful, and kept going up to West Haven to sit with a man who didn't know him anymore. The insurance man may have been, except for Dick's brother, the last one ever to see him.

Word came from Joe Owen in April 1997. Joe was a Marine officer, a big guy, six five, who'd been badly shot up, spent seventeen months in naval hospitals, and wrote a wonderful book, *Colder than Hell.* His letter was brief:

"Dear Jim, Our dear pal, Dick Brennan, died Saturday. His brother Ned called me last night. Said that Dick's passing was a kindness from God. He had been unable to recognize even family members for two years. Ned asked me to notify you, John Ledes and Ace Parker. I spoke with Ace this morning and sent a fax to John.

"Dick Brennan! What a blessing to have had a friend like him in our lives! Semper fidelis, Joe Owen."

And so it was that, at a distance, we all mustered yet again in grief, the long and the short and the tall of us, bonding as Marines do after the firefight is ended, oblivious of caste or class, the wealthy lawyer Ledes, the heroic giant Owen, the Madison Avenue executive Ace Parker, myself, the newspaperman, just a few Marines tabulating our casualties, bringing out the wounded, burying the dead.

And saluting that beautiful innocent, the gallant Marine and our impoverished playwright manqué, Dick Brennan, who one magical night at the "21" Club drew the notice of a famous actress and great beauty, and yet said "non, merci" to Mademoiselle Denise Darcel.

Which is how to remember Dick.

CHAPTER 15

JAMES MICHENER, IN SEARCH OF A NEW NOVEL,

VISITED THE MARINES.

The newspapers our flight attendants passed around during the long flight to Inchon were full of stories from Iraq. With all the excitement, the embedded correspondents riding up there with the troops and getting shot at, I permitted my mind to wander back to the Taebaek Mountains of North Korea, the winter of 1951–52, when we rarely saw a journalist.

War correspondents were movie characters played by Clark Gable or Joel McCrea and not actual people. Well, Richard Harding Davis in the history books. Ernie Pyle, but the Japanese killed him. I suppose there were correspondents covering the Korean War, Maggie Higgins of the *Herald Trib* and Keyes Beech, David Douglas Duncan from *Life,* the wire-service men who actually saw some fighting. But most covered it from headquarters, attending press briefings, and didn't visit frontline troops. There weren't any of what le Carré in Cambodia would later call "warries," the young Fleet Streeters sent out to cover Asian wars, the most junior of them "looking like boy pilots in the Battle of Britain, fighting their borrowed war."

Then came James Michener to stay for a week with the rifle companies of the 2nd Battalion, 7th Marines, traveling I suppose on war correspondents' credentials. Maybe that made him the very first "embedded" reporter ever. We all knew who Michener was, of course, the writer who gave us *Tales of the South Pacific,* a small and wonderful book of war stories about sailors, mostly, and aviators and Marines and Navy nurses during World War II. It became one of the most glorious musicals ever on Broadway, a show I'd seen in college, with its original cast, Mary Martin and opera star Ezio Pinza, and later a blockbuster of a movie.

And, being Jim Michener, a writer who'd done one of the truly fine books of the Big War, he encountered no red tape or other difficulties in his desire to bunk in with some combat Marines. The brass understand positive ink. Ordinary Marines hoped he'd stay with us, that some of his celebrity might rub off, and people at home would read about us. Or we might end up in a bestseller.

Michener was quite frank about his intentions; he was a writer in search of his next yarn. He didn't hang out with our bunch, Dog Company. I can't recall just who got custody of the author, Fox or Easy Company. But men who met Michener declared him a very pleasant gent, properly appreciative of the work they were doing up there along the Kanmubong Ridge, patrolling, raiding, ambushing the North Koreans, and defending against similar enthusiasms on the enemy's part. And attempting to keep from freezing to death in the process. Michener got to see some snow, presumably felt the cold, maybe even heard a random mortar crump in, a few shots fired in anger. And eventually he went off, his notebooks filled.

Over the years, Michener wrote a couple of books about Korea: *The Bridges at Toko-ri,* a heartbreaking yarn about carrier pilots, and *Sayonara,* a grand love story between an Air Force ace enjoying R & R in Japan and a gorgeous Japanese actress. Both books would eventually become films, the first starring Bill Holden and Grace Kelly, the second Marlon Brando. In my idler postwar hours I occasionally found myself wondering, if Michener had gotten to know us at Dog Company, and ended up writing a Marine novel, might I have been played by Brando or Mr. Holden?

In the 1980s when I was working for CBS in New York I interviewed Jim Michener on TV about his latest book. And off-camera after the interview, I asked why he'd written about aviators and had never gotten a novel out of the Marines he'd stayed with that winter. He was surprised I even knew about that, and when I explained I'd been there, he said he had intended to do a book about the war we were fighting up on the ridgelines. But couldn't do it.

"The fliers took plenty of risks and a lot of them didn't come back. But the ones who did, came home every night to a base, they had lives beyond the war. They got leave, went to bars and out to dinner, they got drunk, they fell in love. There was simply better material there at hand for a novel."

He paused, as if to see if I understood, and then when he was convinced I did, Michener said something like this.

"You Marines were great. You lived the hardest life. I couldn't imagine living as you did up there all winter in holes in the ground. But all you ever did was fight. I tried but I just couldn't make a novel out of that."

All we ever did was fight? Not a bad eulogy if you think about it.

CHAPTER 16

Our 747 was deep into Asia by now and nearing touchdown when I thought of one of us 1950-era Marines who might have made a pretty fair Michener story, Jim Callan, who called himself "Wild Hoss," who was shipped out to Korea early on. And I was partially to blame for that, and for what happened to Callan later.

Wild Hoss was a blond-haired kid in tooled cowboy boots, a lean youngster but big shouldered and strong, with a flat mouth and narrow, squinty eyes (all that time on horseback looking into the southwestern sun?). He and his daddy had a cattle ranch there in New Mexico that was habitually going bust and so Jim Callan was saving all his Marine Corps money. After the war he was going back to help his daddy keep the ranch.

Callan made it sound as if the Comanches were on the warpath, circling their ranch just beyond the campfires, and where was the 7th Cavalry when you needed them? So he and his old dad would just save the homestead on their own with young Jim's Marine bankroll.

Wild Hoss was especially popular with me because he let me wear his cowboy boots. I was curious to see if a city kid could walk in them. And since I wore elevens and he had long feet, Callan humored me by letting me try them and clomp around the barracks. Dog and pony shows like that were popular and our pals fell about in mock hilarity, indulging us. I'd just finished reading a wonderful paperback novel by a writer called B. Traven. The book was *The Treasure of the Sierra Madre,* and since it was a great yarn set in Mexico, with lots of gunplay, hunting for gold, and fighting bandidos, I suspected Wild Hoss might enjoy it. Because I was an English major and while in college had worked the four-to-midnight shift as a copyboy for the *New York Daily News,* Callan would take advice from me on literary matters, whereas my opinion on, say, longhorn cattle or the War Between the States would be of no value whatever. So he promised to read the novel and carried it in the pocket of his field jacket and would get it out during a break or at night.

Wild Hoss surreptitiously was reading *Treasure* one warmish afternoon during an especially dull lecture by a dreary but, unfortunately, keen-eyed instructor. "You there, Lieutenant, stand up." Callan looked around. "Yes, you, mister. What's your name?"

Callan told him, sir-ring him to a fare-thee-well. Times like that, a little sucking up couldn't hurt.

"Bring that book up here."

Wild Hoss climbed sheepishly onto the speaker's stage and handed over the garishly colored book with its jacket sketch of cacti and Mexican bandidos. The lecturer pounced.

"I thought so. Is this the latest field manual, small-unit tactics?" he inquired sarcastically.

"No, sir."

"And?"

"No excuse, sir."

"Well, I'll just keep this book, Callan. And you'll report yourself to your platoon leader."

"Aye, aye, sir."

Wild Hoss sought me out later after he'd reported himself, to apologize for having lost my book. "I'll get you another copy," he promised.

"Hell with it. Sorry I got you in trouble."

When we graduated from Basic School early in April, Jim Callan was shipped off on leave with orders to report in to Pendleton and then join the division as a replacement platoon leader. I believed they thought I was still so immature that I could use another four months at Quantico, in effect sending me twice through the same courses, first as a student, then the second time as a teacher. Not a bad idea, either.

It worked out fine because my first command was composed entirely of mustangs, enlisted Marines who'd been Marines for years, had gone through a ninety-day screening, and then been commissioned. Most of them were older than I was, all of them had been Marines longer, and I learned more from them than they ever learned from me. It was some platoon!

Pete Soderbergh was the catcher on our softball team and what they themselves called "our resident genius," despite his affinity for rolling around happily in the playing field mud or dust, which gave him a resemblance to Pig Pen in the *Peanuts* comic. Soderbergh was something of a star in Korea, married a woman Marine, ended up administering a big southern college, and his son Steven makes Hollywood movies. Carl Ullrich was athletic director (at different times) of both Annapolis and West Point and later ran the Patriot League. Archer Parr became a legendary Texas sheriff, and Dr. Sam Hazo the first poet laureate of Pennsylvania.

The skipper was Captain Robert McNeil. The Yankees were in town playing the Senators over the weekend and Captain McNeil was strolling in Washington on Sunday morning when a husky young man with a suntan and a crew cut hailed him.

"Captain, it's me, sir. Henry Bauer from your platoon in the war."

They shook hands, and McNeil, who didn't follow sports very closely, asked, "And what did you end up doing when you got out of the Corps, Bauer?"

"I went into baseball, sir," said Hank Bauer. "I play right field for the New York Yankees."

Our executive officer was Captain Bill Doelger, a tall, lean, rather dashing Annapolis grad who had been an enlisted man before going to the Academy (he would end up a general), and drove a sleek, black, and powerful Buick Roadmaster convertible we all lusted after, and which Doelger spoke of and addressed endearingly as "You big black son of a bitch!" He seemed to share the doubts my platoon had about me and expressed them through customarily clenched teeth.

"I've seen your scores, Brady. So I know you're intelligent. But some of the things you do, man! I dunno, I just don't know."

Yet I'd been left behind at Quantico to train others while a better man like Callan, who'd gotten a bad chit, was shipped out to the war.

He and Bob Bjornsen, the forest ranger, and Doug Bradlee, the Harvard tackle, each of them half a head taller than Wild Hoss Callan, ended up in the same rifle company which was about to jump off against the Chinese. That's how fast the division was losing platoon leaders that spring, one rifle company getting replacements three at a time. Bjornsen was a mustang who'd fought the Japanese, but Doug and Wild Hoss were, like me, just out of college, one month out of Quantico. Still kids, but everyone knew they were going to be swell Marines. No such unanimity of opinion about me.

Letters began to come back to Quantico from the front, mostly from Bradlee, some direct, some forwarded by his dad in Boston.

He wrote eloquently, for a football player. But then, we're talking Harvard.

"The country is very rugged, almost unbelievably so. . . . We are dug in for the evening around the bottom of a ravine for a change. Stream about 100 yards away, babbling over stones, cold and clear. Washed myself and clothes and feel wonderful. . . . Yesterday my platoon was sent up to seize a ridge. We really pushed hard and found the Chinks had stopped on a ridge 600 to 800 yards away. Small arms and machine gun fire came sporadically but we didn't pay much attention and they gave up in disgust. Marines are far and away best fighters in Korea but tired out. I've lost five men in the last three days through heat prostration and exhaustion. Platoon very good. Company commander is good, and whole outfit and whole 1st Division very sharp.

"The spirit of the Corps never ceases to amaze me. Walking to our assembly area yesterday it rained all the way. Much singing, horseplay, laughter, even though pretty miserable actually. Spirits kept high and we were rewarded by a beautiful day when we arrived.

"Have impression of Korean civilians, farmers, as they watch Marines move onto their farms and set up camp. They can only look and hope for the best. No language bridge, so no talk exchanged, except extra rations usually find their way to them. Many houses burn because of thatched roofs. On ridges at night I can usually see two or three burning in valleys below. Usual procedure is to set up in a line around a bowl of terrain. Each platoon tied in with one on each side. Fighting holes are on the front slope, sleeping holes on the reverse side.

"Amazing thing here is that there are mockingbirds exactly the same as in Colorado."

There were no such letters from Jim Callan; maybe he was writing them to the folks back home. Then we got word.

Wild Hoss was dead. Killed, we heard, by a Chinese mortar shell, in June of 1951. No details.

I wrote about him years later in *Parade* magazine. His sister Gloria Callan Toombs wrote me a letter about him, about how his death nearly broke the family, how he had been their hope. It was some letter.

Dear Mr. Brady, For 49 years I have looked at pictures and war stories and TV pictures to see if I would ever hear or see anything about my brother. In the Pa-rade today, there is my brother's name mentioned: Wild Horse Callan of New Mexico. I was in shock and I can only have this thought: someone besides those of us who adored him, remembered Korea.

"Wild Horse" [that was how she spelled her brother's nickname] was really James Callan III from Menard, Texas, a descendant of Texas pioneers and of the Republic of Texas. He graduated after World War II ended from Texas A&M University and moved with all my family to a new ranch in New Mexico. We were newcomers there, having been in Texas since before the Civil War, indeed during the days when Texas was a nation.

Our lives, after the shock and incredulity of his death, were forever changed. There were my parents, Mr. and Mrs. James Callan Jr., and my brother and sister left besides me. Months later, about the time you arrived in Korea, our brother's body returned, flag-draped, and the tears have been flowing ever since.

His grave is in the Callan family plot in Menard, Texas. Only the simple GI stone marks his grave: "Lt. James Callan III, USMC July 9, 1925–June 14, 1951, Korea."

This is all that's left. He was 25 years old. My mother is next to him; then my father and grandmother, all with the same headstones. There is a marble Catholic cross in the center of the plot that says "Callan."

My magazine piece had cautioned against the country's sending off, all too casually, young American soldiers into places like Bosnia and Kosovo (Afghanistan and Iraq II were still in the future), warning of casualties and the human cost. It was that point which Mrs. Toombs addressed.

We shouldn't fight not to win. Even now. We shouldn't put up with defending our Constitution and our Bill of Rights with any thought but to win. Thanks for remembering my brother and the other martyrs. I wonder if any of them knew Jimmie. And how can I find out more . . . ?

I didn't know any more, I told her. By the time I got to Korea, Wild Hoss was dead five months, that wonderful boy with the enduring grin and the squinty cowboy eyes.

CHAPTER 17

EIGHT THOUSAND OF US WERE STILL MIA,
LOST IN THE SNOWY MOUNTAINS.

Our jet was over Korea now, Inchon just off there to the left, sticking out like a dowager's pinkie extended from the teacup of South Korea into the Yellow Sea. Aboard the 747 we were all awake, the businessmen and everyone, even Eddie. The stews bustled, collecting earphones and passing out heated towels. A good flight, and it had gotten me back to Korea.

Year after year, as decades go by, its veterans grow older and Korea remains "forgotten," a savage incident shadowed over by that great historical event of the century, World War II, and by Vietnam.

People who tabulate such things tell us that of the 14 million Americans who served in the Second World War, the veterans are now dying off at the rate of a thousand a day. I have no idea if similar counts are made of Korean veterans. But you figure it out. Of the three Medal of Honor winners there on the football field at Camp Pendleton that sunny afternoon in the year 2000 when we saluted the Chosin Few, only one, Hector Cafferata, is still alive. General Ray Davis and Colonel Bill Barber are gone. And on that day both were not simply alive but hale, vigorously shaking hands, gallant, apparently indestructible men who fought the Chinese at the reservoir. A fight most Americans have now forgotten.

This callous dismissal of Korea is hardly limited to civilians. Even men who fought there recognize our war for what it was, hard but small, inarguably not World War II. Sergeant Wooten, the ultimate old salt, with the career soldier's appreciation of whatever war came along, chided me for my lack of respect and, defending Korea, kept reminding me: "Mr. Brady, it ain't much of a war. But it's the only war we got."

As the jet began its descent, I wondered yet again, Just what did we accomplish here? Korea had its moments, its highs and lows of elation and despair, its glorious wins and tragic losses, and probably was worth fighting. The historians will eventually figure that out.

It was Harry Truman's finest hour, his decision to fight it validating the notion of an actual UN army taking the field against aggression; it finished off the great soldierly career and the overarching political ambitions of Douglas MacArthur, and may have won Ike the White House; it surely saved South Korea; arguably it kept Japan from going Communist; it permitted Red China to make its entrance onto the world stage yet disproved the invincibility of its huge army; Korea reinforced a long and honorable fighting partnership between ourselves and the Brits; it burnished yet again the reputation of our own Marine Corps, adding Korea to the pantheon alongside Tripoli and Belleau Wood, Guadalcanal and Iwo.

But that too is the stuff of history.

For those of us who fought there, especially boys too young for World War II, Korea was something personal. When the Marines went ashore at Iwo, I was a high school junior, sixteen years old. When Hitler killed himself, when the Hiroshima bomb was dropped and an arrogant Japan sued for peace, I was still sixteen. Our bunch, the "Korea generation," weren't the men who won the Big War, weren't Michener's or Irwin Shaw's or Mailer's or Kurt Vonnegut's heroes. Nor were we the men about whom all those Hollywood movies were made. We weren't a generation Tom Brokaw would later call "the greatest." Because we had in some vaguely shameful way missed that war.

Korea would offer us our chance to prove ourselves as equal to the Old

Breed who defeated Japan, our opportunity to cross the great Pacific, to fight and win another war in a strange and deadly place, "beyond the seas."

Korea was to be *our* war.

And now as the men who fought there die off, a few other Americans, young men as we once were, continue to stand sentinel along a demilitarized zone 155 miles in length, today's handful of gun-toting GIs on ranging duty, going out through the minefields and the barbed wire, looking for trouble.

North of the same line lurks a hostile and much larger army. And the only thing between them and us is the DMZ, where Eddie Adams and I had been and were going again.

The DMZ is drawn on the footprints of the past, the ridgelines and high ground blooded by the young men of half a century before, and it is there that today's GIs patrol. Where they don their helmets and their flak jackets, lubricate their weapons, snap to for the sergeant, grouse about the weather and the stinking hills, and curse their luck, drill and run field problems, hope for an early rotation home, and wait for another war. In other words they do what soldiers everywhere have always done. They wait. And they wait. And like the wartime émigrés stranded in *Casablanca*, they wait.

And then every so often, the North Koreans (those bastards!) do something nasty or just plain stupid, and that forgotten little place is momentarily back on the evening news.

Once you've asked if a war was worth fighting, you must also inquire, and what did it cost? I've spoken of the thirty-seven thousand American dead. I have no idea how many of the more than a hundred thousand wounded still suffer. What of the emotionally and psychologically damaged? We'd not yet discovered post-traumatic stress disorder, but I suppose there were some of us who had it. The Vietnam War has calculated such casualty figures; Korea never did. There are also at this writing still another 8,100 Americans missing in Korea, their bodies never found. You hear plenty about Vietnam MIAs, but rarely of the Korea missing. Few theories are promulgated, no deep plots suspected. After the fighting ended in 1953 a few reports began to trickle out, about American POWs, their boots stolen, having been hustled north barefoot through the mountain snow into Manchuria, of others shipped farther north into Siberia. Gruesome stories, none of them proved, emerged about executions, about cruel treatment, even about medical and other ghastly experiments, some of them laid not to the Chinese or the North Koreans but to the Russians. Tales of Soviet doctors and shrinks called in to study torture, who stood up to it longer, more stoically, blacks or whites, the Irish or the Italians, southerners or easterners? The usual wartime atrocity stories, fact or wild rumor? The government in Washington wasn't saying.

Some U.S. pilots shot down over North Korea were stripped naked and tied to barbed-wire fencing overnight in winter, drenched with buckets of water, and left to freeze to death. POWs confirmed these accounts. As for the other missing Yanks, no great mystery about most of them, no paranoia or conspiracy theories. Those men were surely dead in a hard country, killed or wounded and left behind to die, frozen under the snow and ice or drowned in the paddies or lost at the bottom of ravines or their bones bleached white on mountaintops where nobody goes, chewed over by the wolves and bears and the smaller scavenging birds and carnivorous beasts and worms of Northeast Asia. Which is what happens in all wars.

And as Mr. Bush's army, the way cleared by those "shock and awe" attacks, neared Baghdad, a few of us asked, might Korea be our next war, the war after Iraq?

CHAPTER 18

SHRAPNEL WHIZZED MERRILY ABOUT,

CLANGING OFF THE GALVANIZED TIN SHEDS.

The big plane dropped low enough on its flight path to the new In-chon airport that I could pick out Wolmi-do Island and its cause-way to the mainland, keys to the Marine assault on Inchon in September of 1950, Douglas MacArthur's brilliant left hook, and the famous seawall over which the Marines scrambled with grappling hooks and scaling ladders. But I couldn't locate the long concrete pier off which we'd been fer-ried out to the troopship *General Meigs* that rainy night I left Korea.

I could do without the seawall, but that pier meant something to me. It was where three thousand of us were trapped and damned near killed our last day in the war.

A small Japanese freighter, loaded with ammo, had taken fire and was at risk of blowing, with an entire rotation draft of American Marines and GIs squatting just yards away. After a year of war and on the way home, here we were with an ammunition ship blazing merrily away and crewmen leaping from the deck into the Yellow Sea to escape the fire and explosions. The other crewmen, the stubborn ones who stayed with their ship, they were what saved it, and all of us as well.

There was no way on a narrow pier that three thousand men could have gotten ashore without panic, chaos, and people trampled to death, and it was those dumb Japanese swabbies who gallantly hung in there hosing down the fire and tossing ammo crates overboard who saved us, saved the day.

Good men, those sailors.

I was a company commander by then (if only of a four-hundred-man rotation draft company), and when the explosions started I ordered helmets on. I don't know what good that might do but it was all I could think of. While we all just sat there, debris raining down, some of it smoking or aflame, and shrapnel whizzed merrily about, clanging off the galvanized sheds of the pier and ricocheting off the concrete flooring, we had our hats on but no place to go. There was one moment of jollity when a couple of the Army guys closest to the shore panicked and started to run, and the Marines waved handkerchiefs, "Bye, girls!" all the time wishing we too could get off the dock like the doggies but not close enough to pull it off.

In the end, no one was killed, only a few of the Japanese were burned, but Korea didn't give up easily; it surely had a way of hanging on to the bitter end. Near midnight the lighters took us off in a steady rain.

When our 747 touched down at Inchon, having traveled nine thousand miles and never caught up with night, it was midday and sunny.

There were supposed to be some Army officers there to greet us but we didn't see any uniforms. Eddie Adams had a fallback position.

"You can't trust the effing Army. No problem. I've got this pal, see. He runs the Korean Olympic committee (actually the Olympic Convention Center). He's a great guy and knows everybody. He was very close to their last vice president. Or maybe the last president. He's my best friend in Seoul and he's connected. He'll get us up to your Hill 749 if anyone can."

"What's his name?"

"I forget. Jong or Jung or something [it turned out to be Sang Hae Jung]. One of my best friends."

But the American Army hadn't let us down. Two of their officers were there waiting. And so was a Mr. Hong. Not Eddie's best friend but, in this instance, even more helpful.

The Americans were Lieutenant Colonel Steve Boylan, born in Astoria,

New York, and Major Holly Pierce ("Yes," she admitted, "they do on occasion call me 'Hawkeye'") of Star Lake, New Mexico ("right up on the Continental Divide"), who was blond and attractive and a trade school grad, a West Pointer. My, the Army was doing it up right. Sending a colonel and a West Pointer to look after us. Both officers were in very casual civvies. There'd been some ugly anti-American riots (we later learned Boylan had been stabbed by three rioters just before Christmas) and there was no need to call attention.

Hong worked for the Army, facilitating things. He was one of those clever, invaluable fixers you see hanging about seaports and airports the world over. They get things done, know the ropes, cut through the red tape, shake the right hands, know whom to tip, which palms to grease. Steve Boylan and Holly were our babysitters; it was Mr. Hong who hustled us through, got our luggage, and flashed our passports around. I've spent more time getting through airport formalities at O'Hare. When I tried to tip him, Hong shook his head. The United States Army employed him to do these things; it was an honor.

They had an Army car and uniformed driver (so much for camouflage) and they sped us along good highways into the city. I'd forgotten how the mountains sort of crowded into the town, how right down some dull, routine little street of shops, you turned a corner and there rising up before you was a brown hill about the size of New York's Bear Mountain, but without the ski jump.

I stared out in growing fascination as the suburbs sped past and we rolled into Seoul itself. Was it really half a century? Boylan and "Hawkeye" Pierce pointed out the sights. I was wrong about this trip being *The Canterbury Tales*. It was beginning to feel like the mysterious East, pure Conrad! With its warlords and coolies and sailing junks, colonial governors in Palm Beach suits, slinky Eurasian beauties, and White Russian émigré generals driving taxis, sinister fellows from Mr. Moto movies, lascar seamen, and drunken remittance men who could still sing the "Eton Boating Song."

Or so I imagined, excited all over again about Asia, channeling Conrad, while at my side Eddie Adams cursed the traffic.

By now we were in sight of a big river, which I knew to be the Han, running a mile wide at places. From the western bank of the Han River while we were still way out, you could see Seoul rising in the distance, the Seoul skyline—Donald Trump run amok, a very tall house of cards?

"The bridges will be coming up," the colonel said, "where we cross into the city itself."

I had crossed the Han before. Had fought on the Han, April of '52 if memory served. Not that the fighting was much, artillery duels mostly, the Chinese Army on the far shore, us on the near shore on Kimpo Peninsula.

We ran amphibious landings on the Han as we had done on the Potomac near George and Martha Washington's plantation at Mount Vernon. As we had run landings out of Camp Pendleton on the beach at Oceanside, California, where small children built sand castles and ignored the Marines. You give the USMC brass an empty hour and they'll fill it with a small-boat exercise. They're kind of fun, too, more so than trotting up and down hills in the heat. And with amphibious landings sometimes you ran into girls sunning or in the surf. That was fun, too. Landings on hostile beaches, those were less amusing. Ask any old 2nd Division Marine who waded the lagoon at Tarawa.

Later, May of '52, the real fighting against the Chinese began on the other bank of the Han in the low, sandy hills just north of the Double Bend of the Imjin River.

When we crossed the Han this time and got into Seoul itself and the kaleidoscope of midtown traffic, and reached the Westin Chosun Hotel, Eddie's "best friend" was there in the lobby. He embraced Eddie and kissed him a couple of times. I settled for a handshake. With Mr. Jung were a couple of assistant managers and a squad of bellmen, their arms full of flowers. For the next couple hours they were hunting up sufficient vases so that before I was even unpacked, my room resembled Healy's funeral parlor in Sheepshead Bay. I'm sure Eddie's room was even more handsomely appointed. Jung was charming, expansive, well dressed, and pretty fluent in English.

Maybe I've grown cynical, been a newspaperman too long.

"This guy Mafia?" I asked Eddie. He looked at me as if I'd insulted his dear old mother.

"Jung? You're kidding. He's the true bill. Arranged the Olympics here!"

How do you "arrange the Olympics"? I wondered. The two of them were already plotting a number of elaborate evening social events, jabbering away, very graciously including me. And I kept busy thinking up reasons just as politely to decline.

When I go away for the weekend I pack as meticulously as if accompanying Scott to the South Pole. Yet I always forget something. This time it was toothpaste. I returned to the lobby to scout up some in the gift shop.

"Toothpaste, please," I told the young man, articulating very loudly, as Americans do with foreigners, and miming a brushing movement and pointing to my mouth.

"Yes," he informed me, "there are many varieties of delicious pastry. The bake shop is to the left."

There turned out to be toothpaste in the room. But after a fourteen-hour flight, what did my breath matter? I slept until the next day.

Skyscrapers hovered outside every window. Luxury department stores that could humble Saks Fifth Avenue, more new cars than Detroit, bustling commerce and industry, TV screens tuned to CNBC and the latest Dow.

Last time I'd seen Seoul I was armed and in a jeep, and I don't believe there was a building taller than two stories left unscathed in the whole god-forsaken town, and the only traffic was Army trucks and tanks, the only civilians a few woebegone homeless living on the streets and begging food.

Our first serious appointment would be Friday afternoon with General Leon LaPorte, the American four-star general who was in command of everything over here, not only our own GIs but the Republic of Korea (ROK) Army and small detachments of Brits and a couple of other allied nations. I'd read up on General LaPorte in the plane and knew he came from Rhode Island. Had he known John Chafee? I wondered. Reporters are always looking for an edge.

What an odd couple we made to be calling on generals: Eddie with his white ponytail and black clothes and baseball cap, an old Marine buck sergeant resembling the last of the hippies; me an aging lieutenant on a gimpy knee, togged out in Merrell hiking boots and a pink Brooks Brothers shirt and rep tie under tweeds—a pair of old Marine jarheads set down on an alien landscape.

So we began what would turn out to be a cool adventure, a mix of catharsis and elation, alternately giddy and fulfilling, emotionally moving and oddly quite pleasant, with the two of us having ourselves a hell of a time. Whether it was Conrad or Chaucer, it was nice to be back.

To where it all started so long ago.

CHAPTER 19

On the Sunday morning in June of 1950 when the Korean War began, they hesitated to wake General of the Army Douglas
MacArthur at his shogunate in Tokyo. Sundays, the General slept
in. On this Sunday, June 25, the president of the Republic of Korea was
phoning from Seoul to inform the General that his country was being invaded and to request immediate American assistance. There were already 450
U.S. military advisers in South Korea, but Rhee knew, correctly, he needed
more than a few advisers. Told the General was not to be disturbed, Rhee
went into something of a screech.

Would General MacArthur sleep comfortably while Americans were being killed "one by one" in Korea? In fact, few if any Americans had yet been
killed, but the North Koreans were surely coming on fast, and at places quite
dramatically so. In Kaesong, a big border town and railhead, a freight train
rolled routinely at dawn into the sleepy downtown station, the boxcar doors
slid open, and a thousand Red shock troops jumped out and began killing
people.

When aides finally summoned the courage to rouse MacArthur, he listened to President Rhee, promised to send ten planes and a few howitzers and

bazookas, and then did nothing. Rhee was an old man given to crying wolf. Later that Sunday an American journalist about to fly home got to MacArthur and asked for guidance. Should he instead hang around Tokyo to cover a possible war? The General sloughed off the fighting as "a border incident. The Koreans can handle it."

The great man was wrong. This was more than just another "incident." And the South Koreans couldn't "handle it." Not with Russian-supplied Yak fighters strafing the ROK troops and civilians (the ROK Air Force had already been destroyed lined up wingtip to wingtip on the ground!) and with the North's tough peasant army, spearheaded by huge Russian T-34 tanks, smashing through everywhere along the thinly defended 150-mile artificial border of the Thirty-eighth Parallel. The North was very much a client state of Stalin's Soviet Union, as the South was a client, though less well armed or equipped, of Washington.

By Tuesday Seoul had fallen, and the president, his Austrian wife, and their cronies, along with the national treasury in gold, had fled south by two special trains. ROK parliamentarians of the National Assembly, primly but rather admirably, stayed put. They would meet and dicker with the invaders as representing, in Rhee's absence, the legitimate government. None of these innocents ever got to dicker; Communist infantrymen simply herded the legislators out into the courtyard and shot them.

In Washington, Harry Truman declared the North's move was naked aggression against a friendly and at least putatively democratic nation (Rhee was in reality an autocrat), and decided to intervene. As the UN voted to raise an army, the first dribs and drabs of American reinforcements began to arrive, intending to stiffen the fleeing, panicked South Koreans. Surely the mere sight of big, healthy Yanks would cow the oncoming Reds. No sale! These GIs MacArthur had rushed over were not organized fighting units but occupation troops, soft, slack and undisciplined, ill-trained, lightly armed, and pulled together from the bars and drug dens of Tokyo and their Japanese girlfriends' beds. Not surprisingly, they were brushed aside or rolled over by the advancing Red troops. It was still the time of segregation, and one American Army outfit, the 24th Infantry Regiment, an all-black unit with mostly white officers and lousy morale, early on and cynically fashioned a song to accompany its retreats, "The Bug Out Blues."

Even the first two American Army divisions shipped over piecemeal from Japan were badly handled. The commanding general of the 24th Division, the courageous but hapless Bill Dean, separated from his men, was reported missing in action, wandered hurt and hungry around the South Korean hills for a month, and was eventually sold for a few bucks to the Communists by a "friendly" farmer. Dean spent the next three years in a POW camp. Not since "Skinny" Wainwright on Corregidor was ordered to surrender to the Japanese in early 1942 had an American major general been taken prisoner.

That, too, unhappily, was on Douglas MacArthur's watch.

Despite our air power and the admitted brilliance of MacArthur (he was now officially in charge, though still working out of Tokyo barring a few flying day trips to Korea), no real stand was made by the Americans and their battered allies the ROKs until the Naktong River, far to the south of Seoul, along a line that came to be known as the Pusan Perimeter. By then some better-organized U.S. units had landed, including a provisional brigade of Marines, and after stiff, bloody fighting in the sapping August heat, with the North having suffered its first real losses and outrun its supply lines, things stabilized. Serious talk of a Dunkirk sort of evacuation by sea was dropped.

MacArthur was an old man and crazy, but he was still a great soldier, and ambitious. The General had his eye on 1952 and the Republican nomination. He was sure that God had ordained him to lead his country as he had led armies, and to become president. And not that charm-school faker Eisenhower, who had never fought, and had once long ago served as an aide under MacArthur and, ever after, been cruelly demeaned as "the best secretary I ever had."

And along with God, the Hearst papers and Colonel McCormick's *Chicago Tribune* were lining up. Saving Korea, coming on top of his victory over the Japanese and his successful vice-regency of postwar Japan, would swing the party behind him in '52. Now, all he had to do was end this crappy little war quickly to defeat Ike. Ego, arrogance, ambition, war—a volatile mix.

So in September, MacArthur unleashed a powerful left hook spearheaded by the 1st Marine Division. Even the Marines, serial haters of MacArthur from World War II, acknowledged that his scheme to land far behind enemy lines at Inchon, disregarding the risk and its ferocious tides, was a brilliant and courageous tactical stroke. Seoul was liberated after a mule-headed and costly frontal assault choreographed by MacArthur (for political reasons he wanted the city freed three months to the day from its capture).

Now, with winter coming on and Mao Tse-tung threatening to intervene if the UN forces even approached the long border of North Korea with China along the meandering Yalu River, General MacArthur divided his army into two parallel columns and ordered it north at flank speed, laughing off Chinese threats ("a bunch of laundrymen") and discounting the weather and the terrible, mountainous terrain. The war, he demanded, had to be finished off quickly. An aide suggested (the quote was never that of the General himself!) that he wanted "the boys home for Christmas."

The Supreme Commander was in a hurry. And he was in denial. When the first Chinese bodies were brought in, MacArthur's intelligence chief, General Willoughby, scoffed. "Another goddamned Marine lie," he told the press. As the Allied armies hunted down fleeing North Koreans, the temperature dropped, snow now cloaked the northern Taebaek Mountains, the first pitched battles were fought against Chinese regulars. "A few volunteers," MacArthur believed them to be. Or contemptuously said he did.

As November deepened and readings fell below zero Fahrenheit, you could see disaster coming. Over Thanksgiving weekend, up near the Chosin Reservoir, an estimated twelve Chinese Communist divisions snapped a trap on the 1st Marine Division and the 7th Army Infantry Division. To the west, on the far side of the mountain range dividing MacArthur's two armies, other U.S. and Allied divisions reeled backward under Chinese hammer blows. Only a gallant Turk detachment, just arrived in town and lacking interpreters, stood fast, mowing down the attacking "Chinese," only to learn the men they'd slaughtered were panicked, fleeing South Koreans. The next day the genuine Chinese swarmed over the Turks.

Welcome to the party, lads!

CHAPTER 20

SUDDENLY, AND OFF-KEY, SOMEONE BEGAN BAWLING OUT
"THE MARINES' HYMN."

That same November of 1950, the 7th Army Infantry Division was mauled on the eastern shore of the big reservoir, with its two best regimental combat teams smashed, and both of their commanding colonels, Allen D. MacLean and Don Faith, dead. The survivors, those not chivvied out onto the ice of the great lake and hunted down like animals by the Chinese, made their way south and west to hook up with the Marines and some British Royal Marine Commandos, who had begun a desperate, fighting withdrawal toward the sea through terrible mountains, snowstorms out of Siberia, and with the mercury standing at twenty below. Fahrenheit!

Abruptly it looked not only as if MacArthur's White House aspirations were finished, but that it was entirely possible he might lose his entire army, outnumbered and battered and confused as it was. The Marines' epic fight along narrow, precipitous mountain tracks, smashing Red roadblocks as they moved, so badly damaged the Chinese that four of their twelve divisions had to be withdrawn. The great march culminated in an orderly evacuation from Hungnam on December 15. The Americans, though not all of them, would live to fight again.

MacArthur still had his army. But barely. On the sixteenth Truman declared a state of national emergency at home. In Washington and across the nation, it would be a bleak Christmas. The third of January 1951 I reported for active duty to the Marine Corps Schools at Quantico, and Seoul was abandoned to the advancing Chinese. So was Inchon, where in September MacArthur's light had never shone brighter. Now his future appeared clouded. The drumbeating in the Hearst papers fell mute; there was less talk now in the *Chicago Trib* of a MacArthur presidency. But the old man continued to politick, writing privately to Republican House leader Joe Martin letters critical of U.S. policy, most of his arguments rubbish. Importing, to save the day, Chiang's disgraced and incompetent army from Taiwan. Dropping the H-bomb on China. Risking World War III. Truman had finally had enough. On April 11 he sacked MacArthur and named Matt Ridgway, the old paratrooper, supreme Allied commander.

The war continued for another twenty-seven months. But the dramatic dashing north and south were pretty much over. A slugging match ensued, less glamorous but even more deadly. By late 1951 the war had settled into a kind of 1914–18 trench warfare which had bled the Brits, the French, and the Kaiser's Germans into near exhaustion in the First World War. Now it was pretty much the Americans and Chinese regulars who faced each other, slugging it out toe to toe, raiding and shelling and sniping from the trench lines.

From November of '51 to July of '52, I fought in that stage of the war.

As a negotiated truce neared in early 1953, both sides vied to hold on to the high ground along what would become today's Demilitarized Zone. The UN side, our people, manned defensive positions in low hills masking higher mountains and ridgelines from the enemy. The Chinese, under specific orders from Mao in Beijing to "take the high ground," threw their divisions into the fight to capture not only the "outposts" but the higher ridges behind them, so as to win a strategic territorial edge as a political bargaining chip during the uneasy peace that was to come.

This was what they called "the Outpost War," and I fought in one of its first battles—a skirmish, really—on a hill called Yoke. But later it became an organized and ghastly slaughter. You couldn't, not even Marines could, hold low hills like these with little cover against thousands of good infantry advancing, with predictably bloody results, through their own artillery barrages.

Think about that. When we laid down artillery concentrations and followed up the shelling with attacking infantry and tanks, the troops didn't jump off until the shells stopped falling. The Chinese divisions jumped off before the guns stopped firing, coming up the hills under heavy fire from their own guns. The hills had to fall. Only to be retaken the next day by exhausted Marines supported by air, napalm, bombs, strafing. Then to be submerged again the next night by the regimental human waves of endless Chinese manpower. We had six U.S. divisions in Korea; Chairman Mao had forty!

Brave men, really good infantry on both sides, caught up in a stupid, irrational meat-grinder carnage. What they called in the First World War, with a sour wit, "the sausage factory." Night after deadly night, the armies fought and died, night after night, month after month after month. . . .

At ten in the evening of July 27, 1953, the Korean War ended. Martin Russ, a tall young college-educated Marine sergeant serving in the same front lines where I'd fought a year before, would write about the moment in his splendid memoir, *The Last Parallel*.

Marty is today still tall, a bearded, happily married family man, pestered by Parkinson's and somewhat reclusive, who lives at Oakville, California, in the wine country, writing important books (he once worked in Hollywood for Stanley Kubrick helping Nabokov convert *Lolita* into a screenplay). His eloquent description of that last night of the Korean War continues to resonate:

"A beautiful full moon hung low in the sky like a Chinese lantern. Men appeared along the trench, some of them had shed their helmets and flak jackets. The first sound we heard was a shrill group of voices, calling from the Chinese positions behind the cemetery on Chogum-ni. The Chinese were singing. A hundred yards down the trench someone started shouting the Marines' Hymn at the top of his lungs. Others joined in, bellowing the words. Everyone was singing in a different key and phrases apart. Across the wide paddy, in goonyland, matches were lit. We all smoked for the first time in the MLR [main line of resistance] trench. The men from Outpost Ava began to straggle back, carrying heavy loads. Later a group of Chinese strolled over to the base of Ava and left candy and handkerchiefs as gifts. The men that were still on Ava stared, nothing more. So ends the Korean conflict, after some 140,000 American casualties."

Marty Russ's stats have been altered somewhat by subsequent official recount. But his sketch of that night the Korean War ended remains seared in memory, the shrill Chinese song, the off-key, bellowed "Marines' Hymn," the gifts of candy offered by the enemy, coldly rejected by the Marines, the stony stares and nothing more, of the Americans manning the outposts.

These were men who had nothing to smile about, who had lost too much and won too little.

CHAPTER 21

In the spring of 2003, up on the DMZ, Bill Clinton's "scariest place,"
two hostile armies faced off.

Considering that north of that line they were developing a nuclear
arsenal, the former president's description seemed valid. Personally, I found
Korea scary long before Mr. Clinton did.

When in late November of 1951 I arrived in country with Mack Allen, a
courtly Virginia gentleman from Lynchburg with cropped hair and jug ears
(an enlisted Marine in the Big War, later a graduate of VMI and the Harvard
Business School), to report in as replacement lieutenants to Captain John
Chafee's Dog Company up on Hill 749, we climbed the hill on a sunny
morning, accompanying the usual morning resupply column of Korean Service Corps bearers, but guided by Dog Company Marines wounded in the
bad September fighting. These men were now coming back from the hospitals and rehabs, as they said, with an understandable gallows humor, "for a
second helping."

We stuck to the path, under their instruction. There were mines all over
the goddamned hill, they said, theirs and ours.

The division Mack and I joined on the ridgelines that November may have been the largest, most powerful infantry division there ever was. It was big, twenty-five thousand men (the enemy divisions were smaller, ten thousand or so men), heavily armed, mobile, and very dangerous. In addition to the usual three infantry regiments, the 1st, 5th, and 7th Marines, and an artillery regiment, the 11th Marines, there was a fourth regiment of infantry, of KMCs, Korean Marines. There were ROK outfits of dubious reliability; you could rely on the KMCs, trained, organized, and equipped as they were, officers, sergeants, and men, by United States Marines. And the Marines had something no American Army division ever had: an entire air wing, so intimately coordinated with the ground troops that each of the nine Marine rifle battalions had two pilots attached to us to direct close air support. When the men on the ground calling in the air strikes were aviators themselves, temporarily pressed into the infantry, who had been flying such missions last month and would be flying them soon again, you could rely on those strikes.

The men of the division were a seasoned bunch. There were, as was expected, plenty of pimply-faced eighteen- and nineteen-year-old enlisted men, but even they had been fighting the North Koreans and the Chinese for months. Most of the staff NCOs and officers had fought the Japanese, and so had a surprising number of thirty-year-old corporals and buck sergeants, even the odd PFC (who'd probably been promoted, and busted back, several times in his career). There were some old China-side Marines like Captain George Howe with their colorful tales of Shanghai in 1937: the drunken rickshaw races on payday, the famed German brewery up at Tsingtao, the gorgeous Eurasian and White Russian women, a favorite waterfront gin mill where the bar girls sat on the Marines' laps and opened beer bottles with their teeth.

With all these salty veterans on hand, the 1st Marine Division had its ground rules: no freshly arrived replacement—officer, NCO, or enlisted man—was to go forward of the MLR for five days. The idea was to acclimate a new man, to let him orient himself so that he wouldn't get lost or confused in unfamiliar terrain and stumble into trouble.

Or do something really unpopular, like getting killed.

The rule was sensible and it worked. I welcomed the period of acclimation, aware of how much I didn't know, despite summers in the PLCs, nine months at the Basic School, advanced infantry training at Camp Pendleton, cold-weather drill up in the Sierras at Pickel Meadow, where in October, at eleven thousand feet, we ran field problems in a foot of snow. I was still considered, and considered myself, a green man.

Being a replacement, especially as an officer, is a weird, otherworldly experience. You don't know anyone, you don't yet have a job, you don't even know where to take a leak. Everyone else has been fighting; you haven't. The men you're about to command are veterans of combat, men hardened in firefights, while you've never heard a shot fired in anger. Yet, because the Marine Corps has trained you, you know that eventually you'll be of some value. Eventually you'll be one of the "few good men." But you're not there yet!

Even those first sheltered days on the line had their scary moments. Chafee was short two officers, but for the time being Mack was parceled out to the machine guns and I to the mortars, instructed not to give any orders but simply to bunk in with the men and pretty much take our lead from them, do what they did. Two more of Chafee's officers were due to be rotated home, Tex Lissman and Ed Flynn, and we would be given rifle platoons to command once the five days were up. Executive officer Red Phillips was assigned to show us the ropes.

We were out on a lope with Phillips along the snow-covered ridgeline of Hill 749 on that first day when a whiz and a bang crashed through the tranquil afternoon and Red Phillips leaped nimbly into a trench. Allen and I dove in, following close behind.

"We shouldn't have shown ourselves on the skyline," said Red. "They'll take a shot when they get the chance. Remember that. Don't get careless." He looked a little sheepish. The captain did not like replacements getting killed off before he got any work out of them.

"What *was* that?" Mack asked.

"A 76 millimeter. High-velocity flat-trajectory weapon. They do a nice job. If you hear the whiz and the bang both, that means they missed you. An accurate gun, modeled on the German 88 from the war."

"Oh."

A week ago I'd been on the beach at Waikiki. Here on a snow-covered ridgeline in North Korea, guys I'd never even seen were trying to blow me up because I took a stroll on the hilltop.

CHAPTER 22

L ate in the morning of our second day on the line, two Dog Company Marines were killed and two others badly hurt (one lost his
legs). There wasn't even a firefight. Just a single North Korean 82
mm mortar round tossed up almost casually without a ranging shot that
caught the four men lazing atop a bunker. It had been a rare clear day and the
men were sunning themselves. Chafee ordered the other platoons to shift a
few men around to fill in the blanks. He had been seeing Marines die since
Guadalcanal in 1942 and he just looked pained. It is the company commander who has to write home to the parents.

"Well, that happens. Blame the sunshine if you have to lay blame. Truman
himself couldn't keep Marines from getting some sun."

A chopper landed on the reverse slope (you couldn't bring in a helicopter
on the forward slope without taking fire) to pick up the two wounded
Marines, stowing each of them in a coffinlike box on either side of the small
craft to be flown to a medical unit at the Punchbowl. Helicopter time and
space were rare and expensive and restricted to the badly wounded and to senior officers; you didn't waste chopper time on stiffs. The dead Marines
would be lashed up lengthwise in ponchos and carried downhill to the divi-

sion morgue by the next day's "gook train," by the bearers, known as the "chiggy bears." It was cold enough overnight: "They won't spoil," an enlisted man said. It was weird to hear Marines wisecracking about their dead buddies, calling them "stiffs." Evidently, you developed a hard shell.

I was stunned by how fast things happened around here, by how swiftly, even without a battle going on, a healthy young man could die. And up here on the ridgeline, along the main line of resistance with its trenches and bunkers, was supposed to be relatively safe. That was why they had the five-days rule. Those four men hadn't been out on a patrol or an ambush or a duck blind, nothing like that. Just shooting the breeze, and now two of them were dead and one crippled.

The third or fourth night that I bunked in with the mortarmen in a large bunker of logs and sandbags started off quietly. Staff Sergeant Porterfield was in charge, but the chief mortarman was a diminutive but inspired madman who claimed to have pitched in the Southern League. I forget his name, "Dodge," maybe, but not that mad gleam in his eye. "All good mortarmen have that," I was assured by older hands.

I don't know how I expected that combat began—a gradual buildup of tensions, I supposed, muttered warnings, a message from headquarters, perhaps a ranging shot or two, you know, ready or not, here I come! Well, it wasn't anything like that.

I was awakened by voices, Porterfield on the field telephone. "Mr. Flynn is getting gook sound," he said. That must be Ed Flynn, whose platoon actually shared the 749 ridgeline with the enemy, at some places only fifty yards separating the two trench lines. Red Phillips had detailed this for Mack and me; we'd met Ed Flynn visiting him by trench, staying in the trench, heads down all the way.

"They'll kill you otherwise," Red explained. "For a good rifleman at fifty yards, it's no test, putting a bullet through a man's ear. Just call your shot, right ear or left?"

Dodge was already gone from the bunker, out rousing his crews. I got out of my sleeping bag, pulled on my boots, grabbed my helmet and carbine, and went outside to see what was happening. You don't want to be thought of as a guy who hangs back. I first expected it to be nearly dawn but it wasn't quite ten at night, a dark night with no moon but a lot of stars, the starlight reflecting off the snow. There was rifle fire and the heavy *rrrippp* of a machine gun somewhere nearby. I climbed up the reverse slope to see where the fighting was. I could hear Dodge swearing at his crews. Porterfield shouted at me: "Hey, Lieutenant, get off of there."

I slid back down the reverse slope to where Porterfield crouched.

"What are you doing on the skyline? Don't you know those people are firing at you?"

"Well," I said, excited, happy not to be dead but feeling pretty dumb, "I guess they were." Odd thing, I wasn't scared. Too ignorant to be.

Porterfield just looked disgusted. The company needed replacement platoon leaders and they sent me?

"Secure the guns, see-cure!" Dodge shouted. "Secure" was used as a verb in the Marines. Back in Quantico we turned it into a wise-guy joke: "There's no cure like see-cure." Dodge was cursing at one of his crew. He was always cursing at someone. Back in the sleeping bag it kept going through my head, being shot at, being chewed out by a sergeant, the shooting close up and personal, not at a distance as it was with the whiz-bang 76. I could have been hit. Could be dead right now. Was that how it happened, when you didn't expect it? When you weren't thinking? I hadn't yet given an order, hadn't gone out in front of the line or fired a shot. And almost got killed. Twice. I suspected I would dream a lot that night, muddled, weird stuff.

All that training at Quantico, those gold bars on my shoulders, what was I but a stupid kid posturing as a Marine officer? They were tossing around terms like "duck blind"; I had no idea what a duck blind was except back home where people shot birds from them. What had I gotten into here?

We went back to sleep. Some hours later the mortarmen were again up and stirring. "More gook sound?" I asked. At least I could try using the lingo.

They didn't have time to bother with me. I think Porterfield grunted and Dodge cursed a bit, and then we were all outside again. I was just in the way and a bit fed up with their superior airs so I called Red Phillips and checked it out with him and he said okay, so I told the mortarmen, "I think I'll just go down to the CP and see what's going on. Don't worry, I'll stay in the trench."

That was for that damned superior Porterfield. And if I stayed in the trench, I couldn't get lost, right?

I didn't quite get to the command post when the night just sort of exploded and the first mortars hit. What seemed like hundreds of rounds. All I knew was that the explosions seemed to be everywhere and that the night lit up like Fourth of July fireworks. I found a bunker and dove headfirst through the opening to bang up against a couple of other men already sheltering there. I was last man in, and barely so, and someone said calmly, "You know, that's just a poncho hanging there behind you."

I didn't know. Had, in fact, believed I was safer in here. But there was nothing but a bit of canvas between me and the exploding shells. A chill ran up my exposed back.

Abruptly, the incoming ended. Chafee and Phillips later estimated that in fifteen minutes some four hundred to five hundred shells had hit our positions. And no sooner had the shells stopped falling than the North Korean infantry came on. They were good at coordinating these things. But nothing was perfect. As quickly as the mortars quit, the Marines' heads came back up and they moved from their sheltering positions to their firing ports, going over on a proactive defense.

"Now they'll come," someone said very quietly.

"Yeah," said another Marine behind me. It was Chafee's runner. I was starting to recognize individual men.

There was silence, and then, erupting right above us, came machine-gun fire. And burp guns, rifles, and our own mortars chugging out. Dodge and Porterfield were in it now.

The North Koreans, moving slowly as they had to in deep snow coming up the steep forward slope, were targeted just as they reached our barbed wire. I was barely downhill on the reverse slope, a few feet below the ridge. Over the ridge of Hill 749 everyone was firing. On both sides. I threw off the safety catch on my carbine and began crawling on my belly to the ridge, the firing all around me now and confusing me so that I momentarily lost direction, then realized that up was north, and resumed crawling. I was used to the sound of gunfire. Plenty of that at Quantico. It was something you heard a lot of in training, but this was firing for effect. The real deal. And now there was firing below me, behind me on the reverse slope. Burp-gun fire. Atop the bunker I'd just left, a man stood erect on the roof. Damned fool Marine, showing himself. As I'd done earlier. Then the man was gone. He wasn't a Marine.

He'd been a North Korean, trying to shove a grenade down the chimney, and someone had shot him. Hadn't even occurred to me that he might be the enemy. I'd seen him and should have shot him. Boy, how dumb was I? In my own defense, it was night and all pretty confused. Was it always like this?

When dawn broke there was the dead man on the bunker roof and five or six North Korean bodies hanging in the wire.

"Lookie here," a Marine said happily. "The machine gunners got 'em."

That was what the barbed wire did for you, channeled the bad guys so that even in the dark, preaimed machine guns could fire down the outside of the wire aprons along the aiming stakes, could catch the enemy where they bunched up, trying to cut a way through the wire. They were sitting ducks. I went down to look at the bodies closely, not really wanting to but thinking I should. I'd have to do it eventually, why not now?

"Here, Lieutenant, want a souvenir?"

A Marine handed me a small, sodden wad of North Korean currency he'd taken off one of the bodies, one of the "stiffs." I overcame a natural delicacy and peeled off a bill, can't recall the denomination, and shoved it in a pocket. It was still damp. I remember that pretty clearly. Also remember how the faces of the dead men looked not like flesh at all but like wax. And their blood wasn't really red but resembled brown shellac. I wondered if that was the cold. Or the passage of hours since they died.

When it was full light Chafee sent out Red Phillips with a patrol to track the rest of the North Koreans by their blood on the snow. At least one of them had been hit but not killed, and Chafee thought Dog Company ought to try to bring one of them back, maybe the wounded man, to be questioned.

Prisoners are the best intelligence there is, what they have to say, what they've got in their pockets.

"Skipper?" It was the first time I'd called him that.

Chafee looked at me. "Yes, Brady, you want to go along. Go ahead. Just stick close to the exec and don't tell battalion."

It was the fourth day, maybe the fifth that I'd been on line with Dog Company, and this would be the first time I'd been forward of the MLR.

We stepped through the barbed wire and headed downhill. And north. North toward the enemy lines.

We tracked the retreating North Koreans for an hour, following the blood spoor in the snow like deer hunters. Never did catch up. We stayed on their track until we ran out of hill and came out into the fringe of evergreens at the edge of a brief valley that separated the two facing hills, ours and theirs. From here on out, we were playing on the Commie side of the fifty-yard line, Phillips explained. And if we followed the trail of blood any farther, we would be beyond the trees out in the open and draw fire.

"That stream there, mostly frozen, that's the Soyang-gang. That's the stream Bob Simonis crossed by night a week ago and went up there with a patrol and just raised billy-be-damned with the gooks. Good patrol."

Simonis was a quiet, somewhat older lieutenant I'd known at Quantico. Never impressed me one way or another. But Phillips was impressed. You could tell from his voice.

We turned then to begin the long climb back uphill to the MLR. I was sort of glad we hadn't caught them. That fellow who was wounded, he stopped once to take a crap. We found the turd there on the snow, blood-streaked and wormy. The poor bastard was gut-shot and had worms to boot and we were coming after him to kill him if we could. And he still had to stop and take a crap.

That was my fifth day on the line.

CHAPTER 23

I COULD SHOW YOU CAVES THAT
CAN HOLD A REGIMENT OF TANKS.

By contrast, on our third day back in the damned country, Eddie Adams and I would be traveling in more exalted circles, meeting with four-star general Leon LaPorte, commanding officer in Korea and all of Northeast Asia. A three-star named Campbell was originally supposed to have briefed us, but he'd been supplanted by the top guy. Campbell's conversation was to have been off the record and I rejected that in advance. I was a reporter; that's why I'd traveled nine thousand miles to get here. Good omen that he was out of the picture, I thought. General LaPorte's office was being painted, so we met in an Air Force general's rooms, full of aviation photos. Given my experience with the three-star USAF general on television, this did not bode well. But General LaPorte, a short, compact, barrel-chested fellow in full uniform, didn't wear wings. A Ranger tab was affixed to his shoulder and paratroop insignia to his chest. Marines like seeing foot-soldier stuff like that, and the blue metallic combat infantry badge.

Even the difficult-to-please Mr. Adams was smiling.

Eddie and I had been driven to American headquarters at Jongsan in the heart of Seoul and our session with the general. En route we caught up on the military gossip.

Yes, there were always Commie infiltrators trying to sneak in across the DMZ. Our GIs were taught not to overreact. No one wanted an international incident; no one wanted to be singled out as having fired the first shot that ignited a second Korean war. Some of the infiltrators came across without evil intentions, simply to do gravestone rubbings, the way English schoolboys do. What? No explanation. Maybe it had something to do with ancestor worship. Or to prove to the commissars they really had crossed over into the South. In the North, everything was mysterious.

Rummy (Defense Secretary Donald Rumsfeld) had been wondering aloud about a possible U.S. withdrawal south of the Han River to avoid exposing GIs to being taken hostage and used as negotiating chips. The North had a tradition of kidnaping people (Japanese civilians were a favored prize), so this was something to take seriously.

South Korea had just offered to send troops to Iraq. No other Asian country was being as generous. Since the new ROK president was thought to be a lefty, this was seen as a positive sign of friendship toward America. Whether we wanted the ROK troops or whether they would ever be sent was still in question.

For our meeting with the general, I was costumed by Brooks Brothers, Eddie in the usual black leather. Coffee was served and a South Korean four-star joined us. This was General Nam, who was top deputy to LaPorte but who, that next week, was to be installed with appropriate ceremony as the senior man in the ROK Army, their new chief of staff. He had a young, not very competent interpreter at his side, and our interview was in English. Two four-star generals in the room and people are serving coffee to a former lieutenant. Men dream of such moments.

Eddie deigned to snap a few pictures, the first time I'd yet seen an Adams camera in action. He was in his element, an old sergeant ordering two four-stars about, posing them this way and that. I was probably the last working reporter writing shorthand notes in a spiral steno pad and not recording the stuff, so I pulled out the old ballpoint.

I thought, what the hell, how frequently did I get an opportunity like this, and launched right into a shameless sales pitch. *Parade* paid me plenty; this was going to be an expensive trip. It was little enough for me to do as payback. So I started off with: "General, every Sunday some seventy-five or eighty million Americans read *Parade* magazine and I'm going to ask questions I think they might ask if they could be here."

General LaPorte said he was fine with that. And confirmed that the interview would be on the record. No off-the-record nonsense. This was starting very well indeed and I liked LaPorte already. Why had I been thinking negative thoughts about the Army?

"General, the war ended fifty years ago. Why *are* American troops still here, and is it accurate to say they're acting as a 'trip wire'?"

"Good question. U.S. forces are still here because we signed a mutual defense treaty with South Korea in 1953. Our goal is to maintain the peace in Korea and we also insure stability in Northeast Asia." As for being a trip wire, LaPorte didn't like that much. "Pretty inappropriate. Our commitment is based on mutual respect and not the distribution of forces. ROK Army abilities are enhancing every year."

General Nam seemed pleased. Through the interpreter, he began by thanking me personally for "having fought for my country. South Koreans never forget."

I smiled my thanks for his words but wondered, if that was so, then who stabbed Colonel Boylan? Not being a wiseass, I didn't ask this aloud.

Nam continued. "We don't believe we are yet fully able to defend the country alone. It's the combined defense. It's why we [the U.S. and the ROKs] fought together in Vietnam." Then he blathered on at length about his distaste for the term "trip wire." His young interpreter had a very thick accent and I wasn't getting every word, not even in English. I was becoming sorry I'd brought up the subject.

So I asked LaPorte about the auld enemy, Communist North Korea. How dangerous were they? We were both talking conventional weapons and manpower.

His was a somewhat chilling response.

"The North has a 1.2-million-man standing establishment and they are credible. They have twelve thousand artillery and missile tubes, which, even if old, if they're maintained, is a powerful force. They also have one hundred twenty thousand special operations forces in a predominantly infantry army, their navy and air force being limited. They've invested that money in missiles and underground." Which he said meant caves.

And it wasn't just a few Afghan caves, he emphasized, guys in turbans and bandoliers crouching around the old cook pot with steam rising. The North Koreans, I knew from experience, were excellent engineers and prodigious diggers. Opposite Hill 749 was a small, snow-covered enemy-held hill, the snow blackened and scarred from our bombs and napalm, which was said to be virtually hollowed out. The entire hill.

LaPorte elaborated: "I mean caves that can hold a regiment of tanks. I can take you to the DMZ right now and show you their artillery behind the hills that can range this building. All Seoul is under artillery range. They could cause tremendous casualties and damage."

And in all of this, no mention of their growing nuclear capability. I took that without debate. After all, nukes were the government's business; a general in the field doesn't make those judgments.

General LaPorte spoke of the DMZ itself, 155 miles long and four thousand meters in width, with patrols from each side permitted to range out about halfway. He explained the rules of engagement. I knew we had thirty-seven thousand GIs in South Korea.

"How many of them are actually foot soldiers up on the line, running those patrols and manning gun positions?"

His response stopped me. I hadn't anticipated this.

"The South Korean military mans the entire thing except for one outpost and one reconnaissance battalion of about six hundred men, forty percent of them American, the rest ROK. Only two hundred forty Americans man the [DMZ] line but the Second U.S. Infantry Division is north of Seoul with an augmented artillery component for counterbattery fire."

Only 240 U.S. troops actually on line! The Commies have 1.2 million men facing them, 120,000 of those highly trained special ops troopers. And LaPorte doesn't think the term "trip wire" is appropriate?

It was my job to ask questions, not to argue strategy, so I didn't beat that one to death. We told the general that Eddie and I would be going up to that "one outpost" the GIs manned and staying with them overnight in the bunkers. He knew the place, of course, actually knew the name of the American platoon leader we'd be visiting, Jim Gleason. Everyone seemed to know Gleason. He must be quite a guy. In my time four-star generals weren't acquainted with lieutenants. We traveled in distinct social and military circles. I asked more questions, got more answers. Beyond that, LaPorte asked, still playing "good mine host," was there anything else he could do?

Yes, there was. I told him about Hill 749, where all those Marines were killed and wounded, and where I served for five months as a replacement helping to hang on to it. And how to Marines of my time, it was a sacred place. LaPorte listened carefully but admitted he'd never heard of the hill and didn't know just where it was. Feeling pretty pleased with myself and earning an astonished glance from old Eddie, I tugged out of my Brooks Brothers tweeds a carefully folded United States Marine Corps topographic map, scale 1:25,000, dated November 1951, showing that area of the Kanmubong Ridge of North Korea with Hill 749 noted in red ink. I'd kept that map neatly folded for fifty-two years. LaPorte looked at it closely, then passed it to General Nam.

"What have you got up there, General?" LaPorte asked.

Nam studied the terrain. "We have an outpost up there," he said through the interpreter.

The American four-star looked at me. I nodded.

"Then that's where we want to go, General. But they keep telling me that's where no civilian ever goes, that they can't take responsibility. They say it's okay for me to look at it from a distance but that I can't go up the hill. I fought there all winter on that hill and I want to see it again. Go back up there and look around and write about going back to it. I think maybe I'm entitled."

Leon LaPorte consulted with Nam. Then, very carefully, as if it might be important, the general refolded my old map and passed it back.

"Mr. Brady, I'll get you up there if I have to send you in my own chopper."

CHAPTER 24

As we left the two four-star generals, being saluted by officers and MPs, and with a full, bird colonel waiting for us in a chauffeured car and already on a cell phone talking to someone about our upcoming flight to Hill 749, I permitted myself to speculate what "Gunny" Arzt might have thought of his onetime protégé at the Basic School and how far I had come in the world. Probably not much; Arzt didn't impress. But he might have shaken his head in bewilderment.

Kenneth Arzt was a big, thick-bodied first lieutenant in our platoon at Quantico, a spiky-haired (that was the brilliantine) thug with Groucho Marx eyebrows, pasty-faced and rather ugly with jowls, an underslung jaw, and a heavy beard. You shaved close at the Basic School, but with Arzt, the five o'clock shadow began at noon. In Yakima, Washington, he ran an auto dealership following the war with the Japanese, during which Arzt had been an enlisted man, later promoted to lieutenant. When I met him in 1951, Arzt had three distinctions:

He actually mispronounced his own name. "Arzt" became "Arts." When I asked him about that he said, "Everyone says it wrong anyway. Why argue?"

According to him, during the war Arzt had made "sixty-three landings on hostile beaches." Was this possible?

I believe he was the strongest man we had (and our bunch included some big-time college athletes). No one really tested Arzt on strength; his one-armed push-ups were sufficient unto the day. Dropping to the concrete deck of the barracks in his skivvies, Arzt would rip off a quick twenty-five or so with his left arm and turn around and do the same number with his right. Then he would challenge the room.

"Think you can do ten?" Gauging his blocky, powerful body and heavy arms, the big, useful hands, the odd optimist took him on, but no one ever beat the Gunny. And all those landings on Japanese beaches? Well, he had his skeptics.

"There weren't sixty-three invasions during the damned war, Arzt. You know that."

"I didn't say 'invasions.' I said 'landings on hostile beaches.'"

He would say no more, offered no further explanation, but just smiled a menacing, tigerish grin and placidly puffed away on a large black cigar. He occasionally bragged that he had the soul of a born car salesman; he certainly had the style.

For some reason Arzt tolerated me. Even provided me a nickname. To the Gunny I was "Buford." It was a stupid name and demeaning and I disliked it. But that cut no ice with Arzt. In a way, it was flattering even to be noticed by Arzt, who may or may not have been a gunnery sergeant during the war but whom we all called "Gunny." He was older than most of us, thirty maybe, drove a big, powerful sedan, and had lots of money to throw around. The auto dealership apparently did very well.

"Come on, Buford," he would remark on an idle evening in barracks, "we'll drive into Washington and show ourselves to the ladies."

He liked hotel bars and cocktail lounges and the better saloons and anywhere else he could chase "government girls." Which is what in politically incorrect 1951 we called Washington career women.

"You get six hundred young women in the typing pool at the Commerce

Department or some bright little secretary working for an old bureaucrat at Interior, they'll welcome some male attention after a day slaving over the file cabinets," he assured me.

"Schoolteachers are good, too, Buford. You get a frisky, intelligent woman's been educating eight-year-olds all day, she's in the mood for a high-ball and some conversation. And if there's a band or a piano player, perhaps a circuit on the hardwood."

Arzt fancied himself a dancer, and for a large, powerful man he was surprisingly deft, light on his feet, and knew all the steps. Even the Peabody and, I believe, the tango.

I asked him once, but only once, why he took me along on these fishing expeditions, since I knew little of women. He didn't hesitate or go polite on me.

"I have you along, Buford, so that I'm not the ugliest man in the room."

I shared his affection for cigars but made no attempt to drink with him. I'd just sit there with a Coke, admiring the girls, and gaping in amazement as he worked his wiles on the young women of wartime Washington. Occasionally, what looked to me the most attractive women in the room would pick up the vibrations from his antennae, and join us for a "cocktail."

"This here is Buford, ladies, a promising young officer of good family who serves as my aide-de-camp, and often accompanies me on social occasions."

I was realist enough to understand I was not the draw. It was pure animal magnetism and total self-assurance on Gunny's part. The women came, they drank; they listened as well, rapt, to his stories, both of the South Pacific and of Yakima and the automotive trade. Phone numbers were exchanged as, issuing our au revoirs, Gunny grabbed the check and off we went to Quantico and a few hours' sleep before the usual dawn patrol of bugle call and reveille.

There were two schools of Quantico thought on Gunny Arzt. One couldn't stand him, considered him a blowhard, and didn't believe he'd made all those landings. And there were others of us, like me, who took impressed note of the decorations on his chest and got a kick out of him. I don't believe Arzt really gave a damn one way or the other.

One morning they posted a one-hour training film on reconnaissance. That sounded pretty good, and we all were up for that, recon being one of the sexier career tracks for a young officer. Training films were popular anyway because when the lights went down you might catch up on your sleep. People asked Arzt about it. Had he ever seen this particular flick?

Arzt was more opaque than ever. Said he couldn't remember every damned training film he'd ever seen. They were all bullshit, anyway. He might have done a little recon time, he conceded.

You weren't allowed to cut classes at Basic School the way we did in college but no one would have cut a World War II training film on recon.

Arzt pulled me aside. "Don't miss this film today, Buford. You might learn something."

He was telling other men it was "bullshit." Telling me not to miss it. This was becoming as complicated as our evenings in the cocktail lounges.

Maybe 120 of us, an entire company of Marine officers, crammed into one of the usual classrooms, the way little kids attended the Saturday matinee at the Bijou, excited, grabbing the best seats. Rumor had gotten around the barracks that this particular flick might be special. A captain mounted the stage, gave us a few words of introduction to the film, a few airy snippets about reconnaissance, the need for accurate intelligence. Said that, by the way, the recon team we were about to see had actually done all this stuff, during dozens, maybe scores, of landings on hostile beaches.

Come on, Captain, where's the movie?

Lights dimmed. I looked around to see if I could find Arzt. It would be fun to get his reaction. He was out there in the dark but I couldn't find him.

The projector whirred into action and the film rolled. Black and white, of course. This wasn't a Technicolor soundstage at MGM with Walter Pidgeon, and Greer Garson smiling through the tears.

Instead, it was a black-and-white movie starring Kenneth "Gunny" Arzt!

There he was, younger but the same, the spiky crew-cut hair, the heavy shoulders, the face a bit leaner, less jowly, but the arms big, the heavy, powerful thighs. He was on the deck of an American sub, one of a half dozen young toughs in black turtlenecks, watch caps, sneakers dyed black, muscling and heaving at an inflated rubber raft, pushing it off into the chop, balancing with difficulty against the big swells washing over the deck, and into the raft.

After something of a struggle, the Marines got the raft into the water, slung their tommy guns, and got on board. There, paddling on the near side, driving his paddle efficiently and powerfully into the sea, was Ken Arzt's even-then ugly twenty-year-old puss, his head lifting briefly so he could stare into the War Department cameras, give the audience a wolflike, wicked look.

And in the dark of a Virginia classroom, a low growl rose and became a cheer.

"Arzt! Arzt! Arzt!"

And a hundred or more Marine officers were on their feet stamping and cheering. Maybe I led the cheering but everyone got into it. Even men who couldn't stand Gunny Arzt. We were all cheering. Knowing there really had been all those landings on hostile beaches.

The training film itself was stunning in that it featured one of us, but it was sobering as well. That little black rubber raft and a handful of Marines setting off in the dark of a Japanese-held ocean, paddling toward a hostile landfall, and landing on a speck of island in total darkness, silence too, to encounter an enemy which so outnumbered them that the odds were off the board. The navigational skills alone, never mind the killing skills, boggled the mind of an innocent. And Arzt had really done this, or something like it, sixty-three times.

And how many times had other Marines, in other little black rafts, set off from American submarines, and never again been seen or heard from?

The rest of that day and into the night, the Gunny's grin was even smugger, the big black cigar even more complacently clamped between his large, yellowed, but very useful teeth.

"Buford, you learn anything this morning?"

I did, I told him. And not just about recon work. But about believing a good man when he tells you something.

In April when we got our new assignments, most of the men were ticketed for the 1st Division in Korea. A dozen of us were held back to instruct. And Gunny Arzt?

He was being assigned to Recon Battalion, Camp Lejeune in North Carolina, to teach a new recon generation how these things were done. He was a realist, this was a job he would do well, and Lejeune was a post he liked. So you got no hand-wringing from Gunny Arzt over being cheated out of Korea. He and I met one last time and I thanked him for all those nights in Washington, for improving my taste in cigars, for teaching me a little about recon work. And about women.

"So you really did learn some shit after all, Buford," he said, his big ugly face smiling on me like a proud uncle.

"Yes, Gunny. I did. I learned some shit."

He grabbed both my arms in his huge hands, half lifted me from the deck, gave me a shake, whirled, and was gone, a big grinning man moving light and going on to the next landing on the next beach.

Eventually, I went off to Korea to fight, a green young officer still learning the trade. While one of the true, natural killers among us would spend the war in North Carolina training other men to become true, natural killers.

And, now, fifty years later, hanging out with four-star generals and driving about with colonels was Gunny Arzt's onetime aide-de-camp Buford, a young officer of good family.

CHAPTER 25

THE HOTEL HAD A LOUNGE ACT, THREE BULGARIAN
BLONDES DOING SHOW TUNES.

With our journey to "forbidden . . . out of bounds" Hill 749 officially approved by the boss, General LaPorte, I celebrated by indulging myself in a Saturday morning stroll through a big, dusty city park to see a Royal Palace and Museum.

It was sunny and schoolkids ran around in the April sunshine. They wore uniforms like kids at home who attend parochial school. The children were all pretty, boys and girls both, and it was nice to see them running around. Though I kept thinking about General LaPorte's twelve thousand North Korean artillery pieces and missile tubes ranging the city, ranging this park, ranging these kids.

Eddie had big plans for Saturday night with his pal but I passed.

In a way, Eddie Adams's sheer animal energy made me envious. But I decided I'd rather be me than Eddie doing the town. There was NCAA basketball on Armed Forces television and the war coverage from Iraq featured suicide bombers and some experts talking about how we were going to rebuild Iraq and how the Iraqis would instantly all become enormously democratic and love us. I thought to myself, let's win the damn war first and then go to the Marshall Plan. There were also many Korean and Japanese language programs on the local channels and some guys shooting pool. I gave them all a look; I'm easily satisfied.

To the right of the hotel was a big department store, with Korean automobiles queuing up to get into the multilayered car garages underneath. I went inside and rode the escalators and admired the young women clerks in their Oxford gray woolen dresses, very smart. They smiled and asked, in pretty good English, if they could be of assistance. They seemed to be asking the same question of Korean shoppers in Korean. Bloomingdale's should be as customer friendly. I didn't buy anything.

To the left of the hotel was a sort of Buddhist shrine, a pagoda-looking building in dark stone surrounded by a courtesy garden of lawn and heavy trees, with a footpath and benches. With an hour to kill, I sat out there on a bench and read and worked a little on my suntan, still bleached out from the hard winter on Further Lane. Dinner was in one of the hotel restaurants where a trio of Bulgarian blondes performed show tunes. Seoul must be where the lounge acts go that don't make it in Vegas. The red wine was Australian, Compass Rose. Nineteen bucks a glass, and that was the cheap stuff. *Parade* magazine was going to love this swindle sheet.

Sunday morning I walked up to the Catholic cathedral, directed by a boy named Francisco. That was his baptismal name, he said, even though he was Korean. He was going there to the 9 A.M. mass, so we walked along together with his girlfriend tagging along and we climbed a hill to the church. All of Seoul is hilly, and I wondered if my bum knee was going to hold up. Well, it got me to mass.

Outside of church a beggar was asking for alms and I gave him something. It was dark and cool inside the cathedral and most of the women wore white lace mantillas, as you used to see in that big church in Havana across the square from the Ambos Mundos Hotel where Hemingway wrote part of one of his novels.

They sang "Tantum Ergo," which is an old Latin hymn I remembered from Saint Mark's Church in Sheepshead Bay. Quite early in the mass everyone got up and began walking up to the front, and that confused me. I thought it was to receive Holy Communion so I went along but when I got up there, I realized it was an offertory, to give money, and I held up the line while I got out a ten-thousand-won note to put in the basket. That was about twelve bucks, I believe. Behind me people were impatient, the mantillas bobbing, so I scurried in some embarrassment back to the pew.

I wouldn't put the ten thousand on the account, I assure you.

Eddie had come up with another pal, a Yank and an expatriate, and that afternoon he drove us around town sightseeing. Most of the sightseeing was on the U.S. military base of Jongsan, where this guy worked. He showed us some Quonset huts decaying and other fascinating stuff. Eddie and I restrained our enthusiasm. It was a tour of stultifying dullness and then we had lunch in a fast-food joint, still on the base.

This American, John, asked if our eyes stung.

No. Was the meal that bad?

Lots of people's eyes stung, he explained. Seoul is very polluted especially in spring when they get yellow dust from the Gobi Desert and airborne dust from China kicked up in vast clouds when farmers do the spring plowing. Gosh! Just think of that. Rather proudly, I thought, he said Seoul had maybe the second most polluted air of any city in the world. Someplace in Czecho with a lot of steel mills burning soft coal might be worse.

He was a decent, gentle, quite boring man, had been a soldier, and had now been in Korea nearly forty years working for the U.S. military. Sad sort of life, none of your exotic, storied expat glamour. I hoped Adams's nights with Jung were somewhat more exciting.

Eddie smiled smugly but went into no detail.

We met for breakfast about seven each day. That Monday morning, Eddie, perhaps embarrassed by our boring tour of the post, was much more expansive.

As he tucked into his sausage and eggs laced liberally with Tabasco (he used Tabasco on everything), he told me about the night before, choreographed by Jung.

"The daughter of the president was there. Attractive, late thirties, very nice. Maybe it was the last president she was the daughter of. Jung knows everybody."

And he wasn't Mafia?

Eddie assumed a chill dignity.

"Look, here's his card. 'Republic of Korea Olympic Committee.'"

"Anyone can have a card made up, Eddie."

"He's the goods," Adams said stubbornly, like the le Carré character, "to whom all his geese were swans."

I shrugged off the estimable Jung.

"She sang, too, after dinner."

"Who sang?"

"The daughter of the effing president. Very nice voice, pleasant."

"What did she sing, show tunes?"

"No, Korean shit mostly."

Captain Duncan Miller of Seattle and the United States Marines picked us up and we drove over to the U.S. headquarters at Jongsan, where we would be briefed and I was to speak to the men. There were only twenty or thirty Marines in Seoul, with a more sizable detachment down south at an air base that Marine and Navy planes use. And an infantry battalion comes in once or twice a year from Okinawa for maneuvers.

The few Marines in Seoul function, I gathered, much like a cadre if there were ever to be a big buildup.

Mr. Adams swiftly developed a distaste for Captain Miller. I asked why.

"He turns his effing back on me and just talks to you. You'd think I wasn't there. Damned officers!" Old enlisted resentments rankled.

I promised to talk to Miller.

"Don't bother. He'll be busted to sergeant before we're out of here."

Colonel Michael Malachowsky was in command of the Marine detachment. He was from Bushwick, Brooklyn, and during the Vietnam War was an enlisted man in the Air Force. Then he switched to the Marine Corps and, obviously, had done very well. He already knew his next duty post after Korea: the chief-of-staff job at Parris Island, the big boot camp in South Carolina.

"Glad to be out of here?" I asked.

"I will be. You know about Steve Boylan being stabbed and I've been spit at. You get a lot of cold, hostile looks. We don't take the subway anymore.

137

"There's never been as much tension on the peninsula as there is now. There are too many eighteen- and nineteen-year-old South Koreans who believe the U.S. started the Korean War."

He was also impatient with the lack of discipline among the Army troops here at HQ, sentries smoking, reading magazines, the slovenly sort of thing that drives Marine officers nuts. I had the impression the colonel would do very well at Parris Island.

After a briefing by the Marines, we all went into a sort of conference room and I was introduced and talked for a while about how it was fifty years ago when there was an entire Marine division fighting here. Due to my advanced age, I was clearly the only man in the room (Eddie was wandering around somewhere) who'd actually fought in Korea, so I had curiosity value.

Had we fought in this area in what came to be called "the Outpost War"?

Yes, I said. I had, but only at the very start. Did they know of a hill called 229 up near Panmunjom? Yes, they did.

We and the Chinese had a pretty good firefight that started with a reconnaissance patrol sent out from Hill 229, near where Eddie and I would be going the next morning, to spend a couple of days with the recon troops patrolling on exactly the same hills and ridgelines where Marines fought the spring and summer of 1952.

The headquarters Marines knew the ground I meant and so they perked up. Could I tell them about that fight?

"Of course."

So I told them about Jack Rowe of Dog Company and how he lost one eye and half his fingers fighting the Chinese with about sixty other Marines including me on the Memorial Day of 1952.

CHAPTER 26

THEY WERE TOSSING GRENADES, ONE OF THEM AN OLD
GERMAN POTATO MASHER FROM WORLD WAR I.

Colonel Gregory was holding his regular officers' meeting one pleasant spring morning in the lee of Hill 229 about half a mile behind
the MLR. The colonel's staff sat in a circle on the ground or on
sandbags and it was all very relaxed, Gregory standing there in the middle of
us in his fatigues and yellow canvas leggings and with a .45 strapped on, and
going around the circle for the report: the operations officer, Major Dennis
Nicholson; the supply officer; the air officer, Captain Gibson; the communications officer, Joe Buscemi, who had played in the 1947 Rose Bowl; Mack
Allen as the adjutant. When he got to me most mornings I gave the intelligence report: whatever happened during the night, any hint of enemy action
to come, issuing the password.

On this particular morning Colonel Gregory had a specific question for
me. Which was rare, since I believe the colonel and I both understood that I
didn't know much about intelligence. He kept me around, and Mack Allen,
who was also clueless when it came to being an adjutant, just in case there was
a spring offensive and the usual casualties. The battalion would have a couple
of spares, rifle platoon leaders who knew the job.

"Lieutenant Brady, as our fine intelligence officer, can you tell us if there are any Chinese on Hill Yoke?"

Yoke was a smallish hill out between the lines just north of us, a dull-looking pyramidal hill of sandstone with only one distinguishing feature, a badly smashed steel high-tension tower on its summit.

"I don't know, Colonel. We haven't seen any but that doesn't mean they aren't there."

"Well, then, as our fine intelligence officer"—Colonel Gregory could be cutting—"why don't you go out there and look around and come back and tell us?" He cackled when he laughed and he was cackling now.

I said that sounded like a swell idea, one of the more creative ideas I'd heard in some time (lieutenants are expected to agree with colonels), and the S-3, Major Nicholson, was told to set up the patrol.

There was a reason behind Gregory's question, not just a canny old soldier's hunch, or an opportunity to get me off my ass and back out patrolling. It was a division order. The previous Sunday at four, teatime precisely, Chinese artillery in a very well-coordinated attack had fired off an impressive counterbattery concentration, hitting Marine artillery positions all the way along the division line. Did little damage up here where we were but sent us all diving into foxholes and pits as the shells shuttled noisily overhead. Behind us, a Chinese shell touched off some of our stored ammo and killed a couple of 11th Marines artillerymen. Which was unfortunate, but you haven't seen the day Marine infantrymen mourn gunners. Hell, back there they're living it up with tents and showers, and never have to go on patrol. So the infantry wasn't shedding tears.

But it irritated the brass that the thing was so efficiently done. The Chinese must have some pretty good observation posts to pinpoint our big guns. And one of them might be Hill Yoke, from which they might just be able to do a little "peeping Tom" into the rear areas where our 105 guns were dug in. So let's take a closer look at Yoke, Mr. Brady.

Aye, aye, sir.

Jack Rowe's platoon from Dog Company reinforced by a light-machine-gun section was assigned the job of getting me and a couple of my scouts out to Yoke for a look-see. Stew McCarty, Dog Company exec (my old job) decided to come along. He had a new movie camera and thought he might get some good footage, taking pictures from the summit of Yoke looking north toward the Chinese lines. One of my scouts was to do sketches and maps of the area and an ROK interpreter who could patter a little Chinese came along. Just in case. Only forty-eight of us would actually go up the hill, with the machine guns and a dozen men setting up a base of fire on a low ridge behind us, to supply overhead fire if called for. Nice, simple, straightforward sort of job.

The night before, I went up Hill 229 with my scouts to bunk in with Rowe's platoon until we jumped off at 2 A.M. The idea was that the approach march would be covered by darkness and we'd start climbing Yoke itself just before dawn. It was late May but it was cold up there on the hill and I debated whether to wear a field jacket over the flak jacket when we set out and be hot later on, or to jettison the jacket and be cold at first and warm up gradually. I was by now sufficiently salty to make major fashion decisions like these, and I dumped the jacket.

Charley Logan, still Dog Company commander, woke me with a canteen cup of black coffee. I think he liked it that his former exec was still being sent out on patrols. Someone gave me a couple of grenades and I shoved them into the breast pockets of my fatigue shirt. My scouts and I marched toward the middle of the file of men, Rowe's people ahead of and behind us. I remember thinking as we descended the forward slope of 229 and started the march north toward Yoke that we were making a hell of a lot of noise. Marines always did. You talked to them about it, you issued orders; Marines still made too damned much noise. Just before four the head of the column reached the base of Yoke and began the climb up.

The first explosion split the otherwise still night and blinded us momentarily with the flash. What was it? "A mine!" someone growled near me.

The point man, one of Rowe's, was dead. No one was ever quite sure whether it had been a mine or a thrown grenade. But with small-arms and automatic-weapons fire following it up immediately, Colonel Gregory's question had already been answered.

Yes, Colonel, sir. There are Chinese on Yoke, sir.

Dog Company Marines were hustling past me, double-timing up the hill to support their buddies up there at the head of the line. There was more shooting now and some yelling. I added to it, calling Jay Scott and Rudy Wrabel and my other scouts and telling them we ought to get up there, too.

I couldn't find Rowe but Stew McCarty was there.

"Jack's hit," he said. He said he was going to take command unless I objected. Hell, no. Stew was senior to me and it was his company that was engaged. Good, McCarty said.

"Can you take the right flank? We're going up there and get them."

"Sure, you tell me. We'll do it." McCarty was a regular. I hustled over to the right with my scouts and found a sergeant, one of Rowe's squad leaders.

"Mr. McCarty's taken over from Mr. Rowe. Get your men ready, Sarge. We're going up there." Neither of us spent any time talking about Rowe, how he was, what a shame that he'd been hit, that sort of crap. In a firefight there's too much else going on.

"Aye, aye, sir." He was pretty cool. I didn't know his name. Maybe he didn't know mine. That didn't matter, either.

We got organized pretty swiftly and resumed going up the hill, toward the Chinese, but it wasn't going to be easy. There was barbed wire, and attacking infantry hate barbed wire. And to this day I have no idea just how I got over the barbed wire. Flinging myself over it headfirst? Leaping it like a hurdler? No matter, I got over and we were all shooting, them and us.

I'd been in fights before and would be shot at again but this was the first time I'd ever charged up a hill, you know, like old Pickett there at Gettysburg, and we were all shouting. Silly stuff, just noise. I was yelling, "No prisoners! No prisoners!" to impress the Chinese of our serious purpose. I guess we yelled to scare the bad guys, yelled because we were scared. It was half-light now with dawn breaking to our right in the east. The Chinese were having themselves a high old time tossing grenades at us or just rolling them down the steep sandstone slope. Forty-eight Marines went up that damned hill and thirty-two of us were hit. Only one dead, oddly enough, the point man. What happened to Jack Rowe was that he caught one grenade, tossed it back, thought, Well, now, that's good business. But when he caught a second, it went off, getting him in the face and hands. He kept fighting but then while he was lying prone firing, another grenade landed on the small of his back, broke his pelvis, shredded his buttocks. I didn't know that until later.

That first assault I could actually see the grenades flying through the air toward us. One of them looked like an old-fashioned German "potato masher" from *All Quiet on the Western Front*. The Chinese weren't noted for their modern weapons. Another came wrapped up in something. (Later we found they put some grenades in socks, packed in some black powder for extra oomph, and let fly!) I threw one grenade, they threw a few more. I threw a second grenade. More came back. When you are lobbing grenades at the other guy, this is close-range fighting.

We tried to get up the hill one more time but there were just too many grenades and too many Marines hit already. Hurt Marines were all over the damned place but a surprising number were walking wounded, still toting rifles and firing. It's funny, but unless they're gut-shot or hit bad in the head or have broken bones, men with a few holes in them seem able to keep fighting. Long term, of course, they lose too much blood and start to wear down.

McCarty and I lay there on our bellies on the forward slope discussing the situation. I was stunned by how calm we both were. All around us Marines also lay prone, propped up on an elbow, leveling a fairly steady rifle fire at the hilltop and the Chinese. Even the wounded were firing, those who could. McCarty and I agreed that with all these casualties, a lousy recon patrol had had it. The Chinese had stopped us. If we attacked again, there might not be enough of the able-bodied left to get the wounded back. And that's part of why Marines fight so fiercely. They know whatever happens, we'll get them home, alive or dead. We agreed to pull out, the machine guns and the Marine artillery, the 105 guns providing overhead fire to cover us. The 105s had been firing steadily and it was the first time I realized you could actually see an artillery shell coming toward you over your shoulder, black and small and coming fast. I made myself as flat as I could there against the hill hoping to hell there were no short rounds. Rudy Wrabel, a scout from Connecticut, lay on the slope alongside me, firing his weapon. I noticed that he was grinning. I wondered if he knew something I didn't or was just losing it.

"You okay?" I asked.

"Sure am, Lieutenant. It's my first firefight."

He was excited, looked very happy. Some Marines are like that; others choke up and freeze. During this stage of the fight Wrabel saw one man not firing, pointed him out to me. I got up and went over to him and poked him, pointing to his weapon. The man looked up at me. "Rifle's jammed," he said.

I gave him the rifle I'd picked up and had been using. "This one's working," I said. And so was his when I tried it. When I looked back, he was firing. At least I hoped he was but didn't have leisure to inquire. What the hell, you can't hold their hands.

We got out of there eventually, taking the dead and wounded and all our weapons. At one point I had a couple of rifles and three or four bandoliers of ammo slung. I talked to Rowe as they carried him out on a stretcher. He looked bad, very bad, one eye gone and the face all shot up and bloody, the hands, God knows what else. I knew he'd gone to Villanova so I kept telling people he'd be all right, that he was a Villanova Wildcat, you couldn't kill a Villanova Wildcat. It was all bullshit.

Fact was, I thought he was done. I was talking nonsense to cheer him up, if his eardrums weren't burst and he could still hear.

Jack survived to be awarded the Navy Cross, which in the Corps is a pretty big deal, and spent a year in the Philadelphia Naval Hospital, married his nurse, a pretty young Navy JG named Laura, went back to teaching high school and coaching football, moved out west, wrote half a dozen books, got a private pilot's license. In his spare time, he grows avocados, fights brushfires, and kills rattlesnakes out at their big hilltop house in Fallbrook, California. Coyotes take one of their housecats every so often and they're wary of mountain lions. But I've been to their house and it's pretty cushy. He and Laura had eleven children, of whom ten survive. A man I thought finished was living a life richer than most men dream.

And after Rowe had been choppered out and the less seriously wounded carted off in the meat wagons, and we got back, I went into the tent and sat there on my cot, thinking. Years later I wrote of that tranquillity after the fight, "If you were not truly happy at a moment like this when you had just come down off the line walking, perhaps you never would be."

Then someone shouted for me and that afternoon I played some Raiders' Rules volleyball, feeling good to be alive and to have been in that fight up there on Yoke.

That was the story I told at Seoul USMC HQ, and, being Marines, what they seemed to enjoy most was that after a firefight, the Marines went out to play volleyball, Raiders' Rules.

CHAPTER 27

IT WASN'T PRECISELY *M*A*S*H*.

At last the red tape had been cut, the arrangements made, and on the next morning we would be going up to the outposts and meeting the famous Lieutenant Gleason and his recon platoon. And about time! Eddie was getting cabin fever.

"Come on," he said, "I want to get this leather jacket tailored."

We took a cab down to Itewan, the Seoul flea market, and found a tailor shop down an alleyway, where Adams and Good Time Charlie, or some name like that, haggled over price and did fittings. Charlie tried to sell me a business suit, taking me, in my Brooks Brothers tweeds, for what the French call *"un homme d'affaires."* I declined and as we departed the alleyway an attractive woman dashed out of another shop to pursue us up the street crying her wares, "Genuine artificial! Genuine artificial!"

We weren't in the market that season for "genuine artificial" but I thanked her profusely and pocketed her card. Eddie was taking me someplace special for lunch (we were both on expenses from *Parade* but it was thoughtful of him to offer). I expected an exotic Korean dive with raw fish and octopus. But it turned out Eddie's "someplace special" was an Australian Outback chain steakhouse up a flight of stairs, and over steak and beers Eddie recounted amorous adventures of the past in a hotel just across the street, and said that his first night ever in Korea as a young Marine combat photographer, he'd been taken in hand by an old salt and had gotten laid.

I felt rather dull, having no amorous adventures to relate. We topped off our day by buying some jade and pearl necklaces and a chess set with the chessmen shaped like medieval Korean warriors. That was for my grandson Joe, who was a first-grader but already a player, up on the Ruy Lopez defense and all that, though not knowing the terms. He could do it; that was sufficient.

The Seoul of 2003 was nothing like the city I first saw in the spring of 1952. Mack Allen and I had just been promoted to first lieutenant and we were ordered to Inchon and out onto the hospital ship anchored there offshore, the *Consolation,* I think, a big ocean liner painted white with a red cross on the hull. I think it's pretty stupid, but whenever you get promoted in the Marine Corps, officers have to take a new physical. Charley Logan went with us and a lieutenant from Fox Company. Charley had been Dog Company commander since Chafee went home.

Captain Logan wasn't being promoted but was becoming a regular instead of a reserve, since he was planning to stay in the Corps. He was a nice guy and I'd been his executive officer for a time, but he was no Chafee. Charley understood that and one night when we all got drunk he was feeling sorry for himself and began crying, saying he knew he wasn't the Chafee that everyone worshiped.

And now Charley was planning to make a lifelong career of the Corps and John Chafee was back in Providence practicing law.

They issued us two motor pool jeeps and drivers and we set off for Inchon via Seoul. Just south of the Imjin River in the low brown hills (they looked exactly like Orange County, California, around the Irvine Ranch, inland from Laguna Beach), someone took a shot at us.

"What the hell!"

A bullet from somewhere had hit a fender and whined off, ricocheting away. We were all armed and we piled out of the jeeps, even the drivers, and spread out a bit off the dirt track we used as a road. But we couldn't see anyone. Hell of a note. Get promoted and ten miles south of the fighting some dope tries to kill us. We were pretty annoyed, I can tell you. Mack was so sore he wanted to hike up into the hills and find this bird. Whatever happened to the rules of war? You don't mind getting killed up on the MLR but south of the Imjin?

Nothing more happened (maybe it was a dogface out shooting rabbits, we never knew) and we rolled through Seoul and didn't see much reason to stop (the drivers, more savvy than we, assured us there wasn't a single bar and very few women). The place was pretty beat up, which was understandable, in that Seoul may have been the only capital city in the world that had been taken and retaken four times in less than a year. The North Koreans first took it June 28 of 1950, MacArthur took it back in September (the 1st Mar Div leading the bloody assault), it was abandoned to the Chinese January 4 of 1951, and Matt Ridgway liberated it again on March 14. That's how the war went in the beginning, up and down the country over and over, men killing and being killed every step of the way.

At Inchon they had a launch tied up at the pier to take us out to the ship for our physicals. There was a sea running and in between swells the coxswain brought the small boat as close to the ship's hull as possible.

"Okay, you guys, make it snappy." Sailors love telling Marine officers what to do. And when he yelled, "Jump!" we all did it and eventually scrambled aboard the landing stage.

In a kind of vestibule within the hospital ship a sailor in whites stared at us. "What do you guys want?"

"We're Marine officers, sailor," Charley said. "Don't they salute in the Navy anymore?"

The sailor was sulky. "Sometimes," he said.

When we finally got to a doctor, he seemed frightened, or maybe affronted, to see we were wearing leggings and helmets and sidearms. When we turned over our orders, he wouldn't touch the papers. Didn't want to catch anything, I guess.

"Maybe he can smell us," someone said.

"All right," he said. "But leave those guns with someone. You can't take weapons aboard a hospital ship. It's against the Geneva Conventions. And you'll have to take showers. No one's going to examine you like this." He looked at us very disapprovingly.

Gosh, that was a hardship. Having to shower. The doctor kept staring. I looked down at myself, to see if my fly was open. Or was it the smell?

When they finally got around to examining us, Mack passed. The rest of us flunked. High blood pressure. Was that serious?

"Yes, can lead to heart attack, stroke."

Did that mean they'd have to send us home for medical reasons? We asked the doctor. "Of course not," he said.

Not that it was surprising to be told we had high blood pressure. We'd been running around shooting people and getting blown up and staying up nights for months. Then Mack asked if he could be reexamined. Maybe this time he'd fail too and get to go home. We were all laughing now at this jerk and he was getting more and more steamed.

"Goddamned Marines. Give me the papers. You pass, you all pass!"

After we dressed and made our way back to the ship's landing stage, the sea was really getting up. The same sailor greeted us. "Ship's store is closed. They wouldn't sell you anything, anyway. That's for ship's crew."

Ship's store is sort of like a PX. But we hadn't even asked. When the launch came alongside it was having difficulty, the waves higher now and a stiff wind blowing. Darker, too, with night coming. After an unsuccessful pass or two the cox yelled up at us. "Can't do it. I'll bang the son of a bitch and catch hell. Be back for you in the morning."

That was how we came to sleep aboard that night, actual beds with sheets and pillowcases even. It was swell. And that evening we ate in the officers' mess, waited on by Filipino messmen and all, linen on the tables, knives and forks, hot food, steaming coffee. It was briefly like being a civilian again. The mess was full of naval officers, doctors and nurses, mostly. All in their crisp whites. And we were in dungarees and web belts. No guns. And throughout the entire meal, not one nurse or doctor or other naval officer even came by our table to say hello. Not a single goddamned one! Some of the nurses were young and very pretty, and Mack and I hadn't seen or spoken to an American woman since that stopover in Guam in November. I guess Captain Logan and the lieutenant from Fox were in the same case. And not one in this bunch gave us even a smile. Not a Hot Lips Houlihan among them. We were all officers, too, in the same Naval Establishment, we'd actually been fighting. Yet no one even said "Hi."

Perhaps it didn't help that Logan cracked, "That blonde over there is sitting on a gold mine."

I'm sure they'd had plenty of Marines on this ship, men shot up and carried aboard and helpless, and I'm sure they were patched up and competently put back together, all with exquisite care. The difference was we were upright and armed and dangerous, not at all helpless. So they weren't in control. And they didn't care for that.

Bastards. Don't tell me things were all that jolly on *M*A*S*H* either. I like Alan Alda and his show but I don't necessarily believe it.

CHAPTER 28

STABBING AND SHOOTING AND CURSING,

HAVING OURSELVES A HELL OF A TIME.

The DMZ of memory had changed. The Panmunjom of today, where the cease-fire was finally signed in 1953, owes something to Disneyland. They even have tour buses.

On both sides of the line, spiffy sentries stand guard in artificially preternatural poses of supposed martial readiness. In the long main shack of a barracks (really, that's about all it is) where the actual negotiations took place in 1952–53 and where the cease-fire was finally signed, the room is divided in half, one half North Korean, the other South. Goggling tourists are informed with great solemnity that they mustn't step over that line on the floor even now. Wives grab their husbands and pull them close, lest war break out.

World War III is never that remote a possibility when you deal with the unpredictable North Koreans. And no one needs a grocer from Fresno or an Ohio librarian to set it off!

The Panmunjom I remembered was somewhat different.

Every day that the peace talks were in session, a convoy of trucks and cars carrying our trucial delegates (normally, the brass flew by chopper), headed by a flag officer with the wonderful Gilbert and Sullivan name of Admiral C. Turner Joy, plus jeeploads of accompanying press, drove out from our side of the MLR for the little village of Panmunjom along a rural road heading north. A similar convoy of North Koreans and Chinese came south, and they would meet, haggling and dickering sourly in a jerry-built wood-framed and unpainted building furnished with long wooden bargaining tables, and little else, a rustic little one-roomed schoolhouse on the prairie. While all this was going on, we Marines and the Chinese Army were fighting a nasty, and decidedly actual, war.

The "corridor," as it was called, maybe four or five miles in length, about a thousand meters in width, was out of bounds for fighting. So much so that after a time, it began to teem with wildlife—deer, foxes, pheasants—all of whom seemed instinctively to understand that the corridor had become a kind of game sanctuary. While, just about every night, to left and right and less than a mile away, patrols went out, raids were staged, ambushes were mounted by both sides, bloody firefights raged, and men died.

The most amusing aspect to all this more or less deadly stuff was Operation Snatch.

I don't know what martial genius came up with it, but we all thought Snatch was swell and couldn't wait for the inevitable day when, during the negotiations, someone went nuts and began shooting (one side or the other, didn't much matter to us), or the Commies kidnaped the American and UN officers doing the haggling to hold them hostage. Or just plain bumped them off.

To counter this very real possibility of war breaking out during the peace talks four Corsairs remained in the nearby air, circling high and just out of sight; a rifle company of combat-hardened Marines sat locked and loaded in trucks; a battery of 105 mm guns was zeroed in; and a platoon of tanks stood by, their engines idling. The idea was that the Corsairs would dive on Panmunjom, strafing and bombing, the tanks and the trucks would go tearing up the road, the Marines ready to jump out shooting, grab everyone on our side, toss them bodily into the now empty trucks, and shoot hell out of the other bastards, while our artillery would be shelling the enemy lines, covering what was expected to be a very hasty and rather chaotic withdrawal.

Oh, what a ride into Panmunjom that was going to be! And what an even more dizzying ride out! And as part of the show, American and Allied flag officers at the truce table would be grappling with the Commies, both sides shooting and stabbing the other guys, colonels and commissars, majors and captains and maybe old Admiral Joy himself, diving headfirst through the windows of the schoolhouse to get away, the Marines boiling up now, the trucks slamming on the brakes and skidding on the gravel, colliding with each other and running people over, and everyone yelling and shooting and the Corsairs strafing and roaring in at rooftop level, both sides just having themselves a hell of a time.

It was never quite clear to me whether the gentlemen of the press were to be rescued as well. Caveat emptor?

I don't believe there was a rifleman, machine gunner, or platoon leader in the division that spring and summer who wouldn't have anted up a month's pay to go barreling into Panmunjom, blazing away, as we rescued the brass in Operation Snatch!

Eddie Adams and I got to Panmunjom, what is now called the Joint Security Area, somewhat less dramatically. Major Holly Pierce picked us up at the hotel in an Army van. With her was Sergeant Russell Bassett, a public affairs journalist for the Army and reporter for the 2nd Division newspaper.

The Imjin River that we crossed looked the same (we'd skinny-dipped in that river!), except that the old pontoon bridge was long gone, supplanted by modern steel. At Camp Bonifas, part of the Panmunjom complex, a twenty-year-old soldier from Los Angeles, Specialist Robert Rodriguez, briefed us. And who was Bonifas? Rodriguez had the story at his fingertips. Bonifas was an American Army captain hacked and chopped to death by North Korean thugs in 1976. A tree-trimming party, a little groundskeeping, that's how innocently it began, clearing brush and chopping off limbs along the various little pathways leading into the village where the talks took place, and to maintain clear sight lines for the troops assigned to provide security for the negotiators, you had to do the pruning, the tidying up.

Bonifas was there, supervising, I suppose, when a crowd of North Koreans suddenly jumped up from gardening of their own and set upon the Americans with axes, pruning hooks, machetes, beating down the Americans by weight of numbers and cutting them to pieces. It must have been a planned attack, nothing spontaneous about it. The North Koreans are like that; they'll bully you if they can, kill you in a minute. Or maybe these boys were just demonstrating a little machismo, making their bones. The unfortunate Captain Bonifas was, in any event, dead. And as the senior man to die in the massacre, they named this little camp in his honor.

Eddie and I didn't really take Panmunjom seriously. We wanted to see some actual GIs really manning the line and not the "March of the Wooden Soldiers." In charge here was Colonel Matthew T. Margotta, tall, lean, balding, affable. It was with his men that we would be embedded.

The recon battalion that Margotta commanded, he explained, was unique, 60 percent ROK, 40 percent U.S. Exactly the ratio General LaPorte had told us about. "It's a modified light infantry battalion, with a battalion of 155 mm guns attached." The 155s are pretty big. It's not normal usage to have guns that size attached to a mere six-hundred-man battalion. We had them in the war, part of a full division. The colonel said his patrols were permitted to recon out to within twenty-five meters of the center line of the DMZ. I asked him about his men, their qualifications.

"The ROKs have to be tall, have been to college, and speak English. They all know tae kwon do and they sign up for a twenty-four-month tour. The Americans have to be above average in performance and potential and they pull a twelve-month tour."

Margotta liked his command. "We're getting a better class of infantry these days. They're professional." Despite building tensions between ourselves and the North over those nukes, the colonel said there was no increase in the level of alert. "Just normal operational. That has not changed. Maybe our ears are perked a little. I keep one hundred fifty soldiers inside the DMZ all the time plus a platoon on a very short string on ninety-second notice. Those men sleep with their boots on and rifles close."

"And if the shooting starts?" I asked.

"There are options, there are contingency plans," said the colonel. "Defend the key bridges and OPs. But we also have plans to retrograde south." I assumed "retrograde south" meant to retreat. But I left it to Margotta to tell me. Bird colonels like to speak their own lines. "We exercise these plans every three months. We can defend or pull out. My [phone] link is direct to General LaPorte. And every year we have a Defense of Korea exercise and part of that is what we [his battalion] do.

"We have six platoons, four ROK, one mixed, one U.S. Gleason heads that one. They do surveillance and patrolling. His platoon is up at Outpost Ouellette [OPO]. A platoon stays up there ten or fifteen days. His platoon is there but not Gleason. He's running a field exercise. The standard platoon is thirty men, but up here it's much larger, forty or forty-five men in a scout platoon. Gleason's got a great platoon sergeant and great men. And Gleason himself was quite a boxer in college."

The recon battalion isn't up here all alone, of course. Margotta said, "We have the 1st ROK Infantry Division to our left and right and rear."

"They any good?"

"Yes, it's a good division."

Yet I kept hearing him tell us he kept 150 men inside the DMZ all the time. The North Koreans had 1.2 million; we had 150 GIs, good as they were. But this wasn't a trip wire?

Hard not to be skeptical.

We were passed on to a very sharp first lieutenant, another Robert Rodriguez, who showed us around in one of his final chores before being transferred out. He was going to become an aide to a general, he said, sounding pleased about it. Couldn't blame him, either. President Bush the Elder had been here a week or so before our arrival, and Rodriguez met him. "And I got excited and forgot to tell him I was from Odessa, Texas, which is right near Midland."

An amusing sidebar to the former president's visit: atop the big bunker from which Mr. Bush was permitted to gaze out at the "enemy" lines through a scope, they'd laid a flooring of plywood, lest he slip on the concrete roof in the damp morning. Were they getting their ex-presidents mixed up? Were they thinking of Gerry Ford? Mr. Bush wasn't the one who fell down; he was the one who upchucked on the prime minister of Japan.

I tried to orient myself and Rodriguez helped. I wanted to know where

Hill 229 was, from which we had jumped off for that firefight on Yoke. Yoke was now out of reach, he said, out in the DMZ somewhere, a part of no-man's-land, but 229 was held by the ROKs.

"It's up 229 that we do our backcountry runs," Rodriguez said. "Look, you can see it from here."

I could, too. Not that it looked like much. Just another Korean hill. Sentimental journeys are like that. Sometimes the heart goes all aflutter, sometimes not. Memorial Day of 1952 it was where our patrol left from and came back to, just another reconnaissance patrol. And it was where the choppers and the meat wagons waited for us when we came back in, limping. I remembered that.

And today it's just a place where guys run to stay fit, shed a few pounds.

CHAPTER 29

We went now in search of the celebrated Lieutenant Gleason. I'd never heard so many brass hats talking about one first lieutenant. There was some sort of two-day expert infantryman's badge course being run in the hills, and we would find Gleason there, acting as a referee or observing, they weren't sure. The man was beginning to sound like Clark Kent. A Sergeant Major Marvell Dean, from Oklahoma City, took us over, suggested where we might be able to watch the men firing for record on the rifle range. He meant to be helpful and I was courteous, ever respectful of men as senior as sergeants major.

Thank you very much, Sergeant Major, but Mr. Adams and I have been checked out on rifle ranges.

We first encountered not Gleason but his platoon sergeant, Christopher Surtees of Portland, Oregon, who'd been in the Army twelve years and believed, in answer to my question, that the famed British race car driver John Surtees was his uncle.

Oh, yes, we also learned that Sergeant Surtees was the only man in the recon platoon who'd ever been in combat. The Horn of Africa, the Somalia expeditionary force. You remember, that *Black Hawk Down* episode. Where our guys got chopped and the bastards dragged their bodies behind trucks while the populace danced, gleeful, in the streets. Savage and grotesque as it was, Somalia was a vicious riot, a lynch mob, a deadly skirmish and not a genuine war. It is no dismissal of the man and of his professionalism and courage, but that was the extent of Surtees' fighting; and he was the platoon's old salt.

Now we found Gleason in the wooded slopes where the expert infantryman's tests were going on and the men ran field problems on which to be graded. They had camouflaged comm centers under netting where the communications folks worked their phones and radios and computers, and similarly screened areas masquerading as aid stations. On the dirt a "wounded" GI was stretched out and a couple of medics worked on him. They even had phony "wounds" with "blood-soaked" bandages on make-believe bullet holes. Eddie took a couple of pictures as Gleason showed us around, but was not very enthusiastic about it.

I didn't want to be a wise guy so I said, "Mmm, isn't that interesting." It seemed like playacting to me. But the Army, including Lieutenant Gleason, took it all pretty seriously. He seemed to sense that we didn't.

"Why don't you gentlemen ride up to the outpost," Gleason said after a time. "I think I can get away pretty soon now. I'll meet you there."

Surtees showed us around the outpost, a series of big reinforced concrete bunkers that functioned as barracks, a mess hall, a communications center, and the like. Sentries manned their posts atop the higher buildings, with actual outposts atop several of them and a kind of taller crenellated observation structure that resembled Beau Geste's Fort Zinderneuf, tricked up with lots of antennas and wires. Sergeant Surtees explained things and I even climbed the steep interior steel ladder leading to the tower's top. With some difficulty, I must say. Being in one of his rare polite moods, or perhaps just being sarcastic, Eddie complimented Surtees, "Nice view." Out in the distance across the barbed wire to the north there were similar, if less elaborate, North Korean observation towers. We took turns at the scopes and you could see troops over there, could even see them with the naked eye. "Frontier police units," someone explained; "they're not regular troops."

Adams switched to a longer lens and took a couple of shots.

For reasons I couldn't articulate, I was irritated that those people over there on the NK side weren't even proper frontline soldiers but cops. In my time up here on the low hills flanking Panmunjom we had real soldiers, Chinese Communist Army regulars facing us, not the local Immigration and Naturalization Service. This was disappointing.

When we were still negotiating long-distance from New York with the Army and were told we would be "embedded" at one of the observation bunkers, I took them to mean the variety of bunker we'd lived in up in the mountains, low-slung holes in the hillside you literally crawled into on your hands and knees, constructed of sandbags and logs. Not concrete jobbies resembling a Holiday Inn. The platoon sergeant showed us where we'd be bunking that night. Eddie and the ubiquitous Sergeant Bassett would share a utility room off Surtees' own office and bedroom. I said I'd prefer to sleep in one of the squad bays with the men (and be closer to the bathroom facilities). You get to my age, you consider such things as midnight piss calls.

Jim Gleason, a first lieutenant from Carolina, Rhode Island, a town too small to make the maps, was twenty-five, a tough-looking young man educated at Virginia Military Institute, with a broken nose and a Mohawk haircut he said he cut himself. Colonel Margotta told us he'd been a boxer at VMI, so I thought I'd get him talking about himself to start off, and then we could move on to more sensitive stuff like the Army and the tactical position and the potential enemy.

He looked as if he could handle another pug in the ring, but when I asked if he'd boxed intercollegiately, Gleason displayed a nice, candid sense of humor about himself: "My nose kept getting broken. Every time a dual meet was coming up my nose was broken."

What with us here now and with the elder Bush's entourage having just left, did he feel swamped by reporters?

"They get up here occasionally but I duck them if I can. You're different. They told me you were a rifle platoon leader, too, and that you fought here."

It made me feel pretty good, even proud to hear this kid say that, to acknowledge I was a member of "the club." But I didn't say so, just responded to his remark.

"Yes, I did. When I was twenty-three."

Gleason nodded on hearing that. "Two years younger than me," he said.

And by now we were relaxed, being together and talking. So we swapped platoon-leader shoptalk, what scared me, what made him edgy. Because he'd never been in combat and I had, Gleason was deferential, asking me a lot of questions about how it was back then on this same ground. I don't think he was just being polite; I believe he wanted to know. How else do you learn about combat if you've never fought? He deserved the truth, or at least my version of it.

So I told him as truly as I could. About how apprehensive I always was before a night patrol, jumpy and worried. How I dreaded watching the sun going down. That daylight patrols were fine, night patrols spooked me. But that even at night, once we were out there beyond the barbed wire on the move, on the actual patrol, I settled down. I was okay. Once the shooting began, I was fine. In a firefight I focused on the fight, only wanted to do the job. I told him all that, but admitted I never did learn to like patrolling in the dark.

Gleason said he understood that. But with the new night-vision optics they had, "the night belongs to us." That sounded a little cocky when he said it, but if the night glasses were that good, he could afford to be, I guess.

His own particular funk was certain dips in the terrain, narrow corners, blind spots where someone might be waiting, or approaching, unknown to him. Those were the things that bothered Lieutenant Gleason. I realized we shared the same fears of something we couldn't see, me in the dark, Gleason because of the topography.

We sat at a small table in the squad bay and talked. It was casual and quite pleasant and I took longhand notes in the spiral stenographer's notebook. He spoke without self-conciousness and easily, not at all inhibited by my note taking. Men passed by, coming in or going out, but no one disturbed us. Then a man came in and called him outside. When Gleason came back he said: "There's a patrol set for seventeen hundred hours. Do you want to go along, you and Mr. Adams?"

Eddie and me? That was another thing they didn't normally do for reporters, take them on patrol. For a couple of old gyrenes, Gleason would make exceptions. The brass must have okayed it. First lieutenants don't make decisions like that involving civilians. You get a civilian killed, you're in trouble. We went outside and Gleason and one of his squad leaders showed us, on a map and then on the ground, the route the patrol would take, starting out into no-man's-land down a steep sandstone slope the other side of the barbed wire on a footpath that was already crumbling and didn't look climber friendly to me. The squad was forming up, helmeted, flak-jacketed, chatting easily among themselves, while a corporal handed out clips of live ammo.

Apparently the men didn't go loaded except on patrol or when standing watch.

"Once you get past the barbed wire, you lock and load," someone explained. That made sense. Live ammo didn't bother me nor did the North Korean border patrol. But I didn't like the look of that first slope.

Gleason and the squad leader had their heads together, looking at a map.

"Let's give it a try," Eddie suggested.

So we climbed over the wire and started down the first few paces and I went flat on my ass when my bum knee gave way and my feet went out from under me. I scrambled up awkwardly and grinned at Jim Gleason. "I'll pass," I said.

"My guys can give you a hand, sir," Gleason said. I think he would rather I didn't take him up on it. I knew my knee and didn't think I could take the steep slopes down and back up without being helped along both ways. If anything happened, other men would be at risk watching out for me. Or carrying me back. The hell with that. I shook my head.

"Thanks, but no thanks." Not embarrassed to do so, either. My ego didn't need massaging. I'd done patrol time in these same hills when the Chinese were shooting at us.

"I'll give it a go," Eddie Adams announced. That surprised me. Eddie was nearly as ancient as I was and lugging cameras besides. And he didn't seem the volunteering type. There were complexities in Mr. Adams I didn't expect.

I walked down with them beyond the wire to where the steep part began. I liked one big rifleman slung all around with six or eight thirty-round magazines. "Got enough ammo?" I wisecracked, having fun being once again among troops. "I could always use more," he said. That boy might have made a good Marine.

Off they went, Eddie with them, armed only with Nikons, and he made it down the hill, and when the patrol vanished into a stand of trees he seemed to be keeping up. I liked the look of the troops, how they moved, how they took the whole thing seriously. And I found myself rather proud of Eddie. They were out only an hour or so and came back reporting no incidents. After they'd cleared their weapons and shed the armor, Gleason and I sat down again to resume the interview for *Parade*.

I was tempted to say something about the patrol's brevity, remembering going out on an ambush in the midwinter night under orders to stay out there six hours. But I kept shut. This Gleason seemed like a pretty good officer and didn't need old soldiers telling war stories.

Their patrols, he emphasized, were "squad-leader driven. The squad sergeant works out the route, the timing, and he and I go over the terrain visually together and we discuss it and if we both agree, that's how it goes." I asked then for the three sergeants' names, and as he spelled them out, I wrote them down: "First squad, William Baker, second, Andrew Schultz, third Staff Sergeant Brian Joyner."

Gleason said he hoped to stay in the army until he made captain and commanded a company. After that, as a major or higher, he said, "You get too far away from the troops." Did he wish he was fighting in Iraq? "I'd like to be there but right now my role is here with my men, my forty-five men. These are good soldiers. We get top pick of [replacement] men right off the plane."

Any gripes he could talk about on the record? No. I said I was surprised they didn't carry grenades. And did they have any 60 mm mortars? No to both. "They don't let us carry grenades on these patrols. And we don't have any mortars."

Why was that?

The truce arrangements were such that they didn't want any accidental discharges. It was clear Gleason didn't share such bureaucratic concerns.

"A 60 mm mortar comes in handy," I agreed. And no one had to convince me how useful a sack of hand grenades could be.

Jim Gleason was so gung ho I asked why he hadn't joined the Marines or put in for Rangers?

"When I graduated from VMI I thought about transferring to the Marines but the paperwork was too much trying to change my [Army] commission to the Marines. And I'd like to go Ranger but there's only a limited window of opportunity and with my year's commitment here I think I'm going to miss it."

That night we ate with and then bunked in with the platoon in the big concrete bunkers. The place was lined with steel double-decker bunks and was swept and kept pretty clean, though I did see scurrying across the concrete floor something the size of a Florida palmetto bug. It must have been somewhat unusual because one of the men pointed it out to the others and then stepped on it. I kept asking names and hometowns and got them to spell the names for me. Maybe their families would see them in *Parade* some Sunday and take some small, momentary comfort and pleasure in it. Talking to them, getting their names, made me feel pretty good about America, all these big, husky kids in camouflage, some still with paint on their faces from the patrol. Of course, being recon, they were special. Not all our troops may look this good.

These were some of the GIs I spoke with: Calvin Pittman of West Palm Beach, whose dad was a Ranger at Fort Benning; Charles Hill of Detroit, who was a police cadet at the Academy when September 11 happened, and even though he had a small daughter, "I went downtown and joined the Army—I thought it was the thing to do"; John De Meritt from Molalla, Oregon; John Mancino from Seattle; Easton Purkiss from Irvington, New Jersey; James Martin of Bradley, Maine.

I'd forgotten how noisy twenty-year-old boys are, even in their sleep, snoring and calling out, farting and grunting, and when awake, shedding helmets and flak jackets, shucking off boots, slamming assault rifles back into gun racks as they come in from their two-hour sentry duty, shouting and cursing at each other in the spirit of the locker room, the sophomore-freshman rush. But before we slept, I found a knot of eight or ten of them quietly crouching around my cot, sitting on the deck or the upper or adjacent bunks, asking questions. It was nice that they held in some respect an old fart like me, if he'd actually fought in this neighborhood against the Chinese army.

Do you mind, Lieutenant?

No, ask away.

Tell us about the Chinese. How far apart were the enemy lines, ours and theirs? Were there raids every night? Where did your patrols jump off from? Did they have any tanks? Did you get bombed? Lot of mines? Was artillery a big factor back then, Lieutenant?

I found myself being called "sir." Or "Lieutenant Brady." Fifty years after the fact I was playing infantryman again and it felt good. Was that stupid of me?

I told them about the Fox Company raid on 104 and Tu-mari that was a total screwup that morning when four tanks went out with them and all four were disabled in the first few minutes and Fox had to fight its way back as infantrymen always did, afoot. Lost ten dead that morning and they never got anywhere. I told them about the Brits who tied in with us along here, the Leicestershire Regiment.

"They any good, sir?"

"Very good. You could go to war with the Leicesters."

"Where were the North Koreans then? Why were we only fighting Chinese?"

"Lot of the North Koreans were dead. We'd killed them. The rest were up in the eastern mountains, not here."

They asked about the rifles we carried fifty years ago, the C rations we ate, if they'd yet invented choppers, if the Chinese or the North Koreans were the better soldiers. . . .

"What were the Chinese really like?" one trooper asked.

"Well," I said, "they were pretty good and there were forty divisions of them."

"Forty freaking divisions?" someone murmured. We had one U.S. division here now.

Before I could say more, Platoon Sergeant Surtees came in, storming!

He was sore at something, cussing them out, really chewing ass, effing this and effing that! Sounded like Eddie on a good day. The sergeant kept it up, ripping them up one side and down the other, over their Kevlar or something, until he noticed me slouched there against the pillow in the midst of them and backed off. "Sorry, sir, didn't see you there. . . ."

"Sergeant, I was dozing, didn't hear a word."

Later that next morning I would pull Sergeant Surtees aside. "It did me good to hear a platoon sergeant chewing out the troops, Sergeant. To know that's what good sergeants still do."

I liked it too that his men had all gotten to their feet while he chewed on them and, after he'd left, no one whined or sulked or cursed him behind his back, but instead, a few men said, "He's right, you know. We did fuck up."

These were good troops. You could see that. Good troops with a good platoon sergeant, in a scary place. I just didn't like thinking of them as a "trip wire," still less as "meat on the end of a stick."

CHAPTER 30

I suppose you never really get over the old habits, narrow army cots and noisy barrack rooms, but I slept pretty well, waking each time they changed the guard but not otherwise. Got up once or twice and made my way in the semidark to the head. Once when I lay there trying to get back to sleep I remembered that last question a soldier had posed before Surtees came in raising hell.

"What were the Chinese really like?"

When Colonel Gregory made me the battalion intelligence officer, the Chinese became my concern. The live Chinese, prisoners. And the dead.

When they brought in POWs I asked a few quick questions, the interpreter translating, and then by order we shipped them back swiftly to regiment and they passed the lads on to division, where presumably our experts were. There was less urgency with the dead; they were all mine. My scouts went through their pockets; and the interpreter translated letters and documents if any. Six months before I'd been chasing girls at Laguna Beach. Now I was doing morgue duty, pawing over bloodstained service-record books in a lingo I couldn't read or speak.

One poor SOB we dragged in had been in the army since 1937. Fought against the Japs until '45. Then fought in the civil war against Mao and the Reds. In '49 when Chiang bugged out to Taiwan, he and a lot like him were absorbed into the Red Army; he was given a red star on his cap and told he was now a soldier of the proletariat and could address his officers as "Comrade." No end to the fringe benefits the Commies enjoyed, was there?

This former fisherman had been fighting in Korea against us since November of '50. In the army since '37, fourteen years of soldiering, and now he was dead, still a private.

I'd had Marines in my old rifle platoon who were a year out of high school. I fell asleep thinking about that.

About 4 A.M. I got up for good, used the john again, luxuriating in the privacy, dressed and went outside, trying to be quiet. It was still full night, of course, with stars. I can't remember the situation as far as moonlight. I'd lent my pocket flashlight, the one Ike Fenton had urged on us, to Eddie in case he needed a friendly latrine in the dark, so I paused to let my eyes adjust. There was a low stone or concrete wall just outside the barracks bunker and I sat down on it and stayed there. I was opposed to getting shot stumbling around in the dark, either by some wandering hostiles or, even worse form, by our own sentries.

I don't know if I can convey to you in the pages of a book just how it felt. All those years ago I'd sat up on these same hills, looking north, listening and trying to see, knowing the night was nearly ended and wondering what the morning would bring. I was twenty-three years old, a first lieutenant, much like this fellow Gleason. We were both armed, trained, and blessed with good sergeants, good men. The difference was, in my time it was the Chinese Army out there, waiting, not just some frontier police. And night after night, we'd been fighting them. It was a real war, a deadly war, and it wasn't over, not by a long shot, with another year to run until July of '53.

Here in 2003, two other hostile armies faced off. But there was no shooting. Only loudspeakers and insulting signs hoisted and over there a ways, that phony plywood Potemkin village the North had put up for propaganda purposes, all lighted up but empty and still.

Strange people, the Koreans. Both sides. Some of the music the loudspeakers played at four in the morning was quite beautiful, though disembodied and lonely as it bounced echoing off the hills. I don't have an ear but I liked parts of the music, especially the operatic stuff. Then, in between the songs, the shouted insults, the cursing in a language I didn't know. Here I was, sitting in the dark of an outpost that belonged to an American named Gleason that used to belong to me and to other Americans, half a century earlier. And it summoned up memory of that long-ago spring, what it looked like then, what we did, how we lived and how some of us died. . . .

And I was sorry that as I sat propped up on an army bunk the previous evening, with the recon scouts all around me, instead of telling war stories, I'd reminded them that when you're young and healthy and surrounded by pretty good guys of your own totem, even in a shooting war, how it sometimes was fun.

I should have told them about Christmas in Korea, the Christmas of 1951. That might have been a good story to tell to Gleason's platoon. Wish I'd thought of it.

The battalion had been pulled off the line into reserve before Christmas and wouldn't be going back until January 10 of the New Year. We were still training, pulling field problems, most of them at night. It was cold in the eastern mountains and even four or five miles behind the MLR, it was rough country and snow covered. We weren't fighting but still we lost men, still we took casualties. You put a couple of thousand healthy young Americans in uniform, take them nine thousand miles from home, deprive them of women and creature comforts, and put deadly weapons into their hands, things happen. We lost men through accidents, broken legs on the ice, dislocated shoulders, sprained ankles, we lost men to mines planted in the hills, uncharted on maps and forgotten, strewn about haphazardly, and lost some to accidental discharges, Marines shooting their buddies. Or themselves. And not meaning to. But the wounded were no less hurt, the dead no less dead.

Except for people getting hurt or killed, reserve was pretty cushy, living in big eight-man pyramidal tents, with smelly but effective oil stoves, occasional

showers, three hots a day, some beer for the enlisted men, some booze for senior NCOs and officers, a little organized grab-ass, volleyball and football and
footraces mostly. Best of all, no damned night patrols down the forward slope
toward the Soyang-gang and the enemy. I didn't miss those at all.

Christmas was great, a lot of fun. Maybe not for Colonel Gregory, who
was a serious regular and on whose watch all these things happened.

Christmas Eve two Marines stole a jeep, painted "War Correspondent" on
the side, and drove south, "looking for whores," they later said at the court-
martial, as if that excused them. Other Marines played tackle football Christmas morning on the frozen hardpan of the parade ground, no helmets or
pads, just issue fatigues. Lots of bloody knees and knuckles and swollen faces
after that one, you can be sure. No fatalities, however, and some pretty good
football. At midnight to celebrate Christmas Eve, our artillery fired off red
and green flares. The North Koreans, not understanding, and thinking it was
the signal for an all-out night attack, shelled hell out of our lines for a half
hour or so, intent on breaking up our offensive before it could gather mo-
mentum. Marines thought this was hilarious. Not the few guys who got hit,
however.

Christmas Day they put on a USO show on a little stage set up outdoors
on the parade ground after the football stars were finished bloodying it up.
Paul Douglas, who'd been a Marine in the Big War; his wife, Jan Sterling; and
a juvenile from Broadway named Keith Andes did an act from *Born Yesterday*.
Some of our Marines had never seen a stage play before, or even a slice of
one. It was really good, almost great, especially Miss Sterling, who was slender
and blond and who wore a very sexy dress, spoiled not a bit by the issue long
johns she wore under the skirt. This was outdoors, after all, and cold. She still
looked swell.

There'd been a rash of fires our first week in reserve, oil stoves and canvas
tents being what they are. And Colonel Gregory had surely heard about it
from on high, so he named a battalion fire warden to check things and pre-
vent future fires. This was a lieutenant named Duffy who had gone to Holy
Cross and who wore a splendid ginger-colored handlebar mustache. Duffy

was very diligent in his duties, checking out every tent, seeing that the stoves were positioned where they didn't touch flammable canvas. Then, on Christmas Eve, during the night, Duff burned down his own tent.

Maybe that was the most fun we had that Christmas and I was sorry I hadn't told these young recon boys of Lieutenant Gleason's about it.

CHAPTER 31

AT LUNCHTIME HE TOOK SURREPTITIOUS
PHOTOS OF WOMEN'S BACKSIDES.

Gleason was a VMI graduate. So, too, had been Mack Allen. I haven't told you enough about Mack.

I'd known Maurice J. Allen for a long time and considered him unkillable. It was up here on Hill 229 that I last saw Mack before I left Korea. We'd arrived here together as replacements, had fought to hold 749 under John Chafee, had moved up to battalion staff under Colonel Gregory, and now we were both being rotated home. Despite my love for the Corps, I'd accepted with a born civilian's alacrity. Mack re-upped for another three months in Korea.

"Mack, no."

"It's my chance to get a company."

More than anything else, Mack wanted to command a Marine rifle company in combat. And he wasn't going to walk away from possibilities. I went up to his bunker on Hill 229, where he was once again commanding a rifle platoon. To see him one last time and try to argue him out of it. There were no guarantees. And he might get killed.

Mack Allen was stubborn. He wanted that company. It was something he'd wanted as an enlisted man in the Big War, as a VMI cadet, as a Marine lieutenant in the Basic School at Quantico, and even since he got to North Korea last November.

"You're crazy." I felt I might be saying a last good-bye to a friend, a good and decent man, a fine officer.

He was strong, solid, but short, maybe five eight (the Korean urchins who hung around reserve camp called him "Scosh Lieutenant" [Little Lieutenant], with a thick neck, muscular arms, and big hands. He was quiet-spoken and even shy, but he wasn't a fellow you'd want to tackle, not with those shoulders and the cold eyes. That spring we got a football hero of our own, Joe Buscemi, a newly arrived officer. Buscemi was a Chicagoan and at Illinois had played in the same backfield with Jules Rykovitch and Buddy Young, the great running back who'd led the Illini to a Rose Bowl victory New Year's Day in 1947. Young was a world-class track star in the sprints, a fireplug, and might have won the Heisman Trophy that year, and it was Rykovitch and Buscemi who cleared the way for him. Or so Joe said. He and Mack Allen liked to wrestle. No rules, no timekeeper, just the two Marines in their boondockers and fatigues rolling around and wrestling on the dirt. Captain Chafee would have enjoyed it. Mack was giving away maybe thirty pounds but held his own. I used to watch them but, knowing my limitations, prudently never entered in.

Mack had gone north to the Harvard Business School after VMI but he was pure Dixie. He enjoyed telling me, his favorite Yankee, tales of the Old Confederacy. Stonewall Jackson, Lee, Longstreet, they were his heroes. Not Jeb Stuart, dashing but too reckless. I knew the story of how late in the Civil War the South was running short and they called on VMI for help and the whole student body, cadets as young as sixteen, fell in, shouldered arms, and went off to fight the blue bellies. I could see Mack Allen falling in with them, not wanting to miss a scrap. He was still like that in Korea, Harvard B School and all, still a Johnny Reb with a rifle.

Jim Gleason was a New Englander who'd gone to school at Virginia Military Institute; Mack was a Virginian (born in Lynchburg) who'd gone to school at VMI. There's a difference.

Anyway, my premonitions were wrong and Mack didn't get killed. Didn't get a company but got into plenty more fighting, and then one day in Manhattan, where I was back at work helping edit the house organ at Macy's, I got a call. It was Mack, in the big city for a jaunt!

"Come on up!"

I kind of hoped he'd still be in uniform, you know, giving a little class to the place. But he was in a perfectly normal suit. There were lots of pretty girls working in Macy's and some gloriously clever and creative people in the ad department, where I tended to hang out (the house organ being pretty dull), art directors and copywriters, the usual homosexuals, and they all made a fuss over this courtly Virginia Gentleman (in reality a very adept killer) right out of the early reels of *Gone with the Wind*. He'd taken a room at the Hotel Pennsylvania across from the big store.

And a funny thing happened to him, he said, his homely, good face lighting up in wonder. A newspaper photographer had taken his picture and asked him a question and said he would be in the paper the next day.

It turned out to be the "Inquiring Photographer" feature that ran every day in the *Daily News*. They chose people at random, a half dozen every day, asked their question, shot a picture, and it ran next morning on what we now call the op-ed page.

"Do they do that to everyone who comes to town?" Mack wanted to know.

"No," I assured him. "Only the hicks."

He went sightseeing and I got him a date and we went to P.J. Clarke's over on Third Avenue. The Third Avenue El still ran and Mack was entranced by the way the train cast an afternoon shadow on the windows of the bar when it rattled by. When the girls were talking to each other Mack filled me in on the battalion after I left. The fighting, I took it, was getting worse. Up on the outpost line, the Chinese were taking the hills every night, the Marines taking them back by day. It wasn't just raids and ambushes and going out on patrols anymore. It was full-scale trench warfare; it was murderous. It was as if Flanders of 1917–18 had never happened. We were doing the same shit halfway through the twentieth century that had turned Belgium and northern France into an abattoir two wars ago.

"I was happy to go home, Mack. No regrets."

"I know, I know. In the end, even I was glad to come home."

I knew the fighting must be bad, when Mack Allen talked like that.

He kept dropping by the office at Macy's. The advertising department was aswim with girls, artists, photographers, characters: Aldo Biondi, who'd skippered an Army tug during the war and wanted to become a tugboat captain here in New York, but ended up doing advertising. Nat Rose, whose lunchtime hobby was snapping surreptitious photos of young women's backsides. Steve Gavin, the art department supervisor, who was very nearly blind. An artist who specialized in sketches of French poodles fornicating. Rosie the art director. Gomberg the artist, who exchanged reminiscences with Mack from their days in Boston.

Back home in Virginia, offices were serious, solemn places of business bereft of laughter, while here there seemed to be a kind of continual cocktail party going on. One of the young ad department lotharios, who was having a hot affair with a married woman executive at the store, sidled up to me. "While your pal's out sightseeing, would he let us use his hotel room for a couple of hours this afternoon?"

Since Mack was fairly straitlaced, the only one of us who'd bailed out of the geisha house after dinner and before the action began, I said I didn't think so.

He was so wide-eyed, exploring New York, that I had to keep reminding myself what a lethal soldier Mack had been and here he was, taking in New York like the youngsters in *My Sister Eileen*.

He had a job offer, he said. City engineer in some city down south, Florence, Alabama, I think. He thought he'd probably take it.

"Don't want to try New York? Hang around here for a while? Maybe find a job?"

I was walking back with him to Penn Station, where he was taking the train south that afternoon, and he kept turning to look back, at the Empire State Building, at Macy's itself, at the girls hurrying along the sidewalks. He gave me that smile. "Nah, I'm not a big-city boy like you. And I'd miss the South."

I suspected he was restless, that this trip wasn't just to see me but to settle things inside him before he settled down. I knew the feeling. I was restless, too. That winter I would leave the country again, driving up to Mont Tremblant in Canada. The year before I'd been freezing my ass off in North Korea and here I was, going skiing. Ten or twenty below and I couldn't wait to get there.

Were we all nuts?

Up there I met and skied with a girl named Jackie Beaudoin. She was French Canadian, beautiful and smart, skied with considerable style and had money, and one day we drove down in my car to Montreal to attend a cocktail party she'd been invited to. She asked if I wanted to go along. Ninety miles driving on winter roads to go to a cocktail party. Of course! The people were nice, friendly, maybe a bit lefty, and most of them didn't understand why the U.S. was fighting in Korea. "Leave Asia to the Asians," that sort of thing. I was something of a lefty myself, having just cast my first-ever vote for Stevenson. Still, I tried to make the case. Jackie was lefty too, but I liked it the way she sort of stood up for me against her friends when she didn't agree with me either.

For about twenty-four hours I think I was in love with Jacqueline Beaudoin.

Maybe that's how Mack Allen felt about Manhattan. It wasn't really his place or style, but he wanted to gauge the possibilities before he went back.

He took that job in Alabama, got married to a Southern belle named Emma, had kids, went to work for one of the big chemical companies, maybe Du Pont. We corresponded, exchanged photos of kids. When he was in his late fifties, he was laid off by the chemical giant. I don't know the reason. We continued to phone, to write. Then his daughter Janet got on the phone. They thought Mack might have Alzheimer's. There came an invitation to a black-tie Marine Corps birthday dinner at the officers' mess in Richmond. His son-in-law, the major, or the colonel, was taking Mack, and would I come down for the evening? I couldn't go and they sent me a photo. Mack looked fine, the lopsided grin and all, his tuxedo with its row of miniature decorations, the major soon to be a colonel next to him in dress uniform.

Another time, Emma called. He was in the hospital. Then he was dead. The unkillable Mack dead. He'd fought the Japanese, fought the Chinese Army, wrestled Buscemi the Rose Bowl hero. Had once visited New York, and gotten his picture in the newspaper.

We were dying off, the Korea generation.

CHAPTER 32

THANKS FOR WHAT YOU DID HERE IN THE WAR,
AND FOR WRITING ABOUT US.

Dawn broke over Lieutenant Gleason's outpost just before six, its rosy fingers creeping toward me over the broken ridgelines to the east, casting the first low shadows of day, and by now I felt sufficiently secure that I could loosen up my legs, the creaky knee and the other parts, by moving around here on the reverse slope of the outpost hill, without getting myself bumped off.

The recon boys, Gleason's men, would be stirring as, "on the road to Mandalay," the sun "came up like thunder." I tried to remember the rest of the poem but couldn't, and by then the platoon was strolling out of the barracks to another concrete building which served as mess hall. The food was hot, say that for it, precooked in big aluminum pans and kept hot somehow, and pretty punk, dried out and crusted over, much like last night's dinner, so I stayed with the coffee and an apple. Being a throwback (I'd actually liked some of the old C rations of my era), I'd been rather looking forward to Army food, expecting to be issued those new MRE rations, "meals ready to eat," but up here on the outpost, they felt, the men ought to have hot chow trucked up every morning. Hot meals, Kevlar body armor, women soldiers—what was the army coming to?

After the meal, Eddie Adams came in, looking for coffee and tucking into the breakfast eggs and sausage, even without the Tabasco sauce.

"How'd you sleep?" he asked.

"Great," I lied.

There were sentries atop the bunkers and up in the observation tower and some of the men ate more hastily than the others so they could get up there and relieve them for breakfast. An Army bus pulled up just outside unloading some ROK troops. No one paid them much attention. Maybe they were part of the Korean 60 percent that made up this U.S.-ROK recon battalion. They were all tall Koreans, clean-shaven, neat-looking troops, but unarmed. Maybe they stored the weapons up here. In the Marines you drew a personal rifle, memorized the serial number, and locked it to the bunk. I would never figure out the Army.

Eddie took a few photos. I kept trying to include Hill 229 in the background. But the sun got in the way. Eddie seemed annoyed that I kept selecting hills in the wrong direction.

"I'm sorry, Eddie, but that's the hill I want, the hill that figures in the story."

"Effing sun!" He looked a bit sour. Damned writers. They don't know anything about light.

One of Gleason's troopers took me aside. "Here, sir," he said, handing me a metallic blue medallion on a short length of soft leather with a snapper button at the tail end.

"I thought you ought to have this, Lieutenant, for coming up here to write about us, and for what you did here during the war."

It was a tab that Army Forces in Korea were entitled to wear on their uniforms. Or maybe only those who served up here on the DMZ, and he wanted me to have it as a memento.

"Well, thanks."

He looked around. "Please don't tell the other guys I gave you mine."

I guess he was afraid they were thinking he was sucking up. Well, of course he was sucking up. That didn't make it any less thoughtful, and I thanked him again and stuffed it into a pocket. The medal itself didn't mean a thing to me; the boy's gesture and words did.

The Pulitzer laureate, Mr. Adams, didn't get any decorations. He did return my black-rubber-encased flashlight.

Sergeant Bassett, our GI reporter, was bright and chipper. He'd brought up his own sleeping bag and slept on the floor and had no complaints. He took some more pictures of Eddie and me and said he'd like an hour or two with each of us when convenient. Sure. Did we have that much to say?

Meanwhile we'd milked the OPO for all it was worth, Gleason was gone on some errand, and we were flying to the eastern mountains the next morning to go up Hill 749, so someone phoned Major Pierce for us, and told our own personal West Pointer we were ready to get back to town.

"Unless you want to go out on another patrol, Eddie."

"Eff, no!"

He asked me what I thought about life up here on the OPO. I said it seemed pretty posh. "Electric light, flush toilets, hot meals, cots with pillowcases even."

"It's the Army. What d'you expect?" he asked.

"I liked the men. And Gleason sure looks like a soldier."

Eddie had taken a lot of pictures of Gleason, and he looked thoughtful, as if pondering whether Gleason would make a better cover shot than me. And wondering if he could get away with it. The hell with that, I thought. It was my story and if anyone was going to be on the cover it was me.

There were a couple of little plaques on a bunker wall and I went back to look at them and take a few notes. One plaque memorialized eight Marines who'd been killed up here early in '51. The other explained why the outpost was named for Ouellette and who he might have been. It read: "Out Post Ouellette. In honor of PFC. Joseph R. Ouellette, Medal of Honor, Naktong River, August 1950."

I took a moment to say a prayer for Joe Ouellette and those other kids dead now more than fifty years.

The major's car had us back swiftly into the bustle of big-city traffic, and within two hours of leaving the DMZ I was out of yesterday's clothes and into a hot shower. Talk about posh.

Jim Gleason's platoon would be up there fifteen to seventeen days and then break for a couple of weeks and be replaced by ROKs and maybe some other Yanks and then they'd be back up there again for a two-week tour, and that routine would go on for another year.

And the other side would be doing the same kind of thing to its own schedule, and the insult signs would be hoisted and the loud music played, and night after night the Commies would light up their Potemkin village.

And that sort of crap had been going on here since July 27, 1953, when the actual fighting stopped.

You explain it.

CHAPTER 33

"THEY'RE ALL HAPPY AS PIGS IN SHIT," SAID A PLEASED
ENLISTED MAN.

It was almost as wacky as what sometimes went on there at Hill 229 half a century earlier.

Colonel Gregory was my commanding officer when our battalion held this stretch of MLR anchored on Hill 229. He'd been the CO when we were up there on Hill 749 and when we fought on the outpost line. It seemed as if he had always been my commanding officer.

Old Marines eventually die; they just don't fade away, unlike the "old soldier" in MacArthur's famous recounting of the barracks ballad.

Noel C. Gregory had fought on Guadacanal in 1942 and all through the war with the Japanese; he commanded the 2nd Battalion, 7th Marines when I arrived, and when I was being rotated home, he was still in command. I described him in my memoir as being "turkey necked" and, when amused, given to "cackling." He was also sandy haired, tall, skinny, and, I assumed, quite elderly (at the time I thought of most people as "elderly," including a lieutenant colonel who was probably forty).

I always liked Colonel Gregory, much as I disliked his executive officer, Colonel Ed Kurdziel. Kurdziel, younger, more powerful, handsome, and not given to cackling, was your beau ideal of a field-grade Marine officer. But he never (to my knowledge) came up to the line. And it is by that which front-line troops and junior officers judge their betters.

I can hear the voices now, across the half century, the dismissive snarl: "You never see that son of a bitch up here on the line, do you? Answer me that! Never up on the line, that bastard!"

On looks alone, Kurdziel was a candidate for future commandant. But when he was eventually transferred, no one shed a tear. I think he made general of one sort or another, but never commandant. Colonel Gregory used to come up to the line every so often, drop by to say hello. I don't know what good those visits did the war effort, but the rifle platoons and machine gunners appreciated the gesture. Shortly before I was to leave the battalion for home, Gregory and several other staff officers, all of them regular Marines and not Reservists, went up to the MLR on Hill 229 on a little inspection tour. Today our GIs run cross-country there; in 1952 it was the main line of resistance.

While the colonel and his brass were up on 229, four or five of them stuffed inside a log-and-sandbag observation post overlooking no-man's-land and the enemy lines just beyond, the local platoon leader was pointing out the Chinese positions, the routes used by the Chinese in their night attacks. Scouting the terrain, Gregory and his officers queued to use the telescope. There they were, crammed shoulder to shoulder, the flower of the battalion staff, when some Communist spoilsport sent over an artillery shell that exploded on Hill 229 just below the observation bunker, ramming the telescope backward against the eye of the officer then unfortunate enough to be using it, and spraying the rest of them, including Colonel Gregory, with dirt, rock, and shrapnel.

I was down at the command post doing what I usually did those final days of my Korean tour, smoking cigars and playing volleyball (a new intelligence officer, a tall, dashing, mustachioed regular, senior to me, and reliably reported to know something about intelligence! had taken over), when word came down that virtually the entire high command of our battalion had just been wiped out!

Would I have to take command? I always wanted to be a colonel; you didn't have to go out on night patrols. Did I know enough to command a battalion? Probably not. Alas, the reports of disaster were somewhat exaggerated. Perhaps half a dozen people had been hurt, the staff officers plus a couple of enlisted men showing them around. No one was wounded seriously (the man at the scope had a terrific black eye, blue and purple and red and looking sore as hell), and no evacuations were called for. But their wounds were real and undeniable, inflicted by an enemy in wartime, and they'd all just earned a Purple Heart. Which all career Marines value highly because, in the Corps, combat experience counts more toward promotion than any other factor, and a simple Purple Heart confirms as few other things do, yes, I've been there; I've fought.

So it was indeed a jovial, if somewhat battered, party that returned to the command post that afternoon to bonhomie, good wishes, and handshakes all around, and much cackling from Colonel Gregory.

As one of the enlisted men later put it, to general hilarity, "They was all happy as pigs in shit!"

Many years later, in the memoir, I wrote about all this, my assumption being, of course, that Colonel Gregory was by then long dead and would never read the book. Then one Saturday night in East Hampton in 1990 the phone rang.

Some Dog Company guys, Jack Rowe and Jack Vohs and Bob Simonis among them, who lived around San Diego (where good Marines retire to, a sort of elephants' graveyard), were having a cocktail party and phoned to tell me they'd bought *The Coldest War*. They were all in it and they were naturally both fascinated and curious, and I was flattered and enormously pleased. After a chat Rowe said, "Hang on, Brady. We've got a surprise for you. Here's Colonel Gregory."

And by God! it was. You couldn't mistake the voice. So I sputtered out something about what a thrill it was and how well I remembered him and all that guff, "Colonel-ing" him right and left and saying, "Yes, sir," every so often, when Gregory cut right across me.

"I've seen your book, Brady. And I want you to know I do not have a turkey neck . . ."

"No, sir, of course not . . ."

". . . and I don't cackle!"

"No, sir."

"And my attorneys will be getting in touch with you, Lieutenant, and seeking damages."

At that, the old man was incapable of maintaining the charade and burst into laughter which swiftly deteriorated into the auld, familiar Gregory cackle. And I couldn't resist it.

"Colonel, you're cackling now, sir!"

That was fifteen years ago and I believe the old gentleman may really be dead by now but I'm not taking chances and you won't catch me writing anything bad about him, turkey neck or cackling, nothing like that. I wouldn't mind another phone call, though, not after everything Colonel Gregory and I have been through.

Such as our adventures "mucking about" with the Chinese, alongside that distinguished British regiment, the Leicestershires, and how I fell afoul of the Colonel at a cocktail party we gave for the Brits.

CHAPTER 34

THERE'S SOME SON OF A BITCH OUT THERE
IN THE MINEFIELD PLAYING GOLF.

We didn't win the Korean War all by ourselves, you know. Or lose it, either. Or get rained out in the late innings.

There were lots of South Koreans. The KMC, their Marines, were pretty good. About most of the ROK Army, the less said, the better. And a scatter of other Allied units. There were small detachments of everything but the Medes and the Persians.

And then there were the Brits. And the British Commonwealth, God bless 'em. In 1959, long after we fought there side by side, I was sent off to London to work as a correspondent for a couple of years, and I realized that for all our exasperating differences, we really were in ways an English-speaking union.

We first tied in with the British, their Leicestershire Regiment, in April of 1952. By then the snows were melting, the mud drying, and it was a perfectly splendid time for the Communists to try to capture Seoul for the third time in two years. The Chinese were going up against a couple of dozen ROK divisions of varying quality, six American divisions, some other Allied detachments, and, as I say, a very good British Commonwealth division comprised of Englishmen, Aussies, South Africans, Scots, Canadians, New Zealanders, and Irish. The Australians and New Zealanders were understandably popular with the American Marines because so many American Marines had trained, refitted, recuperated (and fallen in love) during the Pacific war in those two gorgeously friendly South Pacific countries. The South Africans? Half of them Boers, half English, and both very good soldiers.

With the Chinese threat to Seoul being taken seriously, in a heavy, wet spring snowstorm, the entire twenty-five-thousand-man 1st Marine Division was pulled out of the eastern mountains and in a single day trucked across the country about a hundred miles to the west to take up positions north of the Imjin River, masking the capital. Not a Marine died in the move and there were only a few traffic or other noncombat injuries (Jack Rowe's truck overturned on a mountain road, and Rowe was annoyed and some of his Dog Company Marines shaken up).

It was in the low, sandy hills of the west that our battalion first fell among Brits. We'd settled into our new positions with the Chinese a mile or two to the north and the Leicesters, as they called themselves, to our east or right. It was a pleasant, sunny day without wind and with no firing. Our three rifle companies were stringing wire and digging in on the ridgelines or taking over bunkers and trenches already there. The machine gunners were setting up their guns and on the reverse slopes the 60 mm mortars were digging in and farther back, the 81s. I had my intelligence section scouts out reconnoitering the line, sniffing out the terrain, while I went over the large scale maps we'd been issued, trying to figure out where the Chinese were and what minefields were indicated along there on the charts.

This low, rolling ground sat athwart the traditional invasion route, between two mountain ranges, to Seoul and all of South Korea. Over the centuries the Japanese and Russians had come this way, the Manchurians, the Chinese of the dynasties. If you invaded Korea, here was the freeway. That's why the brass had moved the Marine division over here from the east to dig in and protect the capital.

Jay Scott, my intelligence section chief, the Yalie who was a Du Pont on his mama's side, had come up with a couple of interpreters, Koreans, who claimed to speak Chinese. I just shook my head. How could Scott or any of us check them out? I told Scottie to find someone at regiment who spoke Chinese and could field-test these birds.

Just then Sasso, a scout from Jersey City, came up at a trot. "Lieutenant," he said panting, "there's some son of a bitch out there in the minefields playing golf."

Sasso wasn't a wiseass or a drinker, nor was he shook. So I went up to the ridgeline with him to check it out. I had some 7×50 field glasses, and by God, there they were. One guy hitting a golf ball, another out there a hundred yards ahead of him shagging flies and caddying. This was on the low ground between the main line of resistance and the blocking position behind and in support, and there were these two out there where mines were marked on the maps, one of them hitting golf balls with a short iron, the other fetching. I gave them a shout and a wave. Got an amiable wave back.

Sasso looked at me. "See, Lieutenant. They're crazy."

It looked to me as if the golfer knew what he was doing (absent the minefield). Nice slow backswing and a full follow-through. The retriever returned the balls with a curious underarm throw. I sat down on the hillside to watch. I'd never seen a golfer blown up before in the middle of a round and didn't want to miss it. After about thirty minutes of this the golfer shouldered his club and ambled toward us. I got up to receive him, assuming he was an officer. Enlisted men have more sense.

"Hallo," the golfer shouted, British by the accent. "Decent weather at last. It's been beastly until today."

"Don't you know the maps show mines out there?" I said.

"Mines, mines!" the Englishman replied impatiently. "People are forever going on about mines. Lot of bloody cock. Wish I'd never heard of the bloody things. Our sappers haven't put one up yet. My name's Lonsdale."

So that was our introduction to our allies, the British.

Lonsdale was a leftenant, his caddy the batman. "Mooney doesn't golf but I say it keeps one in trim, right, Mooney?"

Mooney grunted what I took for sullen affirmation.

Lonsdale said his battalion of the Leicestershires had come out to the wars from Hong Kong. "Splendid duty, that. Nothing but golf, thirty-six holes most days. When they sent us here I took my sticks along. Never know when you'll get in a round."

I explained we were Marines. Lonsdale said he had known a Marine once. "Extraordinary chap. Drunk every morning by ten. Bloody big chap, though. And fit, even when tiddly."

He gave me the fellow's name but I said I didn't know him. "We've been fighting in the eastern mountains."

"Fighting? We arrived a week ago. Bit of gunnery and a few patrols, that's about the size of it. Glad I brought the sticks along."

We would soon have sufficient fighting for both of us.

The Leicesters might be newly arrived but there had been Brits here since 1950, the Royal Marine Commandos up at the Chosin Reservoir with our people and then later on, when the Chinese made their spring offensive in '51, the Gloucestershire Regiment, or as they were called, "the Glorious Glosters." Except that the Chinese, moving fast and by night, caught up with the Glosters when they were exhausted and hadn't put out security and over-ran the position, Hill 235. Two other Brit units, the Fusiliers and the Ulsters, pulled out fighting that night, and so did a Belgian battalion. Not the Glosters, of whom sixty-three men were killed, two hundred wounded, most of the others captured, and not at all "gloriously." For some unfathomable reason our army promptly awarded the Glosters a Presidential Unit Citation.

It puzzled people that no one was court-martialed for what befell the Gloucestershire Regiment. I hoped the Leicesters would turn out to be somewhat more alert than the Glorious Glosters.

They did.

The Brits could fight. They also had style and entertainment value, hosted a good cocktail party, took us in hand and taught us manners. Batmen served the drinks, there were actual canapés, and as we entered the bunker that served as their officers' mess, we were expected, and politely asked, to do something we never did back home in the Marine Corps; we took off our gun belts and hung them on pegs just inside the entryway. It was like Dodge City or Abilene when Wyatt Earp was marshal, setting the rules, and the cow-punchers went along.

Lonsdale and his colleagues, especially the Old Etonians among them, had a language of their own, arch and mystifying and replete with insulting nicknames. Officers were addressed as "Stinky" or "Lout," money was referred to as "wonga." A lot of money was "a splodge of wonga." They also boasted a never-ending store of ribald songs, all of which they sang with considerable brio, every single verse, all of them ripe with sexual innuendo, songs like "The Big Bamboo" and "The Bloody Great Wheel." As I've said, my own favorite was the fanciful tale of "Three Old Ladies, Locked in a Lavatory."

The British were very cool. During one of these little bacchanals, a young officer was called away, retrieved his gun belt, slung it on, and went off into the night.

I noticed and went to Colonel Gregory. Here we were, all drinking, and outside, perhaps a difference of opinion with the Chinese Army was starting. They paid me to be the intelligence officer and I didn't intend to be caught by surprise like the Glosters.

"Sir, there may be something stirring. One of their officers was just called outside. Took his weapon."

"Oh?" Gregory said, and put down his glass.

The British colonel noticed the whispering and came over to old Gregory.

"Is there something going on, sir?" the American asked.

The Brit was exquisitely polite, anxious that we hadn't been disturbed at our drinks.

"Oh, no, Colonel. Nothing of importance. Some Chinese mucking about Harlequin Bridge and we sent a chap down to have a look about."

It was all so understated, no dramatics. Just a chap sent to have a look. Someone might be "mucking about." I felt somewhat deflated.

Marines would have alerted regiment and called for the mortars to stand by, written letters home to dear old ma, handed a prized wristwatch to another officer for safekeeping, that sort of thing. And we considered ourselves "cool"? Not likely, chum. Not compared to His Britannic Majesty's Leicestershire Regiment.

We grew fond of the Leicesters, fought the Chinese alongside them, played soccer against them (they usually won). Our enlisted men swapped for their black "ammo" boots. Or stole them. We junior officers even hosted a cocktail party of our own, less stylish, sans canapés, I regret to say. And which got me into new difficulties with Colonel Gregory when, less than adroit in my social graces, I failed to invite him and was summarily chewed out for it. The important thing about tying in with the Brits, they didn't bug out. You knew you could rely on them in a firefight; you couldn't say that about the ROKs. Not even about some of our own American Army units.

It is on the basis of that, more than anything else, by which soldiers make judgments about the unit on either flank. Would they hold that flank? Could you count on them in combat? Or would they bug out? The answer might mean your life.

CHAPTER 35

I WAS IMMENSELY CHEERED. FLYBOYS, THEY'RE STILL NUTS!

Early the morning of April 3 of 2003, the Army picked us up at the hotel and we drove through the going-to-work traffic of every big city, to the American military headquarters at Jongsan for our chopper ride to the other side of the country, to the Taebaek Mountains and North Korea, to Hill 749.

It was the day and the moment I'd been waiting for.

I was excited but curious as to how I'd feel, what I'd remember. Maybe this was why I'd gotten out of the damned hospital bed and learned to walk again. So I could revisit my younger self, see again the place I'd grown up. We'd come nine thousand miles and to me, if not to Eddie, this was why we'd come. To scale again Hill 749. I wasn't at all sure what my emotions up there would be. I was glad Eddie was so taciturn when on a shoot, thinking about his cameras, fretting about the light, because I wanted to feel the emotion, not talk it out with him or with anyone. But just hold it to myself, whatever it was I was going to feel. Well, we'd know pretty soon.

It was a fine, bonny April morning with sun, which annoyed Mr. Adams, since photographers like an overcast, but it cheered me. At the helicopter pad they passed out earplugs and we watched some ROK military brass trotting out in echelon under the spinning rotors of a big Black Hawk for some mission of their own, half of them losing their hats in the slipstream en route, amid a certain amount of deferential bowing and the ritual permitting of senior officers to board first. It was Keystone Kops slapstick. I hoped our flight wouldn't be quite as freighted with protocol.

But we did have our share of serving officers. Colonel Boylan and Major "Hawkeye" Pierce, of course, our babysitters from the start (plus the redoubtable Sergeant Russell Bassett, our Boswell), and some Marines, Captain Dunc Miller, whom Eddie still didn't like ("Does he have to come along?"), and two USMC light colonels I didn't know, Gerald Burke of Ontario, California, and Jeff Dearolph from Atlanta. Accompanying Major Pierce was a South Korean civilian, a woman in a proper black dress who worked in their office and could translate. And who rode in the rear of the Black Hawk, where during the flight she threw up, quite decorously, into her purse.

When our chopper arrived, kicking up the usual dust, I suggested to Adams that he get a shot of me boarding the aircraft.

"You know, sort of set the stage for our flight to 749."

"That's an effing cliché shot," he responded with his usual tact. "I don't do cliché shots."

I was the only one of us wearing a parka, and in the warmth of a Seoul spring, I felt pretty silly. But I still associated 749 with winter, snow, cold, and that Siberian wind. I consoled myself by concluding that none of the others had ever been up there. What did they know? Mountains made their own weather.

We lifted off at 10:40 A.M. for what the two Army pilots said would be a forty-five-minute ride. I'd logged plenty of chopper time and so too had Eddie, so except for nice views of skyscrapers, there wasn't much to write about the first half hour, but as we bore east and then northeast we began getting into the higher hills, the crests of which were still snow covered, and I felt better about L.L. Bean and its parka, and poked Eddie to show him the snow.

"Yeah, yeah. I see it," he mouthed above the roar of the engines. "Effing snow."

He tolerated me, as you might a precocious and annoying child.

With about fifteen minutes to go we were in the real hills and the chopper dropped down lower to begin swivel-hipping its way through gorges and ravines and mountain passes. Without my realizing it, we had now passed over into North Korea, the part occupied by the ROKs and Americans, and the pilots, who'd made this run before, wanted to stay below the North Korean sight lines and radar. As one of them remarked after we landed: "They'll take a shot at you, the creeps."

The two Marine colonels were hitchhiking. They'd never seen Hill 749 themselves but knew its history, the bloody assault by Marines, and had asked to come along so they could see the place. They expected me to give them a guided tour, based on my memory of what it was like in 1951–52. I kind of enjoyed the situation, General LaPorte never having heard of 749 and all these colonels relying on me to show them around. A civilian enlightening the brass. In the stern the civilian woman was not happy, but the pilots were having fun, and so was I, enjoying the way the chopper swung and swayed (like Sammy Kaye) its way through the passes, the snowcapped granite mountain peaks close in on each side. One of the pilots kept letting the other fellow handle the controls so he could snap pictures through the windshield. I could see Eddie was enjoying it, too, with a cockeyed grin. I was immensely pleased to realize that half a century later, nothing had really changed. Hedgehopping was just as much fun as it had always been.

And flyboys? They're still nuts! But they'd gotten me back to North Korea.

We came in for a smooth landing on a large, flat, and dusty area marked out with a soccer field. This was the Punchbowl, the earthen floor of a long extinct volcano, around which rose the shattered walls of what had eons before been its flanks and which now comprised the jagged heights of Kanmubong Ridge, including Hill 749.

An honor guard of South Korean recon troops, very sharp indeed, was trotted out to greet us, and their colonel, a middle-aged gent named Jeung, led the lads in giving us a formal salute, then ushered us into a sort of mess hall where we were served hot tea and fruit delicacies and a light lunch (including a good portion of raw fish on which I passed) at which the colonel, through an interpreter, welcomed us as men who had fought for his country, and pinned a recon pin to my lapel.

For a moment there, I thought I might be kissed on both cheeks, à la français. I made a little speech responding to his gallantry, and the colonel handed me a framed photograph of a mountain goat, or sheep, I wasn't sure which, standing longhair-coated in the deep snow of the Taebaek Mountains.

"One of the indigenous animals in these mountains," it was explained. I was deeply moved, never having seen one of these beasts in my time, though we heard of Korean tigers still roaming the hills and actually once did see a bear. I also knew of a large snake that insinuated itself into a terrified Marine's sleeping bag in the night. But no mountain goats. I then handed Colonel Jeung my own well-thumbed paperback copy of *The Coldest War,* which I now signed with a flourish. Only copy I had on the trip but I figured, what the hell? He'd been very generous with the mountain goat (or sheep) picture, and I ought to give the book to someone; regretting only that it should have been the classier hardcover edition.

Eddie Adams, having received neither a recon pin nor a goat's (or sheep's) picture, sulked a bit. I suspected Captain Miller might be enjoying his discomfiture.

This was a ROK recon battalion of their 12th Infantry Division and Jeung was in command. He handed us over to a smart young Major Park, who had been to the States and spoke English, and the colonel excused himself to return to his HQ, where, I assumed, he was deep into mapping strategies, and when we went back outside onto the field, above us loomed the old Kanmubong Ridge, a part of which was my Hill 749.

The ridge didn't look as steep or menacing in the sunshine as it did in 1951, when I first climbed Kanmubong to join Dog Company and the Marines who would become my brothers.

That was slightly disappointing; it should still have looked brooding, awesome, hostile.

CHAPTER 36

I glanced around at our little party of Americans, the only one of us who'd ever been here, to whom the place was more than just another piece of high ground, to whom it was a sort of shrine. I can't really think of any other term for a hill that cost so much in blood to take and which we fought so hard and long to hold.

Little in my life compared with having fought to hang on to that damned hill. That holy place.

So I was careful about taking time to orient myself, trying to figure out the terrain, thinking back to when I'd first seen it, snow covered then, a shattered bit of ridgeline nearly three thousand feet in height rising from the floor of the volcano. How had young American soldiers and Marines, lugging packs and weapons, scaled these walls under fire?

Heartbreak Ridge, Bloody Ridge, Hill 749, the crumbling granite relics of a long dead volcano, the killing ground of a generation of American soldiers and Marines, whose survivors in their turn were now dying off.

Major Park, brisk and professional, knowing nothing of shrines, took charge. We all loaded into jeeps with a couple of dozen ROK soldiers, maybe eight or ten jeeps rolling fast out of the Punchbowl along paved roads headed for the Kanmubong Ridge. No more than five minutes later we were halted at a checkpoint. There was a fast stream, the Soyang-gang, I realized, the water high from the winter snowmelt, and a steel bridge over the water, with a watchtower and lots of soldiers, barbed wire and high steel fencing, suggesting Spielberg's *Jurassic Park,* or the wall the natives built across Skull Island to keep out King Kong. Everyone was armed here, businesslike and wary. No silly, ritual standing at attention.

From this checkpoint on, we would be heading for Indian country.

A ROK officer ordered us all out of the jeeps and we Americans had to display IDs (for Eddie and me passports sufficed) and write down our names on a roster. So they'd have a record of those who'd crossed the bridge to be checked against names when we came back. In case we didn't. Or perhaps to foil some cheeky North Korean slipping past them, claiming to be a scribbler named Brady or, more outrageously, the celebrated Eddie Adams.

They passed around helmets and camouflage flak jackets and handed out *Star Trek*–looking assault rifles to the military, including reporter Russ Bassett and Major "Hawkeye" Pierce, both of whom looked quite comfortable handling a weapon. I feared for the moment Eddie and I might be armed as well. Not a great idea. I wasn't sure if these were M-14s or M-16s but did it really matter? I didn't know which end was up anymore. And Eddie? He might start taking exposure readings and shoot himself. Or me! These things didn't at all resemble the good old M1 I could once fieldstrip in the dark.

Major Park explained the flak jackets and tin hats. Not so much for protection, he said, but so that our entire party would resemble ordinary ROK troops and not a party of VIPs on a sightseeing tour, tempting some ambitious North Korean sniper out to make a name for himself.

They raised a boom and we rolled across the bridge over the Soyang-gang. I looked out at the water rushing past beneath us. Fifty years ago it was the same stream but different water. A philosopher might have made something of that, speculating which was the reality, the stream or the water? Our road was climbing now and no longer paved, and because of that, and the increasing incline, we proceeded slowly, grinding noisily into lower gear. Then the road rose even more abruptly, dirt now, ballasted with stone, branching off into the boondocks onto what was little more than a track, a jeep path of crushed rock, scree, and shale, with the slope of the mountain rising to our left, a steep falloff and minefield signs on wooden stakes to our right. The track, switching back from time to time but continuously climbing, rose steadily toward the blue sky of an April noon. We passed no one, soldier or civilian. An empty place.

Feeling strange, I swiveled from side to side and up and down, looking for sign, for familiar things and places, tracking a spoor that might not be there, but found nothing, recognized nothing. I'd expected to feel myself something like at home. After all, five months living on this hill at an impressionable age should have left tracks. I'd climbed this, the backside of the hill, several times, had gone down the forward slope on patrols again and again. Maybe the problem was I knew this place only in the snow months, November into March.

Along one narrow stretch of seventy-five or one hundred yards bordering our way were massive concrete cubes maybe six feet by six feet by six feet, the cubes suspended on wires strung to the right and left of the jeep track. Must have weighed a couple tons, each of them. They were new to me.

"What are those?"

"If there's an invasion they can blow them by remote control and block the trail with chunks of concrete."

Clever, these ROKs. Though somewhat defeatist. If they expected the North Koreans to get this far down the reverse slope, then the ROKs had already lost the high ground, the main line of resistance. Maybe had already lost the war! I hoped no one blew the goddamned concrete while we were passing through. There were more of those signs warning of mines.

Minefields were familiar coin; I knew about mines.

"Infiltrators?" I asked.

"Yes, but every year a couple of civilians wander into the minefields and we find their bodies," the major said.

"Claymore mines," Colonel Dearolph chimed in, trying to be helpful, "plastic explosive laced with buckshot. Good antipersonnel weapon."

That's nice, I thought, always amenable to expert testimony, but having once been blown up by a mine, not totally enjoying the information, think-ing of the buckshot. The road continued to climb.

It took our caravan of jeeps maybe a half hour to get to a level place where the lead jeep stopped abruptly and then we all did. What the hell! Was this it? I didn't recognize anything.

"Hill 749," said Major Park proudly, looking around and smiling at me. But what did it mean to him?

"No, no," I told the major, since we were still on the upward slope and hadn't yet reached a skyline. I spoke slowly, wanting to be sure he understood. "The ridgeline. I want to go to the top."

"Yes, Captain. I know. Up these steps," Park said, gesturing to a steep earthen slope with a track leading upward from the jeep trail and sparsely covered with an unimpressive straggle of dun underbrush, some drifted snow in the shadows and hollows. He indicated the way, head nodding. I got out of the jeep.

"This way to the top, sir." A deferential headwaiter, bowing and scraping.

The ridgeline was right up there? Anticlimactic to say the least. This was the place it took two full regiments of Marines to take, where much of Dog Company had died.

I had thought I'd be excited. Or moved. After all, I had fought here, had lost men here, had saved a few. Maybe it was the spring sun, no snow cover, and a gentle breeze that disoriented me.

Directed by the major, we started up a crude ladder of steps hewn out of the mud of the hillside, rising twenty or thirty feet above the parked jeeps, steps fashioned of old sandbags to the skyline, with a rope hand–line braced by metal stakes as you mounted the steps. Some of the sandbags were rotted away, the burlap bleeding sand into the thawing mud, and the footing was slick and tricky, very steep. Hanging on to the rope with my left hand and having difficulty with my bum left knee, I was reduced to kneeling on the next step up before going on to the one higher, and I'd gotten about halfway when from behind me someone gave my rear end a shove and, above me, one of the colonels reached down a hand and tugged. I'd once bounded up places like this to the skyline, had to be warned off by Sergeant Porterfield before I was shot. I could still hear Porterfield shouting. And now they were hauling me up there like a cripple.

Hell, I *was* a cripple. And a damned fool to have tried this.

Finally, muddied and on my hands and knees, I was there, unkempt, shaky-legged and humbled, but there. Atop Hill 749, on the ridgeline itself, I looked around. There was a clear view of the North Korean mountains to our front. The enemy mountains hadn't changed. To my right, the ridgeline continued to rise another couple of hundred feet toward the blue spring sky. I remembered that, too, how the ground rose and then fell again all along the Dog Company front. Straight downhill in the narrow valley between north and south, the Soyang-gang still flowed between the two small, hostile nations, a single country partitioned by hate.

I was standing erect now, legs no longer trembling from the climb. This was more like it. On my feet and with a view, that made all the difference.

Being a fairly positive sort, the embarrassment of my awkward, halting climb faded and I now felt okay, remembering that first afternoon I was here, when a shell came whistling in, sobering a young man who had never before been shot at. Fifty years and a lifetime later, I was standing on that very same skyline. That had to make you feel pretty good.

Wow! I said. But only to myself.

Around me on the hilltop there was an amiable confusion, with strangers milling about, the bustle of a hotel lobby at check-in time. Major Park snapped off an order in Korean and the dozen or so ROK troopers quickly deployed into a skirmish line of riflemen, dropping down flat on their bellies along the ridge itself and taking over a few shallow firing pits, their rifles ready, loaded and pointed north. Eddie Adams stalked about purposefully, calculating camera angles I suppose, gauging where the sun threw its shadows, fussing with that silly silvered reflecting umbrella to which all photographers are addicted. The Marine colonels looked toward each other, then to me. They didn't say anything. Waiting for me to take the lead, I guess. Hawkeye Pierce was waiting, too. Sergeant Bassett ignored us all and snapped pictures for the division newspaper.

Aside from memory, there wasn't much save the power exerted by place, the spare granite bones of the ridgeline, its only beauty the paucity of beauty. I don't know precisely what I had expected of Hill 749. Some sort of epiphany, startling revelations, the journey completed? I tried taking inventory.

That long and wandering trench in which we stayed off the skyline to avoid enemy fire, the trench where I'd earned my infamous nickname, no sign of that. Shoulder-height to a man it had once been, and now eroded, I guessed, and overgrown. The log-and-sandbag bunkers cut into the reverse slope where we'd lived, the bunker Stoneking and I shared for forty-six nights? Gone. Even the barbed wire was rusted away. You'd think the steel stakes from which the wire coiled and snaked and caught soon-to-be-dead men in its grip, crucifying them, might still be showing. But the stakes, too, were gone. There was nothing up here. I prowled the ridgeline, hunting for . . . what? For Dog Company? For my younger self? The others, following my gimp, kept up easily. Wryly, I realized we were all showing ourselves on the skyline. Good targets. But there was no one firing at us; maybe a man grew to miss even that.

As Peggy Lee sang, "Is that all there is?"

The forward slope facing north was still heavily treed, evergreens of one sort and another. It was up through those pines and cypresses and spruces that the North Korean infantry had come, climbing toward us, with their burp guns and their grenades, and where our machine guns caught them when they emerged from the forest gloom, from the cover and into the gun sights of the waiting Marines. It was down that slope that I had led out by night my platoon's share of patrols and ambushes. Up that slope after the firefights that I had helped carry wounded and dead Marines.

I repressed a small, unworthy shudder, remembering that same forward slope deep as it had been in winter's snow and by night, a place of menace where we lay for hours, under orders and trying to be quiet, immobile, waiting for the North Koreans to come. Sometimes those ambushes went on late into the January night, the men shivering, then trembling, finally jerking about spasmodically, unable to control their bodies in the awful cold. And finally, giving in to my pleadings over the sound-power phone that we were no longer effective, Chafee would let us come back in, realizing that by now we were making too much noise to catch the enemy patrols by surprise. There was no shame or embarrassment. No Marine, no one, could lie motionless in the snow for that long and at those temperatures (twenty below, men said) and not shake. Had there ever in my life been worse nights than those? Not many.

I pulled myself back to the present, swiveling toward the ridgeline and its reverse slope. By contrast, there was only stunted growth, here and on the reverse slope facing south. It was here that the hardest fighting had taken place. Trees splintered by shellfire and the fighting as the Marines attacked had grown back, but sparsely, no healthy good-sized trees. Maybe the vibes were bad, and in this ground, nothing much grew. Too much steel and blood souring the topsoil. That was all there was on the ridgeline, scrub growth and mud and a little melting snow and a nice view of mountains ahead. Not much else. No monuments on Hill 749.

"Mr. Brady?"

It was one of the colonels. Growing impatient, I guess.

"Yes, just give me a few minutes more."

I didn't need monuments to remember.

Without Dog Company men up here, maybe the place wasn't worth revisiting; it was the men who made it holy. If only Stoneking would come trotting along, or Wooten checking the ammo, or Fitzgerald plotting some damned fool scheme to kill people, or a fire-team leader who needed talking to. There were no Marines arguing or cursing or wrestling cheerfully in the snow, a little organized grab-ass to work off steam, no riflemen cleaning their weapons, no midday gook train of bearers heading back downhill toward battalion. Maybe carrying a Marine corpse from the night before. No Captain Chafee here, no machine gunners humping ammo boxes, no Red Phillips, no lone, obsessed sniper squinting through telescopic sights and reckoning windage, no squad leader with field glasses and map studying the route of that night's patrol, no one being chewed out, no working party falling in, no sergeant telling them what he wanted done. And done right effing now! Neither was there a twenty-three-year-old platoon leader who at all resembled me.

Only some tired snow in the shaded hollows.

And a tourist's scenic view of North Korean mountains just ahead. Ridgeline after ridgeline, the mountains marched toward China, the snowy north receding before me. I remembered how we feared that when spring came in '52 they would order the division north, and we would have to go up against those hills. I remembered the residual dread. And the sour wisecrack that, after that, they could hold the next reunion of the 1st Mar Div in a telephone booth.

But they never did order that push north. After Hill 749 and its eight hundred Marine casualties in September, they called off those uphill attacks against fortified, defended mountains. The Marine brass might be slow to learn, but they learned. Unlike murderous bastards like Field Marshal Sir Douglas Haig in Flanders, sending the Tommies over the top again and again, year after year, against the German wire and their massed machine guns, killing young Englishmen in their thousands. The Marine brass weren't Douglas Haig, and eventually they learned. And thanks be to Christ, a lot of us didn't get killed that spring.

And there never again was in Korea an American frontal assault like Hill 749.

CHAPTER 37

I GUESS I JUST WANTED TO BE A
DOG COMPANY OFFICER AGAIN.

The colonels and the others still waited.

I felt pretty good, shaking off the temptation to brood about what wasn't here, the missing trench line, some lost barbed wire, instead of marveling that I was here at all and on my feet, that I'd lived to see 749 again.

As I had so often done up here, I dropped to my belly on the ridgeline to peer north, eyes squinting against the sun, against the glare off the higher, snowy crests. If General LaPorte was right, there were 1.2 million North Korean regulars out there behind those ridgelines. Their infantry would be the real thing, tough and deadly, as they had been those four days in September of 1951 when Dog Company and the rest of them came up the forward slope under fire, killing North Koreans as they came, and leaving behind them the bloody bodies of the Marine dead, their lost young faces pressed against and ground into the earth of the last hill they ever saw.

The good, solid peasant army of the 1950s was dead. Or old and used, like me. The huge new North Korean army had taken over, and the mountains north of where the Soyang-gang flowed could be swarming with infantry, but shrewdly hidden, masked by ridgelines I knew so well, could even name by height.

It was now afternoon. Fifty years ago our patrols would be saddling up, ready to go out when the sun fell. Out there to the right on the Sea of Japan, our destroyers and cruisers would be steaming parallel to the coast, deadly toy ships on a paper sea. To the west where the Chinese were fighting the U.S. Army, you might hear the low rumble of distant artillery. Overhead, against the high blue sky, you would see the white contrails of the jets heading north to the lethal dogfights of MIG Alley. My mind drifted, reaching back into the past.

Up here in the bunkers and the trenches, we had more in common with the North Koreans across the way than with our own American swabbies and flyboys. Mostly, we hated the enemy infantrymen; but not always. Even when we were killing them. There was a certain crude chivalry to the fighting, one poor bastard trying to kill the other poor bastard. Just like us, the North Korean soldiers up in the winter mountains were miserable, cold and wet, filthy and tired, living like animals.

I shook myself, attempting to focus on the here, the now. Looking up, looking around. The colonels and the others stared, waiting for me to convey some meaningful remarks about this place and its history, the loneliness of the ridgeline, the empty void, the sense of menace. I got clumsily to my feet, keenly aware I was standing exposed on the skyline. Let the bastards take a shot. Hit me at this range fifty years later. Nice shooting, pal. There were no shots.

The colonels, Marines and Army both, looked to me. What the hell? they asked with impatient eyes. This Brady was supposed to show us something and there's nothing here!

I felt like a standup comic whose lounge act wasn't going over, tried to grin.

"Well, I dunno. We're here on 749. What can I tell you?"

Now that the awkward silence was broken, they all had questions. Where were our bunkers situated, where ran the trench line, where had been our machine guns, where on the reverse slope were the mortars set up? Show us the observation posts, the company CP, the minefields, the barrages. Career regulars make their living knowing such things. I knelt down and pulled out my

1:25,000 scale map of the Kanmubong Ridge, laid it flat and unfolded on the ground, holding it down against the gentle breeze, my finger tracing out, as I knelt and the others crouched behind me, the MLR, the main line of resistance that I remembered.

How much barbed wire did we have out front? Strung or concertina? Where was it that the enemy came uphill toward us? When we fired at the North Korean infantry, did they turn and run or keep on coming? Those were things the colonels wanted to know. I tried to reply. Told them what I remembered, cheerfully made up the rest.

Eddie was playing film director, having me stand or kneel or walk, moving me around so he could get a shot with the North Korean mountains in the background. The colonels and Major Pierce and the others wandered about, looking over the ground, using field glasses to scope out the North Korean lines. The ROK recon troops stayed in their firing pits, weapons ready. Major Park kept watch over all of us. He knew he was responsible. Adams was trying for the single perfect shot that would work on the cover of a magazine, that would tell the whole story, convey everything I felt, signal where I was, and why.

I posed for Eddie's cameras. No longer a platoon leader trying to figure out the route of tonight's patrol. But shooting a profile, giving Eddie the proper angle, a hired mannequin.

They were all fine people and had helped get me here. But I really didn't want any of them with me on 749. There were too many intruders here with no attachment to the hill, no knowledge of it, no memory of its dead. There were no colonels on 749 in my time, no ROKs. No Eddie Adams bustling and cursing, setting up his effing umbrella.

In some wild, sullen, and surely impractical way, maybe I should have played a lone hand. Come up here alone. This wasn't a tourist attraction; it was a place that belonged to guys like me who'd fought here. But could I have done it physically on my own? Yes, damnit, if they jeeped me to where the fixed rope and sandbagged stair began, just left me there, I could have crawled those final yards on my own. Hands and knees, I could have made it to the ridgeline, would have gotten up. And then would have been here alone with the ghosts. All I'd need, a canteen of water, one day's rations, a good down sleeping bag, to stay overnight, scrounge a shallow hollow on the ridge as darkness fell. To lie there staring up into the bowl of the night at the stars, then to sleep, and to wake finally in the chill morning with frost or maybe a little drifting snow on the sleeping bag, slightly stiff, creaky, ready to get up and see to the men, as Dog Company stirred and woke once more around me, making coffee and grilling a little sweet-smelling bacon in a mess kit over the sterno, grateful another night had passed during which we had not died.

Maybe I just wanted to be strong-legged and young again, an officer of Dog Company.

Every battlefield belongs first to its dead. At Verdun, Fort Douaumont, Pétain or Foch or someone remarked that if all the men, Germans and French, who died there were buried on that field, there wouldn't be room to lay them out; they would have to be buried standing up. I remembered a 1994 D-day memorial piece I did for *Parade* in Normandy, not about the sunny seaside American cemetery at Omaha Beach but the Kraut graveyard down the road a few miles, dark-stoned, Teutonic, bleak, with two German soldiers buried in each grave, two names carved on each gravestone, one body laid lengthwise atop the other to save space, to cut costs.

Battlefields were expensive; you got the graves cheap.

CHAPTER 38

GOING AFTER SIMONIS.

Major Park tried to be helpful, giving us a tour d'horizon. "That's the river Soyang there below us, you know. What we call the Soyang-gang."

He handed me the field glasses.

"Yes, Major. I know the Soyang-gang. I've been there."

I had, you know.

I heard the firing before I was really awake, part reality, part nightmare. Stoneking was already up and he handed me a canteen cup, hot with coffee, very strong the way he made it.

"Mr. Simonis is catching it," he said.

This was January of '52 and Bob Simonis, who'd done that dazzling raid back in November, catching the North Koreans by surprise, had gone out again with a patrol last night and was due to be coming back in at daybreak, about now, maybe with some prisoners.

Except, from the sound of the firing, maybe he wouldn't be coming in.

I pulled on my boots and parka and hustled down to the CP. Chafee had torn his hand muscling barbed wire and it got infected and he was down at battalion being patched up, so Red Phillips had the command. All along the trench line and from the firing pits, men were directing rifle fire at the enemy hillsides across the river, the other side of the Soyang-gang. Not expecting to hit anyone at that range but to keep their heads down, and let Simonis know he wasn't forgotten, he wasn't alone. Red briefed me.

"They were coming back in and got halfway across the valley when they got caught. I talked to Simonis on the radio. He's got dead and wounded. Mortar fire mostly, I guess. They're down there at the bottom of the hill waiting till the fire dies down. Our artillery is firing a mission in support."

"Why don't I take some stretcher bearers down there? Help get them back home?" I was still a new boy on the block, a probationer, but I wasn't walking on eggshells anymore. Going down there to try to help Simonis was the right thing to do. I didn't agonize over it, just said what I thought. And Phillips seemed to agree. Without Chafee there, maybe Red was looking for constructive thinking wherever he could find it.

"Good idea. I'll get some men."

Red went with us through the barbed wire and for a few yards down the forward slope. Then he grabbed at my arm.

"I appreciate this. Get them back. I appreciate this."

Going down was easy. The day was sunny and full light by now but there was plenty of snow on the mountain and we glissaded down, the boys whooping it up a little, like kids on Flexible Flyers going sleigh riding. Marines could wring laughter out of the city morgue. Our artillery had by now zeroed in and was firing concentrations on the NK mortar positions.

The shells flew over us, outgoing mail. Noisy but welcome.

It took us a half hour to get down. There on the flat but pulled back into the trees for concealment was the Simonis patrol. Two men were dead, another just about dead, and there were others wounded. Out of a dozen men. Bob Simonis was fine, very cool. He was working the radio and he threw me a wave and a grin. I remembered Bob at Quantico, how quiet he was. The badly wounded man was a big black Marine, maybe six six. I'd seen him around. Didn't know his name but how could you miss six six? They put him on one of the stretchers we'd carried down. The firing had ended. Our artillery counterbattery fire had the North Koreans pulling in their horns. Bob signed off and we organized ourselves to start back up the hill. It was about 8 A.M. and sunny. Nice day for a winter's stroll in the country.

It took thirteen hours for us to get back into the lines, and along the way another man died. We were mortared and sniped at, and along with the slipping and sliding in the snow and dropping the wounded and getting them back on the stretchers and begging for choppers to get us out, and being turned down, it was about the worst day in my life. At one point, afraid that the North Koreans were coming after us, stalking us in the snow, following the blood spoor the way we had tracked their wounded, the man gut-shot and with piles, back in November, I was silently cursing our own wounded for bleeding!

Didn't the bastards know we were being tracked?

The men were cursing, too, frustrated with the stretchers and how they kept folding up, how on these steep slopes the wounded kept slipping off the stretcher and had to be hoisted up again. Cursing, too, at the choppers.

We knew choppers didn't ever land on the forward slope. They'd be meat for the Reds, direct fire or mortars or both. But Marines lugging their dead and wounded buddies needed to vent rage on someone. It was just as irrational as my raving at the wounded for bleeding.

The deep snow was what nearly defeated us. The snow and the degree of slope. The temperature was probably about freezing but sweat ran down the faces of the stretcher bearers, the other men, too, because they were hefting the rifles and BARs and gear of the men at the corners of the stretchers. I took a turn at the stretchers, then as a rifle carrier, then back to the stretchers again. I hated those damned stretchers. Why couldn't someone have anticipated situations like this and gotten us a couple of old-fashioned toboggans like those the ski patrol uses at Stowe, Vermont?

The big black wounded Marine, Caulfield, I think they called him, was talking to himself through the groans. The bearers kept dropping him or the stretcher folded and they had to yank him back into position. Since he had a number of wounds, it was impossible to move him without hurting the man. A young Marine who'd been listening to Caulfield talk looked up from his corner of the stretcher. "Lieutenant," he whispered, "Jesus, he thinks he's Jesus."

Bob Simonis took his turn at the stretcher. He was calm, not frustrated, and these were his men who were dead, his men wounded. I envied Bob his quiet control. A good man. Whether it was a brilliant raid or a fouled-up patrol, Simonis took both as they came along.

Even before three, the sun began its fall toward the mountain crests. An increased sense of urgency came over us, maybe even over Bob himself. By night the North Koreans could come after us without fear of our guns, and moving fast without wounded or dead to slow them, they might catch us. In the dark we would move even slower. Would the North Koreans come after us? Were they coming even now? Might they catch us?

Men started looking back over their shoulders. Thirsty, the canteens emptied, those of us who had carried a canteen. I had no canteen and was grabbing fistfuls of snow and eating it. Not very satisfying. With night would come the bad cold. It was colder even now, and to sweating men, cold was dangerous. And with the cold might come the Commies on our trail.

Night came early in January. By four it was dusk, by five it was full night. You couldn't use a flashlight out here, even if you had one, because they'd take a shot at the light, and the bearers stumbled, got up, rearranged the bodies, the dead and the ones still hanging on, bleeding, fell down again and got up again, and went on.

Simonis came up to me. "Caulfield's dead. We might have saved him if we got him back sooner. But we just couldn't." It was just past six.

"I know," I said. What else do you say?

Seven P.M. came, eight, without an attack. Twelve hours since we began our climb. We were close now. Simonis talked steadily on the radio, telling them where we were, cautioning them again that we were coming in. Hell of a note to be killed by friendly fire after a climb like this!

We reached the first strands of friendly barbed wire just before nine.

One of the less seriously wounded had ridden piggyback on the back of another Marine and now he slipped off, got up, bounded across the barbed wire and into the lines, moving faster than any of us.

"That son of a bitch!"

The man who'd carried him was cursing steadily. I looked at him, and thinking he'd found a sympathetic ear, he let loose. "Lieutenant, I carry him the last thousand feet and we get to the bob wire and he bounces off my back like the Easter bunny and over the bob wire and into the first chopper, shaking hands and passing out cigars. And I won't be able to walk for a frigging week. I think I got a rupture."

Red Phillips greeted us. He looked relieved that we'd gotten back. With Chafee not here, the responsibility was Red's. There was a reinforced squad with him, armed and saddled up, ready to go down to meet us if we needed help. Or if the Commies caught us. Simonis began to make his report so I got out of there and started off walking the quarter mile or so to my bunker, alone on the hill following the trench line in the dark, tired but not afraid, knowing that I'd been of some small help to Simonis and his men.

Stoney looked up when I crawled into the bunker.

"So you went and got in a firefight," he said.

"Yes."

CHAPTER 39

I SHOULD HAVE STOPPED THE JEEP.
GONE BACK, TAKEN ONE LAST LOOK.

dams and I had our pictures for the magazine, and with the afternoon wasting, Major Park looked to me for instructions. He
understood that all this had been for my benefit, and not for the
Marine colonels or Hawkeye and Steve Boylan.

"Ready, Captain?" he asked.

The Disneyland tour bus must be waiting.

"Yes, Major." If I'd expected some sort of epiphany on Hill 749, I wasn't
going to get one.

We jeeped maybe a quarter mile northeast to what we'd called the Nose,
a jutting hunk of ridgeline (854 meters in height) that protruded out over the
Soyang-gang. Another of our old strongpoints, it was now the linchpin of the
ROK defense along this stretch of line. Clearly, the major wanted to show it
off to his captive audience of Americans, a kind of Maginot Line in miniature, a reinforced concrete bunker three stories deep with an observation
tower rising thirty or forty feet up from the bunker roof. There were sleeping
quarters and a computer room, closed-circuit and cable TV, and I gave them
all a pass. Chat rooms where the chat is in Korean held little appeal. Colonels
love stuff like that.

It occurred to me that in a quirky way, Major Park was somewhat ashamed of Hill 749, and wanted me to see this.

What intrigued me about 854 was a .50 caliber machine gun precisely where we'd sited a .50 caliber in 1952. Same damned place! Our machine gunner sighted in the gun by day, firing tracer rounds at the firing port of an enemy bunker a mile away. Then, during the night, and obsessed, he would crawl out of his sleeping bag to squeeze off one blind shot into the blackness, in hopes a North Korean might be passing en route to the latrine and get his head blown off. Maybe these ROK recon boys had similar intentions.

The old marksman in me found a perverse delight that two generations of mad snipers had come up with exactly the same scheme to kill people.

Topside, on a dusty miniature parade ground that doubled as a basketball court, Eddie had a platoon of recon soldiers doing a mass martial-arts and kick-boxing demo.

"Make a great picture," he grunted.

"Sure."

Talk about cliché photos, I thought.

The Koreans lunged, parried, high-kicked. Eddie was out of his mind.

"Effing great!" he shouted. No language barrier. They knew he was happy and they smiled back. Major Park said the ROKs up here did three months on, three months off, no leave. Picked men who volunteered. He pointed out a bulldozed path scarring the enemy hillside opposite.

"Their patrols use it. We watch them, they watch us." He handed me his field glasses.

Sure enough, there were a couple of men moving. North Korean infantry. I focused the field glasses, held them steady on the North Koreans. From here with an M1, I could kill those men.

"I remember that second bastard," I said. "The way he walks."

"Yes?" Park said dubiously.

"Only kidding, Major. It was his old gramps walked that way."

The major didn't know what the hell I was talking about.

Then it was time to go. The Black Hawk would be coming. We shook a lot of hands and I tossed up a shot at the basketball hoop, just to show what sportsmen we were.

I used to make those shots.

Riding in the jeep on the way down I kept shut and concentrated on watching Hill 749 slip past, wanting to take back a few meaningful impressions, stuff to tell Pierce Power and Sergeant Fitzgerald and Chuck Curley, something personal for me to hug tight. As we passed the sandbagged stairs up which I'd crawled, I turned my head slowly, trying to keep the hill in sight for a bit more. I considered asking them to stop the convoy, to give me another few moments here, but didn't want to play drama queen.

In the larger scheme of things it was only an obscure hilltop in North Korea, poor and barren. But good men had died here and others in their turn had fought, beating off the enemy counterattacks. So that in the spring and in every spring since, for fifty years, a chunk of North Korea stayed ours, and stubbornly so, a validation of our courage and resource. Foolish the fight may have been, but it was well and bravely fought, the hill was held. So that all this time later, an aging American could roam this ridgeline, limping as he went, to look out at the hostile mountains of North Korea.

Let the politicians and statesmen negotiate, let governments contend, let the propaganda loudspeakers blare. I was still up here, an old Marine in a flak jacket and tin hat. Brady's back, you bastards. Back on Hill 749. That was the picture Eddie should have made.

The chopper would be waiting. As the old choppers used to do for us, their rotors turning slowly, waiting for the wounded coming down off Hill 749.

At the Soyang-gang checkpoint we handed back our flak jackets and tin hats and a ROK officer checked off names and counted heads. The ROK enlisted men kept watching us and then turned, alert and ready, to resume their watch on the Soyang-gang. Was it really "the scariest place in the world"? They behaved as if it were. I shook the hand of some guy who didn't understand why, asked if the family was okay, and thanked him, all in an English he didn't understand.

This time at the Punchbowl there were no honor guards, no tea or framed mountain goats, just a message that the flight was running fifteen minutes late. So I could after all have gotten out, taken a final look, maybe sneaked a furtive piss on the old hill, the way Hemingway claimed he did on an Italian battlefield, burying a thousand-lira note and taking a crap so that the sacred ground had his blood, his wealth, his waste.

How reluctantly we let slip our youth.

Colonel Burke and I strolled the dusty field in the late-afternoon shadow of the ridge.

"If the balloon goes up," he was saying, "this is going to be an infantryman's war again. Near Seoul, you can maneuver a bit and use tanks, but not in these mountains. Too tough here."

Tough? You ought to see it in the snow months, I thought, but didn't say. Colonels didn't need my war stories. I liked it that a professional like Burke appreciated how hard a country this was. It wasn't just my romanticizing the place. If you were an infantryman who fought here, Kunmubong Ridge didn't need exaggerating. It wasn't just war stories or, as the Army brass used to say dismissively, "just more Marine bullshit."

Ask the GIs who went up Heartbreak Ridge, next door, if it was bullshit.

I looked back at the heights with a fierce pride, possessive and very nearly smug about it.

The Black Hawk came in as the sun descended toward the Kanmubong Ridge and would soon be backlighting Hill 749. It was late afternoon, day fading and night coming, when the patrols were preparing to go out, when the Dog Company Marines would be looking to their weapons. And then, as full night took over the mountaintops, we would saddle up, a dozen young men armed and ready, and step through the barbed wire once more, and then, warily, head north.

Toward where the enemy waited . . .

CHAPTER 40

"THE BODY CAME OUT IN TWO PIECES.
THAT WAS WHEN I THROWED UP."

I said there was no epiphany up there on 749. Maybe I was wrong.
Maybe I really had found something.

It wasn't the mountain I'd gone in search of, but the men. And for a
few hours and against all odds, I'd been again an officer of Dog Company,
with all those glorious young roughnecks out of Quantico, and the men of
the 1st Marine Division, up there on the ridgeline with me. They, too, had
traveled back in time to 749, scrambling up the sandbagged steps those last
few yards, as I had. We were together again, the crips like me and the wild
buckos, the dead and the living, mustering once more on the ridgelines of the
past, not aging and halt but young and strong. Not only Chafee and Red
Phillips and Stoneking and Fitz, but Pierce Power from Regis High School
and Doug Bradlee from Harvard, Wild Hoss and Joe Owen and Carly Rand
and our lost soul Brennan, Mack Allen and Gunny Arzt and the other Marines
of yesterday. They'd been with me in spirit as I stalked the Kanmubong
Ridge and were still with me now on the landing strip of the Punchbowl, as
I climbed clumsily back aboard the chopper.

I knew that I was seeing Korea for the last time, would never again climb
Hill 749.

That realization, with its intimations of mortality, brought into focus men I hadn't seen in half a century, but men I would never forget. As we strapped ourselves into the Black Hawk, preparing to fly out of the North Korean mountains a final time, the engines caught and coughed into life, and one of the Marine colonels, Dearolph, I believe, looked over at me.

"Was it how you thought it would be?"

He was a colonel and a good man and I owed him a response.

"Oh, yeah. Terrific."

It hadn't been terrific, but I had been again and briefly a Dog Company Marine.

"Guess it brought back memories," the colonel said pleasantly.

"Plenty," I said, shouting as the engines revved.

The rotors were whirling now and the chopper shook and then began to lift, rising into the afternoon sky, kicking up dust and riding a giddy spiral out of the Punchbowl. The roar of engines and the wind whipping through the cabin as we gained speed absolved me from saying more.

Fine with me. Memories aren't necessarily in the public domain. The Black Hawk lifted on a zigzag course south and toward the west, then changed course, bore steadily west, no longer dodging the enemy radar. But I wasn't seeing the fast-vanishing granite and the last gray snows of North Korea but instead a kaleidoscope of names and half-forgotten faces, good friends and near strangers, all of them Marines of another time, a different century.

Seeing 749 again had brought them back. Guys like Charles Curley, that pest of a machine gunner who remembered every little detail, and drove Dog Company men nuts trying to get us to reunions. I mentioned Curley before. Nebraska born, brought up in Glendale, California, lives in upstate New York. "I migrated to Olean after I brought my buddy's body [Tom Speaker, Dog 2/7] here for burial in 1952." Marines used to do that, maybe still do, take the dead men home to their families, riding in the railroad baggage car with the box. I'd asked Curley to write about what he recalled of Hill 749 and afterward.

"Sept. 12, 12:30 A.M. woke up to the chatter of small arms fire. Fought the night before, again that morning, that day and all the next day and part of the night. Item Co. had 22 men left [the usual Marine Rifle Company had about 225 men at full strength], How Co. had 44 and Dog Co. had 60 casualties. Notice"—he sent me a photo—"how tired we were. No sleep for two and a half days, no food for two, no water for about three."

I knew that was a stretch; you couldn't go three days without water. Well, fresh water, he conceded. "We slept for 18 straight hours in this reserve area [the Punchbowl]." Butrica, his buddy in the photo, "was my best man at my wedding 50 years ago."

After the war, Curley said, he "worked at a chrome plating company but when I got laid off, I went back to California where I already had put in one year at Pepperdine. After graduation I moved to Olean as physical director at the YMCA, then taught Phys. Ed. 24 years at Allegheny College."

I knew he'd given money to a college. Had the impression he'd won the lottery, hit it rich somewhere.

"Oh, Lord, no," said Curley. "Sometimes it was tough paying the bills and I never made much, but every time I got a pay raise, I'd take 50 percent and save it. I set up a program and worked it out. The stock market went up, sometimes it went down, but there was compound interest. And I went to Pepperdine and gave them five thousand upfront and said they'd be getting a hundred a month as long as I lived for them to set up a scholarship in the name of De Wert"—Navy corpsman Richard De Wert of Taunton, Massachusetts, shot to death treating and rescuing Dog Company Marines—"who was awarded the Medal of Honor. God was good to me. I got hit twice and here's a guy who's not even a Marine, who gives his life to save Marines. I also made an endowment in the name of Dog Co."

Didn't give anything to St. Bonaventure's, the local college at Olean? I asked.

Said Curley, "I offered the Bonnies a similar deal and they laughed at me and so I walked out."

Duke was there in memory, too, our only black guy, who helped save Fitzgerald and me when we hit the mine, was forever moaning that he needed a bout. If he had a good fight, all would be well. Stoneking, who lacked patience, purposely overmatched him, Duke got hell beat out of him, and for weeks after was easy to get along with.

Our other Duke, Colegate, was a big blond kid killed accidentally on 749 by one of our machine gunners. The machine gunner, who was a minister's son, took it pretty hard.

But later that spring the minister's son had recovered sufficiently that he and another man shot up and terrorized a small village and raped two South Korean women. I was assigned as investigating officer with Mack Allen, neither of us lawyers. We got a corpsman to take a urine sample from the suspects to determine if there was semen in the sample. Yes, there was! Mack and I thought we had the bastards cold. Until the two rapists got themselves a smart young JAG defense counsel who explained away the semen as possibly masturbatory, and they beat the rap.

Colegate was dead and the minister's son went free.

John Evans was our only Native American, inevitably called "Chief," a wonderful Marine in a fight, loved by his pals but stubborn. He was pissed off at the world and anyone who outranked him. You couldn't reason with him, couldn't effectively punish him. Make him shovel snow all day, he did it. Then sulked some more. I couldn't handle him; neither could Stoneking, who wanted to fight him, whip his ass. I wouldn't let Stoney do it. We eventually got rid of Evans when division sent up a call for military police applicants, and with Chafee's blessing we gave the Chief a four-star recommendation as the finest Marine since Presley O'Bannon took Tripoli. No one loves the MPs; let them handle the Chief.

There was Captain Bob Baker, a Marine pilot sent up as forward air controller, who got in trouble with Colonel Gregory. At the morning officers' meeting one spring day in '52, when each of us gave his brief report to the colonel, Baker instead got up and recited a little poem:

> *Hooray, hooray, the Fourth of May,*
> *Outdoor fucking starts today.*

Colonel Gregory didn't like raw language, and that same week Baker was transferred, and promptly buzzed the battalion HQ. As we dove for cover, his plane clipped a length of comm wire strung as an antenna between hilltops, and crash-landed. People said appreciatively that Baker was in the grand tradition of such Corsair drivers as "Pappy" Boyington.

Our other air officer, Ramon Gibson, a more civilized type, was the handsome, dashing son of an American diplomat and his Mexican wife. Pilots needed flight time each month to earn flight pay, and Ray Gibson got his by flying an OY observation plane to Kimpo on an ice run, ice for the battalion mess. To make it look official he took me along to check out the Chinese Army.

When they started shooting I asked Gibson, "Can they reach us?"

"Don't worry, Brady. We're at six thousand feet. They can't reach us with anything small. And doesn't make sense for them to fire big stuff and let us know where their guns are."

To make up for scaring me, Ray let me fly the ship for a while. I could drive a car; how hard could it be? After the Marine Corps, Ray became a test pilot, was still a test pilot in his seventies! Wrote a book about it, *The Way I Saw It,* a memoir published by Brown Books in Dallas.

Then there was mortar sergeant Porterfield, with whom I shared a bunker my first nights on the line. Later, in a reserve area when men were drinking, we got into a nasty slanging match. A dozen years ago Porterfield and I met at a Dog Company reunion, and we shook hands, had a drink. He was by then a sitting judge in some jurisdiction in California. When he died I wrote his wife, explaining how happy I was to have met Porterfield again and been forgiven. A silly letter, I'm afraid. And, understandably, it was never answered.

And there were others. Wooten, the platoon guide, a brave, resourceful, and wonderful man who had known the good and the bad of life and delighted in my youth and occasional follies, nursed me along.

"Mr. Brady, you are a character, suh."

He pronounced "character" in two syllables, as "cack-ter." I loved that wry old man, can hear him now.

Wooten knew about demolitions, and when Fox Company lost a couple men in a firefight, he volunteered to get back a Marine's body frozen in the ice of a stream feeding the Soyang-gang. We always tried to get the bodies back, and Marines knew that, counted on it. The Commies had laid an ambush for two Marines with jerricans on a water run, and in the firefight, one of the Marines fell into the stream, the other ended up as a POW.

So Wooten went down there with an armed escort and when he came back into the lines, looking pretty bad, I asked if they got the body. Yes, they did, Wooten told me. "Except when we got it blowed, the body came out in two pieces. That was when I threw up."

In that same firefight we lost a brand-new officer to a mortar. The guy spent four years at Annapolis, half a year at Quantico, and he was dead before his first five days on the line were up. His nickname was "Lucky."

Sergeant Wright, one of my squad leaders, was a rodeo rider out of Montana, black-haired, very lean, mean as rawhide, hard on his men, so much so that three of them laid for him one night. Two of them held Wright while the other just beat hell out of him, breaking his nose and some teeth, blacking his eyes and busting him up pretty bad. Stoneking told me what happened but when I questioned Wright he held to the Marine code and told me he'd slipped on the ice. Good sergeant.

Lem Shepherd, whose daddy was a general, later to be commandant of the Marine Corps, had gone to VMI, where they were all terrible fire-eaters, including Lem's brothers. Not him, though. He had this real Dixie accent and he'd whine about his situation.

"Mah old man and mah brothers are out of their minds. They couldn't wait for another wah. So they could get mah ass in the Marine Corps." But Lem Shepherd was only making sport of his kin, their military ardor, and in the end, like most of us, he went to the "wah."

A few officers didn't. But they were no longer spoken of at the bar of Waller Hall. Or at other places where Marines gathered to drink and to tell lies in the soft, sweaty southern nights in garrison posts smelling sweetly of Dixie.

At Princeton each graduating spring, the university recalls Allen Macy Dulles, Princeton '51, who made it to the war. They make an award in his name to the undergraduate who best exemplified Princeton "in the nation's service or in service to all nations." Daddy would become head of the CIA and his uncle was the secretary of state under Ike. Lieutenant Dulles was hit in the head by a mortar fragment and almost died. He didn't die, but he was never quite the same. Princeton alumni told me he was still alive, now in his seventies, living in a convalescent facility of some sort where they took good care of him, and friends and members of the family visited. I wrote him once but got no response. A Princeton grad reduced to the simple tasks and games of childhood because instead of going into public service in the family tradition, he went to war.

These were a few of the Marines of my time, and coming back in the Black Hawk chopper that cool April evening half a century later, they were with me again, the reason I returned to the ridgelines, as a surrogate for the ones who could no longer make another journey "beyond the seas."

And in their names, to shout a last hurrah for all of us.

CHAPTER 41

WHEN HE RETIRED, SENATOR CHAFEE THOUGHT HE'D
LIKE TO TEACH INNER-CITY BOYS TO WRESTLE.

After Korea, as of course after all wars, our little band of brothers dispersed, as we all went off to carve out civilian careers, start families, or simply to make a few bucks. We often lost track even of the Skipper, the man around whom our lives, our world, had revolved for those perilous months. I could still see Chafee, tall, lean, the fat pared by the steep hills and slim rations, the hawk nose burned by the mountain sun, tireless and busy, hopping nimbly into and out of trenches, crouching warily on the skyline, calm and cool, the amused smile as he regarded a dubious quantity like me.

Over the years and decades that followed the war I kept up, intermittently, with Captain Chafee. Nothing planned or organized, but he had been important to me at a pivotal time in my life, and whenever I could, and when appropriate, we met or corresponded.

On one occasion, the very first since Korea, I literally bumped into Chafee, or more precisely his wife, Virginia, on a ski trail at Stowe, Vermont. Ginnie Chafee and I sort of sideswiped each other and we both fell. Neither was hurt, we both bounded up, exchanging apologies, when a tall man appeared at her side, inquiring of his wife if she was okay, then turning to look narrowly at me as the villain in the case. It was Chafee. The mustache was gone but otherwise he looked pretty much the same. We exchanged compliments, discussed whether we might get together later for a drink (we couldn't), and we brought ourselves briefly up to date. I was a correspondent in Washington covering the Senate for Fairchild Publications; he was practicing law in Providence. And after handshakes and insincere promises to stay in touch, we skied off.

In the early sixties, when we were living in Paris, *Time* ran a piece about "up and coming" politicians in the Republican ranks who might be factors in the next elections. One of them was the governor of Rhode Island, John Chafee. I scrutinized the thumbnail-sized photo and concluded it was "my" Chafee. Funny, he'd never seemed the politician type. But I got off a brief note saying how impressed I was that someone I knew had his picture in *Time*. That, for some reason, seemed more meaningful than his being governor of the smallest state. That's how journalists think.

He wrote back. Invited my wife and me to visit them at the state house some time if we were ever in Providence. I liked his official stationery. I'd never known that the state's official title was "The State of Rhode Island and Providence Plantations," dating back in some fashion, I supposed, to the time and style of Roger Williams.

Our next exchange was a tragic one. In 1968 the Chafees' youngest child, their fourteen-year-old daughter, Tribbie, was killed in a horseback-riding accident. By now I had two daughters of my own and I wrote Ginnie and John a long letter. Can't remember what I said, something about how I don't know how I would have handled the loss of either of my girls. Not very helpful, was I? Years later when I was interviewing Meredith Vieira for *Parade* magazine, I asked the Providence-born broadcaster if she'd known the Chafees.

Indeed she had. Had been a classmate of Tribbie's.

Meredith said that a few weeks after Tribbie's death, John Chafee came to the school and talked to the assembled kids. He knew how upset they were, how happy Tribbie had been there, and tried to cheer them up by talking up the positives of her life, and about the school, her classmates, their friendships.

"Here he was, the one who'd lost his daughter, and he was trying to comfort us. There wasn't a dry eye in the assembly when he'd finished. I've never forgotten that day or what Governor Chafee did and said."

Chafee served a couple of terms; then, following a loss (he was a Republican in the most Democratic state in the country), they gave him a Washington job as secretary of the navy. But the pull of elective office was still there, and when an opportunity to run for the Senate came along, John grabbed it. And won. Kept winning, too, four terms in all.

One evening on the *CBS News* Dan Rather reported that a congressional fact-finding group, in Israel visiting the West Bank that day, had come under fire. When they rolled the tape you could see congressmen and senators and citizens alike all scrambling to escape the sniper, scurrying away. All but one, a tall, trim, tieless fellow in a blue blazer and khakis. He was sauntering across this dusty town square until he got to the shelter of a shop or restaurant doorway, where he stopped and resumed looking around. That was all there was of the tape, and no one in the congressional delegation was identified.

But I thought I'd recognized the fellow in the blazer, the one of them so cool under fire.

The next morning *The New York Times* reported the story on an inside page and listed members of the congressional group. There it was, "Sen. John Chafee, R., R.I." Being shot at never does quite grow on you, but after a certain amount of soldiering, you adjust to it. Chafee clearly had.

When my memoir of Korea, *The Coldest War,* came out in 1990, it was dedicated to those who'd died in Korea. But "if it has a hero," I wrote, "it is Capt. John H. Chafee." John was delighted, and told me later he'd read parts of it aloud (not the parts about him) to his family around the dinner table. And when I went down to Washington to plug the book on talk shows, he invited me to his office in the Senate Office Building. He'd bought a half dozen copies of the memoir, full price and at retail! He asked if I'd inscribe them to other senators who'd fought in Korea: John Warner of Virginia, John Glenn of Ohio, Warren Rudman of New Hampshire. Warner (also a Marine) and, I think, Rudman, who'd commanded an Army company, came to say hello and congratulate me. It was a gracious gesture by our host, whom I still thought of as "the Skipper," and said something about the Chafee style, I thought.

In more recent years his letters and remarks when we met had gradually taken on a note of sadness that old-fashioned good manners were eroding in the Senate that he respected and loved.

"Contentious," one of his favorite critical adjectives, came up more frequently.

I attended as his guest a formal dinner put on by something called the Alfalfa Club, composed of senior and congenial Washington politicos including the former president, Bush the Elder. We had a splendid evening and I got a kick out of the way people, including the former president, made their way to Chafee's side, drawn by his easy grace and affable ways, the good old New England WASP manners.

It wasn't always a smooth ride. *The Wall Street Journal,* anything but a liberal sheet, profiled favorably the "moderate" Chafee during the heated debate over health care early in the Clinton years, citing how he'd lost his job as the GOP Senate whip, the party's third-ranking role: "When young conservatives drove John Chafee out of the Senate Republican leadership in 1990, the Rhode Island patriarch just seemed to get busier."

The *Journal* reported how in his reelection campaign of '94, conservatives put up an anti–gun control candidate against the two-war Marine combat veteran. At the time, this seemed something of an absurdity. John Chafee "soft on guns"? Colleagues of both parties sprang to Chafee's side. Said Alan Simpson, the Wyoming Republican, "You don't want to spend any time trying to detonate John Chafee. He has too many friends here." And Democrat and Medal of Honor winner Bob Kerrey chimed in, "They'll have to put a new party together if Chafee is described as 'unprincipled.' " Bob Dole, another wounded veteran, remembered how Chafee helped make him the Senate leader.

As for me, clearly, all these years after the war, I was still in his thrall. I once asked John what he might do after the Senate.

"If I have the energy and still have my health, I'd like to start a wrestling club for boys in the inner city. You can work off a lot of anger wrestling. And I think I might still be able to teach them the sport, show them a few holds."

Other wealthy men, heavy with honors, deservedly live out leisured lives at the golf course and the country club. Chafee was going to teach poor boys to wrestle. That, too, tells you about the Skipper's style.

CHAPTER 42

I never thought of myself as a hero."

Of all the war story clichés, that's got to be the hoariest of all. In my case it was literally true, had been for nearly fifty years. I did a competent job in Korea, got over being scared, didn't do anything stupid or gutless that got men killed or screwed up operations. And as I sailed for home on the old *General Meigs,* I understood how fortunate had been my timing, missing the slaughterhouse fighting when the Marines took 749, and being rotated home just as the mindless, bloody attrition of the Outpost War began, with the Chinese swarming over the hilltops every night and the Marines taking them back the next day. That fighting, most Marines might agree, was as empty-headed as the First World War's Ypres and Vimy Ridge.

By contrast, the fighting I'd done had been small beer indeed; I had no illusions about my heroics.

Nevertheless, the Marines promoted me to first lieutenant in Korea, later in 1958 to captain in the Reserves. Then while I was working in Paris as a foreign correspondent with a wife and two small kids in the early sixties, I got an official-looking letter from the Marine Corps. Good Lord! Are they actually promoting me to major? I was thrilled but convinced someone had gone mad.

Instead, they were throwing me out! It turned out to be a Dear John letter.

Because I never took correspondence courses, didn't go to summer camp or attend lectures, I was being honorably discharged. Romance was supposed to bloom in Paris, and here I was, seduced and abandoned. I considered writing an irate letter telling them what a valuable man I was, living in Europe, hanging out with Coco Chanel and parlez-ing French with André Malraux, and hadn't I been Colonel Noel C. Gregory's crack intelligence officer? Half the Americans we knew in Paris (oh, I could name names!) were CIA, and yet the Marine Corps didn't think it wanted me around, locked and loaded, just in case the Soviets reached the Seine? In the end I got over my sulks, forgave the Corps for its callousness, and didn't post that letter. As they began calling up Reserve officers for Vietnam, I was just as glad.

When I came home from Korea I wore the usual campaign ribbons, quite attractive really with their tiny metallic battle stars. Certainly my family was impressed. But I had never gotten a medal (the Corps being parsimonious in doling out the hardware). Deep down inside I wondered that maybe for that fight on Yoke, they could have put me in for a letter of commendation, which is the most humble of awards, but nice to have.

You know, like in the old days at the Khyber Pass where Faversham, or some other decent chap from the Grenadier Guards, was "mentioned in despatches" (as the Brits spell it). I'd always wanted to be "mentioned in despatches." In my most secret moments, I thought maybe I'd earned it. But no luck. And over the years I accepted things as they were and never lost sleep.

When I was interviewed in Korea last spring by Army public affairs sergeant Russell C. Bassett, the story began with a surely overbaked quote from me: "If you have been in combat, there is almost a secret fraternity handshake between guys that have actually fought and known combat; there is nothing like it in the world."

The quote smacked of histrionics and I was an ass to have said it. But there really was a fundamental difference between the Marine Corps and the other services, where a relative few ever actually fight and no stigma attaches if you haven't. In the Corps, there are only two categories of Marine: those who fight and the others—the latter evermore to be snubbed as "real echelon pogues."

Combat doesn't make you a better man. It does make you different. I know wonderful combat soldiers who were lousy human beings, have known men who never fought who were admirable people, ethically, morally, even physically superior to those who fought.

The men in this book, with rare exceptions, fought.

Some years ago on a book tour, in D.C. to do the talk shows, I encountered Stew McCarty. McCarty was a regular, had retired as a full colonel, and we'd been in that fight together with Jack Rowe on Yoke back in '52, later helped get Dick Brennan into the VA hospital. He'd come to buy my book and get me to sign it, and afterward we went for coffee, talked about mutual pals, and then Stew asked me an unexpected question: "Did you get a Silver or a Bronze for the Yoke fight?"

I was flabbergasted. "Stew, I didn't get a Silver Star. Didn't get anything. Why?"

He looked at me. "I don't understand that and I should know. I wrote you up for the Silver Star myself."

"Didn't get it."

McCarty just shook his head. "Jack got the Navy Cross, his sergeant got a Silver, I was up for a Silver and got a Bronze, and you didn't get anything?"

"No sir."

"Would you mind if I looked into this?"

"Oh, hell, Stew, it's been forty years. But sure, if you want."

It took a year or more but McCarty, who apparently has connections, called to tell me he'd tracked down the original paperwork. Would I check it for accuracy?

"Send it along," I said. I was uneasy about all this, didn't know what else to say. You read every so often about some old soldier getting a belated medal, eighty years after the Battle of the Marne or some such. And it always sounds corny and somehow fabricated.

But when McCarty's letter arrived with its neat little package of documentation and the draft version of the letter he proposed to send to the commandant, I was knocked out.

Years before, I'd written my own account of that bloody dawn on Yoke in *The Coldest War,* but it is a weird, out-of-body experience to read how someone else who was there, and a colonel at that, saw that same fight and what I'd done.

McCarty's "summary of action" accompanying the citation was a stunner; had I actually done these things?

For gallantry and intrepidity in action while serving as the Intelligence Officer (S-2) of the 2nd Battalion 7th Marines in action against the enemy in Korea on 31 May 1952. Lieutenant Brady was part of a reinforced platoon reconnaissance patrol of Dog Company, 2nd Battalion . . .

Is intrepidity a noun? I wondered. And read on.

. . . an entrenched enemy force of estimated platoon size opened fire on the patrol with an anti-tank grenade, hand grenades and small arms fire. When the assault on the trench line was ordered, Lt. Brady led one squad in the attack on the right flank of the line. The attack was stopped by intense enemy fire and by a heavy volume of hand grenades causing numerous casualties. Lt. Brady reorganized his flank of the line, directing the base of fire with small arms and hand grenades against the enemy position.

I remembered that part. If you run up a hill when people are shooting at you, you remember it pretty vividly.

When it became necessary to withdraw the patrol because of the number of casualties, Lt. Brady was directed to take command of all able-bodied and walking wounded . . . and organize a collecting party to evacuate the seriously wounded from the hill. While performing this task, Lt. Brady was trooping the line, completely disregarding his own personal safety, moving under an intense barrage of hand grenades and small arms fire. His actions were critical to the successful withdrawal of the patrol. The patrol was able to break contact and withdraw with all of its wounded and dead and all of their weapons.

I did like that part about how I was "trooping the line" and "disregarding" my personal safety. Though as I recalled the moment, I don't believe I was "disregarding" anything, and certainly not our Chinese colleagues rolling down those hand grenades. But by now, McCarty was getting to the good parts.

The engagement was an intense fire fight within 10 to 15 yards of the enemy trench line, and was a hand grenade and small arms duel at close range, lasting one and a half hours. Of the 49 men in direct contact with the enemy, there were 33 wounded and one killed; a casualty rate of 70 per cent. The actions of Lt. Brady in efficiently evacuating the seriously wounded probably resulted in fewer casualties overall and undoubtedly saved the lives of the most seriously wounded by returning them to friendly lines for prompt medical care of their wounds. His outstanding leadership and complete coolness under fire were an inspiration blah blah blah . . .

As I put down Stew McCarty's letter, I attempted to square my recollections with his version. They differed in detail. I never thought there was a full platoon of Chinese up there, maybe only a squad. But the things he said I did, I guess I did them. Funny, though, that part about being cool. That was true. Once the fight began I wasn't scared at all. Not even when we all went crazy and dove over the barbed wire and sprinted uphill into the firing and the exploding grenades.

Wait a minute. I was scared when our own 105s began firing at the hill crest just a few yards in front of us, scared of short rounds hitting me right in the small of the back.

McCarty's account never mentioned that.

I also knew how stupid I had been, shouting as I ran toward the Chinese, "No prisoners! No prisoners!"

Other than that, I was in McCarty's debt and in no mood to carp.

When I read the great military historian Sir John Keegan's classic book *The Face of Battle,* which won all the literary prizes that season, I was terribly disillusioned about Keegan when he confessed on the very first page, "I have not been in a battle; not near one, nor heard one from afar, nor seen the aftermath."

I knew, and Keegan never would, that whatever else I would ever do in my life, on Yoke I had grabbed a wounded man's rifle and charged up a naked Asian hillside against an entrenched enemy firing at us. Millions of men serve, and well, as soldiers of their country. Only a relatively few experience that sublime spasm of joyous insanity running through hostile fire toward the enemy. And neither time nor age nor any man could take that away from me. Medal or no medal.

Sir John, old boy, you missed something.

CHAPTER 43

"YOU RUNNING SOME SORT OF SCAM ON US, BRADY?"
DON IMUS DEMANDED.

In East Hampton, the phone rang on my kitchen wall. It was General Jim Jones, commandant of the Marine Corps. I'd interviewed him for *Parade* magazine so it was all rather relaxed. This was maybe a year after McCarty sent in his paperwork. Then the general's voice changed and became "official."

A review board, he said, had investigated McCarty's belated pitch for a medal, and, said the general, they were awarding me the Bronze Star with combat V for valor. Could I travel to Camp Lejeune, North Carolina, to receive it at a Korean War commemorative celebration of some sort.

So, after all, I was going to be "mentioned in despatches."

But September 11 came along and Camp Lejeune was scrubbed. They had other things on their minds. Instead, in November at the annual Marine birthday black-tie celebration aboard the carrier *Intrepid* on the Hudson River in New York, they did the deed, with a major reading the commendation and General Jones pinning on the medal and my kids and some pals and Stew McCarty watching. And when the general asked if I wanted to say something, of course I did. I've spent my life "saying something." Try getting me to shut up.

What I said was I was thrilled to have the medal but it really wasn't necessary. For I already had my commendation, the privilege of having commanded Marines in combat.

And I sat down.

The euphoria, such as it was, didn't last. On Veterans' Day I was back on *Intrepid* at six in the morning with Andy Rooney and Tom Brokaw and a few others doing the *Imus in the Morning* show. It was a splendid exercise in humility.

Imus was in grand form, showing off a pistol he wore holstered on his hip. Please do not ask me to explain this. Then he launched into his interrogation.

"Are you running some sort of scam on us, Brady?" Don Imus inquired pleasantly. "You're supposed to get a Silver Star and you end up with a Bronze?"

I should explain that Imus was once a Marine (a field music who blew the bugle, and drove a deuce-and-a-half truck, in an artillery outfit), and he knows this stuff.

I attempted to dispel the confusion. It only got worse.

"So in the end you didn't take the hill," Imus said.

"No, the Chinese beat us."

"That's why you didn't get the Silver Star, then?"

"Well, they routinely trade down these things . . . ," I said lamely, and producer Bernard McGuirk jumped in:

"You didn't take the frigging hill!"

"No," I said.

"Bernie's right. You didn't take the hill! Case closed. Get out of here!" Imus said genially. I was summarily dismissed and they brought on Andy Rooney to tell his war stories.

That Christmas a folk musician named El McMeen in Pennsylvania sent me a new CD of his songs. One of them was called "High Ground," and the liner notes said the song "was inspired by the James Brady book about the Korean War, called 'The Coldest War.' The eerie atmosphere of tension and release as Brady's company, on the high ground, defended a line, led to my tune oscillating between a minor and major key." I got in touch with the composer, who told me, no, he wasn't a Marine. But he had read my book. Gracious man; lovely, haunting tune.

Then, on October 16, 2004, at a regional library in Ohio, an astonishing (to me) thing happened. Financed by Rotary International, they dedicated a giant (9½-foot tall) sculpture of eighteen oversized books considered by the community to be significant. They ranged from the Holy Bible and *Don Quixote* to *Huck Finn* and *Gone with the Wind* and *A Passage to India,* with a bow to *The Grapes of Wrath.* Only three living authors were represented, J. K. Rowling for her *Harry Potter* series, Harper Lee for *To Kill a Mockingbird,* and the author of a novel called *The Marines of Autumn,* James Brady.

And never before having been part of a sculpture or mentioned in a song on a guitar player's CD, I was (I guess) now immortalized.

The Navy Department and the Marines were still busily celebrating Korea as half-century anniversary milestones came and went, and I found myself invited to North Carolina and Camp Lejeune. (Clearly, the old love affair had heated up again, either because my books about the Corps were selling or I was getting some mileage out of the medal, modest though it was.) I was still gimping but I got to Charlotte, where a top-wing puddle jumper of indeterminate vintage carried us to Jacksonville, and a showery landing so bumpy and mud-splashed that some old fart in the stern shouted lustily, "Drop the tailhook!" and I knew I was in with the right crowd.

The festivities at the football stadium featured the commandant, General Jones; the secretary of the navy; lots of generals and admirals (even one from the Coast Guard); and Hector Cafferata.

If you have led a sheltered life, you may not know Hector. But the Marine Corps does. He is a bulky fellow with a considerable limp. ("I just had two hip replacements. Had 'em simultaneously so I wouldn't miss two hunting seasons.") Hector is celebrated through the Corps for having, as a private in Captain Bill Barber's Fox Company of the 7th Marines, fought the crucial battle of the snowy Toktong Pass the night of November 27–28, 1950, in his socks. Under a full moon, the Chinese descended so unexpectedly that Hector never had a chance to tug on his boondockers. But together with two PFCs, Robert Benson and Gerald Smith, he was credited with wiping out two platoons of Chinese regulars, and today wears the Congressional Medal of Honor.

"President Truman pinned it on, the little shrimp, and was standing on the toes of my shoes when he did. Ruined the damned spit shine."

Following the formal events, a small group headed by Lieutenant Colonel Ward Scott (until recently a full colonel serving somewhere on the Horn of Africa) and including Hector set out for the officers' club.

"I like officers' clubs," Hector confidentially informed me. Having never risen higher than corporal, it appealed to his finely attuned sense of the ironic.

At the bar Hector bellied up, calling out, "Set 'em up!" and the game was afoot. The barmen, enlisted Marines, were delighted. They knew Hector.

With his love of hunting and his deadly riflery in Korea, I'd assumed Hector was a country boy from somewhere out West. Not so. "I was a Marine-happy kid," he told biographer Larry Smith, "out of Boonton, New Jersey," and here he was now, the old corporal with a couple of new hips, drinking with Marine officers as proud and excited to be with him as he was to be at their club. He lives now in Venice, Florida, and not long ago ran his Volvo into an eighteen-wheeler, totaling the car and smashing his wrist. But he assures me he's fine, just fine.

Later that evening, still guided by Colonel Scott, we found our way to a Tex-Mex barbecue joint just outside the Main Gate in Jacksonville, for dinner. There were twelve of us at the table, and when I looked around, I saw that three men who'd fought in Korea—Hector, Navy pilot Tom Hudner, and General Ray Davis, who in Korea as a light colonel had commanded Hector's battalion—all wore the pale blue ribbon of the Medal of Honor. Three diners out of twelve. Moved, awed, and decidedly humbled to be in the presence of great men, I was conscious of my modest Bronze Star.

In the spring of 2000 I'd gotten a phone message at *Parade* to call the White House. I'd been in the White House plenty as a reporter, so I wasn't knocked out by that. But what I heard stopped me. The young man at the White House (well, he sounded young) identified himself as one of Mr. Clinton's speechwriters. The fiftieth anniversary of the start of the Korean War was coming up June 25. The president would be making a speech that Sunday at the Korean War memorial in Washington and this fellow had been assigned to write it. He'd read two of my books, the memoir that had come out ten years before and a new novel, *The Marines of Autumn,* which had just been published.

Would I be willing to help him with the president's speech?

I was flattered, I said. Honored to be asked. Thought about it briefly. But I couldn't do it. I tried to frame my words courteously but definitively.

"My differences with the president are so many and so deep I'd feel like a hypocrite to help write his speech about the war."

The White House speechwriter said he understood.

I was sorry, thanked him for having read my stuff, and told him to lift anything he wanted from the books. Just leave me out of it.

I suspect my book publisher, sensing the promotional possibilities, could cheerfully have killed me.

Revisiting Korea and the war, I pondered all these things.

CHAPTER 44

I LAY THERE HELPLESS AND DESPAIRING
AS KAFKA'S GREGOR SAMSA.

We were going stateside, back to New York, Eddie and I, and waving us off at the Inchon airport gate was the unflappable Colonel Boylan with his stab wounds. While we were flying home, he would be returning to the same Seoul streets where three young men he never knew had tried to kill him. At the airport, too, were the gorgeous West Pointer Major Holly "Hawkeye" Pierce, to go on leave with her mom; the ubiquitous Sergeant Bassett; and the efficient if inscrutable Mr. Hong. The Army had done its part for a couple of jarheads, and more than its part. Where, I wondered, was Eddy's "best friend," Jung, the man who organized the Olympics, knew the president, and greeted us with flowers? The East keeps its secrets; perhaps best not even to inquire.

As Mr. Hong hustled us through the formalities for our flight home, my mind went back to those first few nights at New York Presbyterian when I'd lain unsure if I'd ever walk or function normally again.

Then, testing myself, forcing the issue in the middle of the night, I'd struggled out of bed to get to the bathroom using a walker and without buzzing for an orderly, and had fallen in the dark, lying there helpless and despairing as Kafka's Gregor Samsa, an outsized bug on its hard shell of a back, feet and antennae flailing. Unable to crawl or even turn over, humiliated and ashamed of my weakness, I squirmed half naked along the floor until, with my good hand, I found and tugged at a dangling call button, and nurses and orderlies came running, righteously chewing me out for stupidity. That was fifteen months earlier; I'd come a long way from that doleful night.

Here I was, riding choppers and jeeps, fraternizing with generals, crawling up hilltops, hanging with the troops, being cursed out by a Pulitzer winner, boarding jets for fourteen-hour flights.

The midday plane to New York lifted off into the improbably blue spring sky over the Yellow Sea, out of the same port of Inchon from which I sailed aboard a troopship the rainy night of July 6, 1952. Now, in 2003, I was quite sure I would never see Korea again. As for Eddie, he didn't know it yet, but within the year he would be diagnosed with Lou Gehrig's disease. He wouldn't be returning to Korea either.

Sergeant Adams and I, a couple of old Marines who had been here before, who'd heard the guns and knew the ground, were going home, our wars behind us.

CHAPTER 45

"WHAT A MAN! WHAT A LIFE!"
CRIED ZECHARIAH CHAFEE FROM THE PULPIT.

In *The Sun Also Rises,* Hemingway's Jake Barnes and Bill Gorton are fishing in Spain, where they meet an Englishman named Wilson-Harris. Over the trout streams they strike up an acquaintance. And when the Americans have to return to Pamplona for the running of the bulls, the three men enjoy a farewell drink.

" 'We've had a grand time, Harris.'

"Harris was a little tight.

" 'I say, really, you don't know how much it means. I've not had so much fun since the War.' "

Maybe you know how Harris felt. War doesn't so easily loosen its grip. I believe there are plenty of men who feel like that about their wars. I know I felt that way about Korea: that never before, or after, had I lived so intensely, done so many strange, unexpected things, or in small ways in a brief, compressed time, accomplished so much.

Now we're dying off, my generation of soldiers, and it'll be the turn of others to write their stories, to tell lies about their war.

No war really just ends. The shooting stops, and the soldiers who are left eventually return home. But the ties go on; the bonds forged in combat, in our case the Marine bonds, they endure. Then, after sufficient time has passed, enough years, the men who survived the battle, who cheated death, begin to die off, the company of the young diminishes. The phone rings, you receive an unwelcome letter from a wife or a son, or read in the obituary pages, about a man you knew, a fellow your own age who was there at the same time, and now is gone.

As 2004 ended, the Christmas cards arrived. From Lee Mead, another Sheepshead Bay boy, who won a Navy Cross with the Chosin Few, who scrawls a "Semper Fidelis" from Smithtown on Long Island. From Fredericksburg, Virginia, old Chinaside NCO George Howe, who fought in Korea as a captain and whose son is in Afghanistan, writes, "We are not well anymore. Wife has memory loss. I quit driving November 16." Sergeant Fitzgerald's wife, Sam, tells me, "John had a brief hospital stay . . . remnants of his police wounds." But Fitz was also shopping for a new boat. "He's searching for a good trawler," she says. A card from "light machine gunner" Robert Knight in Grand Blanc, Michigan, notes he is also a Dog Company Marine who "left the battalion and Hill 812 as you arrived." And Colonel Robert Taplett's wife, Pat, reports from their home in Arlington, "Tap's long journey (86 years and one week) ended at seven in the morning, Friday, December 17. A great husband, loyal American, great father and grandfather, and a real Marine." It was Tap who commanded a battalion at the Chosin Reservoir.

And so it goes. Another small piece of yourself is lost, a bell has tolled and another of Donne's clods has been washed away, and we are all the less.

As taps again sounds somewhere in America.

Following my return to Korea for that famous "second helping," I resolved to stay more assiduously in touch, to look up friends, to write notes of my own and to respond more swiftly to letters received, to be less brusque on the phone, to cultivate patience. Of course this opens me to any number of practiced bores. But it's a slight risk worth taking.

Because the Marine Corps is so relatively small, you tend to know, or to know someone who knows, almost everyone in the Corps. You notice the

USMC bumper stickers: "Good night, Chesty, wherever you are!" on the rear window of a pickup truck or a Mercedes. There is a shock of recognition, a sort of bush telegraph binding Marines together over distance and the years.

Donald Clement of Salisbury, North Carolina, called, a man who had just read my fifteen-year-old *The Coldest War* with its dedication to John Chafee. Clement had been on Guadalcanal with Chafee, a couple of young privates in the 11th Marines. They exchanged phone calls every August 7, the day they'd landed on the Canal. "I must be the only guy around who knew Chafee as a private," he told me. On Memorial Days there are nostalgic calls back and forth between Fallbrook, California, and East Hampton, to and from Jack Rowe and me, remembering Yoke. Having read my lionization of the late Captain Ike Fenton in another book, a Marine named Fred R. Neuman in San Clemente, who served in Korea in Baker Company, 5th Marines, protested that Ike "wouldn't have made a pimple on Tobin's ass," referring to Captain John Tobin, the company commander who was burp-gunned and replaced by Fenton. I get pedantic critiques on decimal points in my writing about the Corps and its weapons. Ron Wynkoop of Phillipsburg, New Jersey, is something of a Dog Company historian and photographer and keeps files on everything. And there is endless chiding of me from John Ledes at the Yale Club and Chuck Curley from Olean.

Captain Chafee would raise hell with you but never complained.

I wish Chafee had made that trip back to Korea with me, seeing it through his eyes as well as my own. What a grand adventure it had been for Eddie and me, in strange ways, what fun. Chafee was a wiser man than either of us, and there were great talks we might have had, questions I always meant to ask.

I last saw him in Washington the October of '99. I was there for a couple of days to do an interview for *Parade* and called ahead to tell John that I had an evening open and ask if he and Ginnie could join me for dinner at the Jockey Club in the old Fairfax Hotel on Mass. Ave., along Embassy Row. Could they not!

They'd come up to New York for my daughter Fiona's wedding earlier that year and I hadn't seen them since. John complained of a creaky back but was otherwise okay, appalled at the "contentious" mood of the Senate and wondering, did the country really need a tax cut? He thought not, believed the money could be used more constructively. He spoke highly of Olympia Snowe, the senator from Maine, and of several others. We spoke of the coming millennium, looking ahead as he always did. Ginnie was in splendid form and I recalled again the story of how they'd met. John arrived at a dance one night to find a friend of his with a glorious blonde, and when introductions were made, he was informed there were two more dazzling sisters coming, just like this one, and he'd called out to his pal, with a joyous gallantry, "Well, save one for me!"

And they did. And that was how he met Ginnie, one of the three glamorous Coates sisters. We had cocktails and called for menus and a wine card, and over the meal John asked what I was writing. A bit hesitant, I told them.

"Well, I've done another novel. *The Marines of Autumn*. It'll be out next spring."

"And when can we read it?"

"That's the thing, John. I've stolen my hero from real life. Stolen a lot of him from you. You're kind of the hero. Under assumed names, of course."

In my business I'm accustomed to defensive press agents and PR people running interference, shielding movie stars from the media. "Did you clear this? We'll have to run this past the lawyers. Who gave you approval?"

And here was Senator Chafee turning exultantly toward his wife and demanding: "Ginnie! Have I ever been in a novel before?"

"I don't think so, Johnnie."

He was as proud and as pleased about that book as if he'd written it himself. I promised him an early set of galleys and we had another cocktail on the basis of it, and went on to a wonderful dinner, three old friends over a meal and a glass. I'll always be glad we had that meal, glad too that I told him about the book and his role in it, how he'd inspired my fictional Tom Verity.

That was Tuesday night and on Friday John fell ill at their home in McLean. Ginnie, who understood such things, rushed him to the Bethesda

Naval Hospital. On Sunday he died, apparently of a cardiac. The Skipper was dead, just seventy-seven years old.

He would never start that wrestling club for inner city kids.

Fiona and I drove up to Providence for the funeral. Half the Senate was there, the commandant of the Marine Corps, every personage in Rhode Island, a Marine honor guard, President and Mrs. Clinton. Whatever one thinks of the Clintons, there is a powerful symbolism to a president's attendance. Fiona and I sat way back to the right. A Senate colleague, John Danforth, spoke, followed by one of the many Chafee kids, Zechariah, an attorney.

Zechariah. I love those old New England names. Zech got into the pulpit and then he cried out, in a strong, steady Chafee voice, "What a man! What a life!"

And a mournful occasion turned almost jubilant. What a man he had been! What a life he'd led. And so it went until Zech got to talking about his father's time in Korea.

". . . and now a description of Captain Chafee in the winter mountains of North Korea from a book written by one of his lieutenants . . ."

And he began to read a few lines from *The Coldest War*. I lost it then. Fiona gripped my right arm. She's my firstborn and she steadied me. "It's all right, Poppy," she whispered. "It's all right."

And after a while it very nearly was.

CHAPTER 46

I LOSE MY HEART, AGAIN, IN SAN FRANCISCO.

There were other friends to bury.

In the early October of '03, I flew west on an American Airlines jet to San Francisco, invited by the Marine Corps to participate in what was billed as the "final" commemoration of the fifty years since the Korean War ended in 1953. No one took that "final" very seriously. Old soldiers not only "never die"—the young doing most of the dying—they rarely miss an opportunity to recall bygone wars and nostalgic battles with the appropriate mix of solemnity and robust good cheer. And who ever turns down a chance to visit San Francisco?

The big event was at high noon on a Friday in Union Square. But I strolled downhill from Sutter Street early in the cool, sunny San Francisco morning to check out the place. If you've never seen it, Union Square is a kind of urban plaza more than a park, crafted of white stone, granite I suppose, ringed with tall, tailored, and very elegant emperor palm trees, with the St. Francis Hotel at one end, a church at the other end, the modern, glass-fronted Macy's on one side, Tiffany and Saks Fifth Avenue on the other side. It's a swell place. Nothing like it in New York or L.A. On this day there would be several thousand Korean War vets on folding chairs facing a little stage where the grandees (I was surely the lowest ranking of the bunch) would be seated facing the audience. The first vets were wandering into the square now but it was too early to sit down so I went instead to the hotel at the top of the little square.

The St. Francis was a sort of shrine, in a small way like Hill 749, and being a Catholic, I'm accustomed to visiting shrines. Wasn't it here that Carly Rand and Ledes and Dusty Rhodes and the rest of them hatched that disastrous scheme to fly to Reno the night before going to the war? I wanted to see it again, to remember them, and to remember Brennan and Wild Hoss and Bradlee, who'd been invited on the flight but had bowed out. Where Bradlee had said, No thanks.

I told you a little about Doug Bradlee before, about how because of the alphabet we had bunked in next to each other from the very start in the summer of '48 when we both joined the Platoon Leaders Class and how he was a Harvard man who played football and came from an old Boston family.

When we were at the Basic School I took him home one weekend to our little redbrick row house in Brooklyn's Sheepshead Bay. I'd forgotten to tell my mother and we'd gotten in from the train about midnight, so her first view of the distinguished Bradlee—the only Harvard man to enter our house, I assure you—was the next morning in the upstairs hallway, where she encountered a six-foot-four, broken-nosed redhead in his skivvies looking for the bathroom. But it was okay, once I explained this was Doug, about whom I'd written home so much. She took over and served up a swell breakfast. In the dining room and with paper napkins (customarily we ate breakfast in the kitchen, no napkins).

My girl at the time, Sheila Collins, got Doug a date that Saturday evening with a tall, sassy friend of hers who worked at the phone company, and we went down to the Sheepshead Bay waterfront for dinner along Emmons Avenue where the head boats go out each dawn and local people keep their boats moored, and the bars and local restaurants elbow the bait-and-tackle shops for space. Bradlee was delighted to realize that a part of New York City looked like this, reminding him of New England. Over the meal he told about pulling lobster traps during summers up on the north shore of Boston

at Gloucester and telling tall tales about the fishermen and lobstermen he'd
gotten to know and things he'd learned from them that Harvard may have
overlooked. And with his Pinckney Street breeding and St. Mark's and Harvard manners, he charmed Sheila and her phone company pal, who was turning more playful and less sassy as the evening filled.

Early that spring of 1951 the Quantico brass pulled Doug aside. The commanding general of the base at that time was a jock, less colorful but in the
grand tradition of General Smedley Darlington Butler (later the police com-
missioner of Philadelphia), who used to lead the cheers and the Marine band
at Quantico football games, wearing his dress blues over which he sported a
long, handsome fur coat, and who once ordered his Marine spectators to
charge the opponents' grandstand after what Smedley considered poor
sportsmanship by the other team.

Nothing to be ashamed about there; good athletic teams are positive influ-
ences on peacetime military bases. Let off steam, dispel boredom, inspire es-
prit de corps. But in wartime, the zeal to field a winning team could be
pernicious. When they called Bradlee in, they told him the team looked
pretty good for the upcoming season; they already had some talent and it
looked as if Washington Redskins quarterback Eddie LeBaron might be playing, but they could use a big tackle.

Doug wasn't interested.

The Marine Corps doesn't take no gracefully. The general became in-
volved. Patiently, he pointed out that Bradlee might owe something to the
Corps he'd joined, that now might be the occasion to start paying off.

Yes, Doug said, he understood that. He'd joined the Marines to become,
and to serve as, an officer. And now that the country was at war, to go out to
the division as a platoon leader.

Of course, of course, does you great credit, Lieutenant.

What it came down to was straight bargaining: if Bradlee played on that
autumn's Quantico team, he wouldn't be needed in Korea until after the season, and then could pretty much write his own ticket to Korea as a platoon
leader or anything else.

When he declined, with thanks, and our Basic School course ended early in April, Bradlee was one of the first ordered to ship out. And the Quantico team had to play the following season without the starting tackle for Harvard. In one of his first letters from the division, Doug promised me, "We'll keep things going until you get here." It was a promise he wouldn't keep.

I was still at Quantico, commanding a platoon in the new Basic class, when his father, Malcolm Bradlee, sent me a Western Union wire.

"WORD RECEIVED DOUG'S DEATH IN ACTION 3 JUNE NO FURTHER DETAILS."

That was all. People told me later Mr. Bradlee never really got over it. Doug was their only son.

Bjornsen, who was with them, wrote me it was a mortar shell that killed Doug. Wild Hoss Jimmy Callan was killed that same week, Bjornsen said, also from a mortar while on the attack, jumping off against the Chinese. A bad week for our bunch. *Marine Ops (U.S. Marine Operations in Korea,* volume 4) devotes a chapter to the early June fighting on what became known as the Kansas Line, summarizing, "The cost in Marine casualties had been high." Wild Hoss and Doug paid some of that "cost."

We were all pals from Quantico but it was Doug Bradlee that I loved. Someone up at St. Mark's School in Southborough, Massachusetts, where he went to prep school and played hockey and football, asked me to write a note about him for their memorial service of June 17, 1951. So I wrote:

"He became one of my closest friends, someone I always wanted to be with in the good times or the bad. He was independent and brave and gentle, all at the same time. When he was ordered overseas and I stayed here, I felt a sense of loss that he tried to assuage by saying he'd keep things going over there until I could catch up. Now I never will catch up."

Professor John H. Finley of St. Mark's presided over the chapel service, and on July 28 Mr. Bradlee sent me a copy of the memorial leaflet about Doug. It included excerpts from letters he'd sent, such as this from San Francisco before flying out:

Frisco was fun. I went to Palo Alto for the night with Jim Brannaman. His father runs a combination filling station and garage. They have an old not very Californian looking white clapboard house with a homemade barbecue fireplace in the back yard, plus garage so filled with junk and tools it warmed my heart to the core.

Had a very interesting talk with Champion as the evening wore on. He's the man who has three children, two Purple Hearts, and fought through almost the entire last war. He was a lieutenant on Iwo and Okinawa after coming up through the ranks. Very mild, quiet, slim guy who was a refrigerator repair man in Muskegon, Michigan. He was considering moving and I told him my liking for old timers in New England, the rather reduced but satisfactory scale of living of lobstermen. He likes to work with his hands, too.

Sounded just like Doug, the wealthy Harvard boy whose heart was "warmed to the core" by the sight of a garage full of junk. I knew very well from knowing him over the past three years that he loved the lobstermen's life. And here he was in California counseling a refrigerator repairman from Muskegon on a possible move to New England. That part about Champion's "working with his hands," that, too, smacked of Doug. I knew his automobile, a sedan of a vintage so ancient that the floor in the front had rusted through so that as you drove, you could see the pavement ribboning by under your feet, and Doug had cobbled up a jury-rigged floor, fashioned of four-by-fours that he'd sawed and hammered and bolted into place.

That was the same car that got him to Colorado and his first postcollege job teaching and coaching boys at a prep school out there; also got him back east to Quantico when his academic career was interrupted by a call-up of reserve officers.

It was also very Bradlee that the people who drew him were working stiffs, filling-station guys and fridge repairmen. He had written something the previous autumn when his call-up had come in but he hadn't yet gone on active duty. "I hate the attitude of looking always for the easy way out." That must have been part of the reason Doug said no to the general when they offered him a spot on the Quantico football team that would keep him out of combat at least until the following year, when, who knew? the war might be over.

Another letter home was posted from Bradlee's transpacific flight as a replacement to the division.

"I keep thinking of Kon-Tiki as we fly along. . . . The ocean is very blue. Sometimes we fly over white cloud banks which extend for miles and miles to the horizon. I feel content and very appreciative of the sunshine and good company, the little things which mean so much."

I wondered if his plane too had stretchers attached to the walls instead of seats, as ours did. And whether Doug had, like us, occasionally stretched out to enjoy the luxury of a good nap in flight thousands of feet high above that "very blue" Pacific.

His letters from Korea were read. Including that line he got off about the mockingbirds being just like those in Colorado. Doug died before he wrote any more.

In a thoughtful, slightly earlier letter to his family, he had written:

As I once said, try not to be overly upset by my present mission. I have felt during the last seven years or more that I might have been cut out for things away from the beach and country club—not away from business into schoolteaching, but really away. I didn't figure on its being in this form, but this might be a good foundation.

I look to the world of the spirit and the world of human relationships as the most important thing. No peace treaty, no international government, is any good at all without the spirit underneath it. I look to the principles of a Christian life, not stopping at a "gentlemanly" Christian life but working toward a saintly one.

I hope one day to find and work toward God.

The Chinese killed him when he was twenty-three. I often think of all those young boys he never got to teach, how many young lives he would have touched and helped shape, all the good Doug might have done.

I stood considering these things amid the tall marble Corinthian columns of the lobby of the St. Francis Hotel in the October morning more than fifty years later. Just off the lobby to the left, up a broad red-carpeted flight of stairs, was the St. Francis bar, where, I assumed, they'd invited Bradlee to join them on the flight to Reno and he'd turned them down. To go instead to Palo Alto with Jim Brannaman, son of the filling-station man, to gaze upon and enthuse over a garage full of junk. But when I got to the door of the bar it was too early and there was no one there. No boisterous young giants in Marine Corps forest green, nor their ghosts, conjuring up one last night of glorious mischief in America.

There was only a fellow in running gear cooling out after his morning jog on the top step of the lobby stairs leading to the St. Francis bar, talking on a cell phone to someone I couldn't see.

CHAPTER 47

IN THE BAR AT THE TOP OF THE MARK,
THERE IS ALWAYS ONE CHAIR KEPT VACANT.

When I walked across the street to the ceremonies about to start in Union Square, former secretary of state and of the treasury George Shultz and his wife were up front with Al Gray, a former commandant of the Marine Corps; a three-star admiral; the South Korean consul general; Tom Hudner, who wore the Medal of Honor; and Major General Ray Murray, who commanded the 5th Marine Regiment at the Chosin Reservoir and led them out, smashing the damned Chinese Army as they came. Ray stands six two and is still ramrod erect, celebrated for his daily rounds of golf.

"How's your golf, General?" I inquired, wanting to be polite.

"I quit three weeks ago," he said, sounding sore about it.

The yips? A bum knee?

"No, but I used to play every day. Now I hurt all over the next day. I need a day off between rounds."

Ray Murray is ninety years old.

I met the admiral and was invited to visit his headquarters at Coronado, down near San Diego. "That's mighty handsome of you, Admiral. I like Coronado a lot."

"Nice duty station," he agreed.

There was a very decent gent from the VA named Denver Mills and he introduced us and we all got a big cheer. Even me. They gave him a script which said I was a former Marine officer who fought in Korea, that I wrote bestselling books, but that I was most celebrated for interviewing movie stars for *Parade*.

That was what earned me my cheer and I recognized they had their priorities straight.

The mayor of San Francisco, an engaging rascal named Willie Brown, was to start the ceremonies but he was fifteen minutes late so the Marine Band from Twenty-nine Palms had to play a couple of tunes twice. Then Willie showed up, very dapper, sporting an exceedingly well cut dark blue suit topped off by a wide-brimmed brown fedora worn with a certain dash. He spoke with a brief eloquence and then the Korean consul droned on for a time and Al Gray got up and gave us a stem-winder of a speech that had the guys cheering and ready to re-up and invade Syria. (Hell, Al had them so stirred up they'd have tackled Finland!)

Tommy Hudner wasn't a Marine. He graduated from Annapolis and flew as a naval aviator off carriers in Korea and later in Vietnam and retired as a captain, a four-striper. We'd met before and so we sort of hung together. Marines are gracious that way, y'know, forgiving Tom for not being a Marine. He won his congressional medal up in North Korea December 4 of 1950 when the 1st Marine Division was fighting its way out of the mountains. Tommy and his wingman were flying close air support, strafing and napalming the Chinese, earning the gratitude of those sorry foot soldiers making their way from the Chosin to the sea, when the wingman's plane was hit and he went down, pancaking to a crash-landing on the snowy slopes of the Taebaek Mountains.

Hudner circled, flying low, trying to see if the downed pilot was still alive. When he saw that he was, but was apparently trapped in the cockpit, and that smoke was starting to wisp out of the broken Corsair, Tommy Hudner made his decision. As Larry Smith describes the scene in his book, *More than Honor,* then-Lieutenant Hudner circled once more and aimed his plane at the same mountainside where his wingman, Jesse Leroy Brown (the Navy's first black aviator, according to Smith), sat trapped in a plane afire, and Hudner came in as slowly as he could and purposely crashed his own Corsair onto the hill, skidding, bouncing, and sliding frighteningly into the Korean landscape.

But he couldn't get Jesse out; in the end, the flames beat him.

Thomas J. Hudner Jr. was awarded the Medal of Honor. Half the Navy, the fighting half, thought him a hero. How the hell do you crash your own damned plane to save another pilot, even your wingman? What kind of raw courage does that take? The other half, the Naval Establishment, thought Hudner should have been court-martialed for destroying government property.

The Navy may have had its doubters but Marines love unconditionally; they loved Captain Hudner. Even forgave him for being Navy, for being a fly-boy, returning each night to the womb of the great carrier, to the officers' mess, to movies and hot joe, to steaming showers and a warm bunk. Marine infantrymen were dying, shot to pieces or freezing to death on those icy mountain roads, with the Chinese Army coming fast. And there were Tommy Hudner and his wingman, and other pilots in other Corsairs, flying close air support, dodging ack-ack, scraping the mountaintops, killing the Chinese, helping the Marines on that long, hard road to the sea.

Or, as Marines poetically put it, "You don't forget shit like that."

Hudner might have made a pretty good story for Jim Michener.

Or maybe he did. When he wrote *The Bridges at Toko-ri,* maybe Michener knew about Thomas Hudner, and how he crash-landed his plane in Korea. And could have died.

Pete McCloskey was there, too, at Union Square that sunny noon in the audience, not up on the stage where he belonged. Sitting in the audience with the other vets but recognized by most of us.

If you don't remember who Pete McCloskey is, you should. He was an eight-term congressman, but more to the point, he was a Marine. And by the by, the nemesis of TV preacher Pat Robertson. In Korea McCloskey was a ri-fle platoon leader wounded twice and awarded the Silver Star and the Navy Cross. Later in both their careers, Pete was sued by Robertson, his Basic

School classmate at Quantico, for things Pete said about Pat's using his senator father's pull to keep him, Pat, out of combat. McCloskey fired back; Robertson, running for the presidential nomination at the time, eventually withdrew his suit, paid the legal costs; and Pete McCloskey stood justified.

Following the Union Square ceremonies McCloskey, in rustic brown tweeds, gave me a bear hug. I know and love Pete. Most Marines do.

After the speeches and the medaling ended, a lone bugler played "Taps," the beautiful, mournful dirge carrying on the air across the little plaza, and as it often did, bringing me close to tears, and then we stood, turned, and headed toward Powell Street, where the Marine Band had formed up. Along the sidewalks civilians stood to see us pass and little boys capered about, and off we went, the aging detachment almost in step, to the strains of "The Marines' Hymn." I walked besides a woman who was telling me about her son, the Marine. I couldn't quite make out if he was dead. And if so, how. So I just kept saying, "Well, you must be very proud." And "Isn't this some turnout?"

Whatever I said she took it as appropriate, and then we turned into Sutter Street and I dropped back a few paces to march alongside a fellow on crutches, who didn't talk to me. It was simpler that way.

That night we gathered in the theater of the Marines Memorial Club, and George Shultz, who was a Marine before he ever became a cabinet officer, introduced the new commandant of the Marine Corps, General Michael Hagee (pronounced with a hard *g*), who told us about Iraq in the dicey weeks after the organized war was over.

In one of the uneasy provincial towns where civilian hostility and ambushes had become the plat du jour, a young Marine corporal was leading a squad-sized patrol down one of the town's narrow stone streets when coming toward them was a small funeral procession, the body borne on high, mourners firing rifles in the air, the usual appurtenances of a funeral in the area (the equivalent of an Irish wake).

According to Hagee, the corporal, "not having any three-by-five file cards in his pocket to consult," did what Marines are supposed to do; he thought it through and made a decision.

The corporal ordered his Marines to reverse their rifles, carrying them muzzles down, and to remove their helmets until they had passed the funeral cortege.

The Iraqis, usually sullen, smiled and nodded their heads in appreciation as the two groups passed without incident.

I never visit San Francisco without dropping by the Mark Hopkins. And now I walked the three steep blocks up to Nob Hill, sturdy-legged, suntanned California girls jogging past me as I paused every so often for breath, retaining slim hope that somewhere along here between Camp V and Camp VI, I might encounter a friendly team of Sherpas. Like Mallory on Everest, I had no luck but unlike Mallory, I eventually made the summit.

Atop the hill there is an attractive little park where I encountered nine Asians doing a slo-mo ritual and arm-waving dance to the music of a small tape recorder on a park bench. A pretty young girl in shorts sat nearby reading a paperback edition of *The Grapes of Wrath*. Middle-aged men walking rather precious dogs spoke to other, similarly interested men on their cell phones. "Pete-ah here. With the dogs. Do join us." I enjoyed the park, its denizens, the wonderful views.

And its Mark Hopkins Hotel, where I'd spent my last evening in November of 1951 before I flew out to the war. I'd had a beer or two there, at the Top of the Mark, the restaurant and small bar on the roof of the hotel with a backdrop of the Golden Gate Bridge, with a good bit of San Francisco Bay and a sliver of the Pacific in view. At its bar, I'd considered the meaning of life, hoped I'd be a good officer, wondered if I'd be killed, tried to analyze what I really felt on the eve of departure, very much in the mood of "the Minstrel Boy to the wars has gone."

This time it wasn't much different. I was old now but still mulling the same questions. The view remained spectacular, San Francisco was just as lovely, and I was still a Marine, if somewhat superannuated. The wine was as good as I remembered the beer to have been. The same Marine Corps plaque on the wall of the bar carried the same message from the Top. It was a gracious little tribute to the thousands of Marines who'd sailed from San Francisco for the islands of the Pacific war, telling each other they'd be back, would meet again "at Top of the Mark." And the inscription ended, as it always had, with a pledge from the Mark Hopkins Hotel that, here at the Top, there would always be one empty chair for a Marine who had not yet come home.

No Marine can read that plaque without emotion.

On this particular early October evening, as the sun fell toward the bridge and the brown coastal hills and the great ocean beyond, there was a baseball playoff game on the tube and two girls, one of them from Boston, were rooting for the Red Sox. Only she pronounced it as they do up there, as "the Sawks." There were a couple of young men heading their way and I decided not to get into a defense of the Yankees. Alone on another stool was a useful-looking fellow in his fifties, well set up, wearing a well-cut suit, but with a decidedly familiar crew cut.

Inspired by wine and the setting, I said, "You a Marine?"

He was. Name of Bill Sudderth, out of Tyler, Texas, in town for a family wedding. The crew cut wasn't nostalgic. "My hair was thinning so fast I decided, why not make it be my idea?" he said. Oil and gas was his business, the drilling side of things. "I'm a small-timer," he said.

I doubted it. I don't believe he was at all small-time.

We exchanged sketches on our time in the Marine Corps. No, he'd never sailed or flown out of San Francisco for the wars. Had never been to war, in fact.

"I spent most of my time as a corporal fighting. In the ring. Fought welterweight." I think that was what he said; I wasn't taking notes. Must have been pretty good. Fought a man for the Marine championship at his weight who went on to fight on the Olympic team. "Black fellow from Louisiana name of Maurice. Retired later on and went into business down there. Does very well."

"Did you give him a good fight?" I inquired.

"I sure did. But what I remember most is how hard he hit. When Maurice hit me in the face, the soles of my feet hurt."

I told him that in my last novel a Marine boxer gets to go to the

Olympics, the year it was Hitler's turn, in 1936. Bill Sudderth didn't know my work but he promised to get hold of a copy.

Nice man. In New York, liberals like me are supposed to despise everything Texas oilmen stand for. I concluded, and not for the first time, how stupid we can be.

The weekend of the Army-Navy game, I read in *The New York Times* that a Naval Academy football player, the linebacker Eddie Carthan, told how, with the Iraq war on, graduating seniors at the Academy were looking forward to active military duty.

"A lot of the football players want to go Marine Corps," Midshipman Carthan said. "They don't want to sit on a boat or fly overhead. They want to be on the ground, eye to eye with the enemy. It's the killer instinct mentality football players have."

I remembered Doug, Doug Bradlee, who also played football. Some things don't change, do they?

I had one more touchstone in San Francisco before flying home to New York. This was Taffy Sceva.

CHAPTER 48

HELMING A CATAMARAN ALONG THE BEACH AT WAIKIKI . . .

Of all of us who enjoyed pretty good postwars coming home from Korea—Chafee elected governor and senator, Mick Trainor promoted to general and becoming a Fellow at Harvard, Bjornsen dispatched by the Interior Department to help reforest the known world, Jack Rowe falling in love with his nurse and having eleven kids, Ted Williams batting .300 for the Red Sox, Dick Brennan dazzling Denise Darcel at the "21" Club, John Warner marrying Elizabeth Taylor, Pat Robertson becoming, well, Pat Robertson, my living in Paris and writing books—perhaps the most favored of our Korean generation jarheads was Taffy Sceva, who went to live in paradise and made money at it.

To Sceva, who'd fought in two wars, just about everything was "cake." Everything was a "piece of cake." But for Taffy, life was too full of living to waste time and breath on the nonessential, so "piece of cake" was boiled down to plain "cake."

Climbing the High Sierra was "cake." So was navigating a yacht across the Pacific. Even the war was "cake." Nothing bothered Sceva. Not even the Marine Corps' mulish insistence on messing about with his name.

The Marines have any number of curious obsessions, a proper middle initial being one of them.

I first met Taffy Sceva at Quantico in the Basic School, a broad-shouldered and grinning redhead who'd served under the legendary Chesty Puller as a scout in the Pacific. During the fighting on Guam he'd been wounded and given a battlefield promotion from corporal to second lieutenant. In 1951 he was married, the father of three, and back in the Marines heading for Korea. His straight name was Nathaniel Sceva and he had no middle name. So the Marines issued him one. His official name now was Nathaniel (n) Sceva. That (n), he explained, stood for "none."

We thought of calling him "none" but settled for "Taffy." He was a New Jersey kid, a cousin of Joyce Kilmer, the celebrated soldier-poet of the First World War, and on turning eighteen while an undergraduate at Lehigh in Pennsylvania, he enlisted in the Marines. After the war he was invalided to Klamath Falls Tropical Diseases Hospital in Oregon (he had malaria on top of grenade wounds), fell in love with the Pacific Northwest, took a degree in agriculture at Oregon State, married Barbara Anderson, and went to work at Olympia Canning in neighboring Washington, where he learned to sail, before being recalled for Korea by the Marines.

He was one of the more gung ho among us. When we graduated from Basic School and some of us were pulled out of the replacement drafts to Korea to command and instruct the next Basic School class, Taffy protested. He wanted to go to Korea. Well, so did most of us (or so we claimed), but Taffy really meant it. He was indignant that they were having a fight and hadn't invited him! Sat down and wrote a personal letter of complaint to his old boss, Brigadier General Lewis B. Puller, reminding Chesty that he'd fought under him against the Japanese, and begging Puller to pull a few strings and get Sceva into the damned war.

"What did your wife say about that?" Taffy was asked.

"Didn't dare tell her," he said.

Eventually we all got to Korea. Taffy joined Fox Company and I went to Dog Company and up on the Kanmubong Ridge our companies fought side by side all that winter and into the spring. His company commander was Rex Wells, who owned a small trucking company in Provo, Utah, and mine was John Chafee of Providence, a lawyer and a Yalie (though we didn't know that yet). Taffy loved Captain Wells, I loved Chafee, and late in the winter we were both promoted to executive officer of our respective rifle companies. In Marine lingo, Taffy was Fox 5, I was Dog 5. At Quantico we'd competed for shortstop on the softball team.

After the war he went back to the fruit cannery, but at age thirty-two, thinking there might be a better way, he bought a fifty-seven-foot yacht, *Westward Ho,* gathered up family and pals, and set sail for the South Pacific. In 1958 they settled in Hawaii, he and his second wife, Elaine Pfeiffer, raced 210s, and Taf became commodore of the Trans-Pac Yacht Race.

Then, the stroke of genius!

Sceva and partner Herb Bessa launched a big sailing catamaran, the *Manu Kai,* and went into business cruising up and down Waikiki Beach in front of the Royal Hawaiian Hotel, taking tourists and honeymooners, for what I assume were outrageous fees, on two-hour cruises to Diamond Head. I've seen a photo of Taffy at the helm. Fletcher Christian, postmutiny, couldn't have looked as smug.

The rest of us were riding the subway to office jobs in Manhattan and Sceva was helming a catamaran in the sunshine off Waikiki Beach.

"Cake": it was all "cake."

In 1980 Taffy and Elaine moved to San Jose, where they played good tennis, skied, and sailed, and he climbed in the High Sierra. Pretty nice life. Or, in Taffy's words, "cake."

We kept in touch. Whenever I had a new book coming out, Taffy promised to put it on the bestseller list, get all his exalted connections to buy a copy. We exchanged snapshots, some of them showing Taffy hefting a backpack with mountains in the background, a big grin on his puss, photos on the tennis court or of a house they kept on the beach in Hawaii, Christmas cards, stuff like that. If you've fought next to a guy, you don't need to be dropping by or composing epistles to the Corinthians.

Recently, he'd been ailing. Cancer, he said. Over the past few years he was in and out of hospitals. Cheerful, enthusiastic as ever, in hospital or out, even describing his treatments, chemo and radiation, the stuff that would get him through this business, as "cake."

"You're a liar," I said, "that, or unkillable." That was another of many things Taf seemed to be, unkillable.

He cheerfully agreed without debate. "Maybe I'm both."

I hoped so. Too many of us were dying off. We didn't need another, didn't need a Taffy (none) Sceva.

The week before I flew to San Francisco this last time, I phoned ahead. Could the Scevas get out of the house and up to San Francisco for an evening? Dinner on me. Or on one of my expense accounts. No, Elaine said. He wouldn't be up to it. When she put Taffy on the phone he didn't sound right. Not the old, shouting, buoyant Taffy. I accused him of slacking off, suggested he probably had a climb planned for the Sierra. No, he said. It was the chemo, the chemo and the radiation. He was always tired now. I kept trying to ignite a spark.

"Still playing tennis, mixed doubles?" Even I could handle mixed.

"No more." His voice was flat, un-Taffy.

I promised to call when I got to the Coast. In case he'd changed his mind. Sure, Taffy said, that'd be swell. "Cake." It didn't have the usual ring.

After I flew out and the ceremonies were pretty much wrapped, I called San Jose again. Elaine and I had a talk. Taffy wasn't good, she said. That was the first time she'd ever said that. When he got on I identified myself as "Dog 5," addressed him as "Fox 5," as "Nathaniel (n) Sceva," gave him a ration of nonsense about what I was up to and what the Marine Corps had organized for this commemoration, throwing out familiar names, remembering the war. Talking nostalgically about it, about the ridgelines.

He perked up. "We sure had some fun, didn't we?"

"Yes," I said. "I'm glad we didn't miss it."

He seemed to be making an effort, trying to make it sound as if none of this mattered. For the first time I could recall, not everything was "cake." And after a while he said quietly that he wasn't doing so well.

I toned down the kidding. Got serious with him, talked about the realities.

"What is it, Taf, the chemo and the radiation? Or the cancer itself?"

"It's the cancer."

"Oh, hell, Taffy."

His voice changed again, fainter but more intense.

"It's coming close now, Jim. Getting close."

I knew he was saying good-bye. We both knew it.

I couldn't talk for a moment, just sat there on the side of the hotel bed holding the phone. It was coming closer to all of us, I thought, but didn't say. He was seventy-nine and had cancer. I would be seventy-five in a few weeks and I'd had a stroke. The Quantico class of '51 wasn't doing so well. Life was closing in on us. Death was.

Finally, I just said, "I love you, Taf."

"I love you, too."

I think I said so long. Or God bless. Something. I couldn't talk anymore.

On the late morning of a November Friday, 2003, I was in East Hampton working on this book when Elaine phoned. I knew from her voice, low, a bit choked. Is it bad news? I asked.

"Taffy died last night. I tried to get you then. I've lost my best friend."

I told Elaine how sorry I was, how much I'd loved Taf. Then I started to choke, but that wasn't what Elaine needed. So I pulled myself up and told her what I believed, that with all the fighting Taffy did in two wars, he might have died fifty years ago but hadn't. He'd lived to sail yachts, climb the High Sierra, have kids and fall in love with her; a cheerful, redheaded man, good at what he did, whether running fruit canneries or sailing catamarans off the Royal Hawaiian, killing Japanese or Commies. But I bit off that last part.

"Was he at home? In his own bed?"

"Yes," she said. "Not at the Veterans' Hospital. And at the end he asked for his Purple Heart to hold."

What would I ask to hold when death came?

CHAPTER 49

LE REPOS DU GUERRIER . . . THE WARRIOR AT REST.

Our war behind us, Korea far distant, the old soldiers dying off, the rifle platoon leaders, never numerous at best, were being whittled down, not by the North Koreans or the Chinese, damn them both, but by the years.

Elaine called one more time. They were having a service December 6 at the Catholic church there in San Jose. Would I write a few lines about Taffy someone could read? With a magnificent resilience, she was working on the arrangements, promising to send the obituaries I'd asked for, and a copy of the service. A woman in charge. If I were wise enough, I might have attempted to console her with those words from Aeneas: "A joy it will be one day, perhaps, to remember even this."

That same Thanksgiving weekend following Taffy's death there came to East Hampton a pale blue envelope with the finishing-school handwriting of Virginia Chafee. One of her sons now sat in his father's Senate seat and was already making a serious, solid impression on Washington, on the Senate. But it was not about Lincoln Chafee that his mother wrote.

A guided missile destroyer named for her husband had lately been commissioned up at Newport, Rhode Island, and now she wanted to share with me her first and maybe only view of the new ship under way, the USS *Chafee* heading out to sea for Hawaii, where it would be stationed.

Ginnie and John had a little place they called "the Pickle House" at Pojac Point, on the Rhode Island coast at the slim entrance to Narragansett Bay, and she stays there when the season and the weather are right. In her brief but rather wonderfully crafted note from the Pickle House, she wrote about that morning the *Chafee* went to sea:

On Monday I went in the early morning to Fort Wetherall, across from Fort Adams and Hammersmith Farm, to see the ship finally on her way to duty in the Pacific. The point of land there is high and wild, the passage out, narrow. The blue water was sprinkled with Cat's Paws—the start of a beautiful day.

Suddenly and silently the high prow, then the whole ship rounded a promontory! I wanted to run back and forth waving—there she was! Many hands were on deck at attention, all serious and on watch. Small patrol boats were on lookout as well. Soon the Chafee *became smaller while heading to the horizon.*

Another goodbye.

When I returned home everyone had left—so quiet there.

In Jim Michener's story *The Bridges at Toko-ri,* when its naval aviator protagonist has crashed in North Korea, and been hunted down and killed by the enemy infantry, the admiral who sends the pilots on missions from which some won't return stares out at the carrier deck, where, already, other young Americans are scrambling into other planes for yet another fight. Marveling at their courage, he asks rhetorically: "Where do we get such men?"

I thought about that now. Thought too of Ginnie Chafee, of Taffy's wife Elaine, of Patricia Taplett and the other Marine wives, of Wild Hoss Callan's sister, Gloria Toombs, of Artemise McKenna, a mother who lost three boys to war and yet continued baking and sending cookies to Dog Company, and of the other sisters and mothers, and realized we might well ask: "And where do we get such women?"

Of course I think about them, the women and the men both, the aging and the dead of our Korea time. But I also find myself recalling Lieutenant Jim Gleason and his platoon, twenty-year-old Americans out there patrolling "the scariest place" in today's Korea, as we once did, the same deadly hills.

Raw meat on the end of a stick.

Sound like a dove, do I? Well, maybe I've earned the right. Of course there are times when the nation has no choice, when Americans have to fight. I understood that. Was that way myself in 1950, once I got over my nerves. Most young soldiers are ferocious warriors, gung ho, can't wait to get to the fight. And once in the war, we're fighting for the country, sure, but even more for the guy next to us. We're caught up with killing and not being killed, with doing the job and winning. We don't start out as pacifists or peacemakers. That comes later, after the battle, even with Marines. Half a century ago I was as hawkish as the next guy.

It's war that turns men into doves.

In East Hampton another autumn was ending, as I got in a few last hikes along the beach, doing pretty well on the bum knee, before winter's first snow fell and icy wind off the ocean shut me down till spring. How fortunate— even blessed in Joe Owen's words about Dick Brennan—to have been a Marine, to have known such men, fought beside and not fled or failed them, the Corps. Or myself. I must write soon to the Pickle House, thanking Ginnie for her lovely description of the USS *Chafee,* an American warship going in harm's way. To ask if I might use her eloquent words in this book.

And to assure her it was quiet here on Further Lane, that at our house, too, the warriors were at rest.

INDEX